SILENT INVADERS

RAF C-47 Dakota aircraft turning away after releasing their gliders. Horsa and Waco gliders lie in the fields below; Normandy, June 1944. *AP Photo/U.S. Air Force*

SILENT INVADERS

Combat Gliders of the Second World War

GARY A. BEST

FONTHILL

Fonthill Media Language Policy

Fonthill Media publishes in the international English language market. One language edition is published worldwide. As there are minor differences in spelling and presentation, especially with regard to American English and British English, a policy is necessary to define which form of English to use. The Fonthill Policy is to use the form of English native to the author. Gary A. Best was born and educated in the United States and now lives in southern California therefore American English has been adopted for the text narrative in this publication.

However, to complicate matters, the quotations are from both British and American sources, and the author and publishers believe this should be kept as near as feasible to the original written source. In consequence, the indented quoted material is a mixture of both British and American English.

Fonthill Media Limited
Fonthill Media LLC
www.fonthillmedia.com
office@fonthillmedia.com

First published in the United Kingdom and the United States of America 2014

British Library Cataloguing in Publication Data:
A catalogue record for this book is available from the British Library

ISBN 978-1-62545-000-5

Typeset in 10pt on 13pt Sabon LT Std
Printed and bound by CPI Group (UK) Ltd, Croydon, CR0 4YY

Contents

Foreword

The use of cargo gliders during the Second World War is an oft overlooked chapter in the history of the conflict. Airborne operations were a major element in the strategy and tactics of the Allies, especially the Americans and the British. Cargo gliders (combat gliders in the jargon of the pilots who flew them) made airborne operations possible. No gliders, no airborne troops behind enemy lines. Period.

A number of books written over the last four decades tell the history of the military operations the gliders participated in. Others discuss the training program or the research and development aspects of the gliders. None have been as balanced, comprehensive and well-illustrated in regards to the whole cloth of the program. In this book you will read about the entire program, from conception to technical developments, from how to fly them to who flew them. This work will become a standard in the field as a result of this breadth. All those who have an interest in the Second World War glider program, or in Second World War airborne operations in general, will need this volume in their library.

Professor Best approached the field operations of the glider pilots in a novel way. Rather than write hour by hour, day by day accounts of the major missions the gliders flew, he produced a readable blend of traditional narrative history which sets the stage for his individual personal narratives. And the narratives themselves are a compilation of individual experiences, which give a broader overall feel for the "life and times" of the pilot. It was important to do this, to make it clear to the reader that these men had many shared experiences, but also many different outcomes as they went into battle. Some pilots did not live to complete their landings, while in the same Landing Zone, at the same time, another pilot touched down without a scratch. The reader will know that there are no "cookie-cutter" experiences in combat; shared experiences yes, identical ones, no.

Donald Abbe, Ph.D.
Curator, Silent Wings Museum
Lubbock, Texas

82nd Airborne load a 75 mm howitzer into a CG-4A Troop Glider during training at Oujda, French Morocco, North Africa a month before the Sicily invasion, Operation Husky, 11 June 1943.

Preface

Silent Invaders, Combat Gliders of the Second World War, is primarily a book about the men who piloted gliders and those who flew in them. To the extent possible it is written in a continuous narrative, often combining first person accounts from more than one person so that those experiences will have multiple perspectives of the same scene, battle, flight, landing, and related experiences. Unit names, flight and squadron numbers and other identifiers are, for the most part, not identified, outside of a larger descriptive framework so that one is able to concentrate of what an individual saw, heard, felt, or accomplished.

William F. Dawson, editor of "The 'All American' Paraglide", the VE Day—May 1945 supplement to the 82nd *All American* Airborne Division newspaper provides a good example of the lack of name and unit specifics in his editorial column: "Specific mention of units and individuals is avoided whenever possible so that all material may have universal appeal." I followed this example in describing the events that took place involving the glider men who contributed to the content of the narrative throughout the text. In some instances, names or unit identifications are so inextricably associated with a specific operation that omitting them would limit the overall description of the action in which participants were involved.

Although memories of many events in our lives tend to fade or lack specificity, those who talked to me about their war related stories were very clear about what they did and where their participation occurred. The sequence of events may not have always been accurate in the retelling, but the sights and sounds of flights and battles remembered by the glider men involved remain sharp and in some cases painful.

It has been said that truth is stranger than fiction. The recollections provided here are true as remembered, for in fiction there is no equivalence.

Gary A. Best
August 2014

They were the personification of bravery.

(A-18-21-HQIXTCC)(1-APR-45) GLIDER RECLAMATION 82858AC

CG-4A Troop Glider being recovered at Wesel, Germany 1 April 1945.

M45 Quadmount Anti-Aircraft machine gunners make their temporary living quarters under the wing of a Waco CG-4A Glider, 1 April 1945.

PART I

The Machines

1
The Beginning

At the 11th hour of the 11th day of the 11 month of 1918 hostilities between Allied forces and Germany were terminated bringing an end to the First World War. The agreement signed earlier that same day set the terms for the armistice that included in addition to the cessation of hostilities, the withdrawal of troops to behind Germany's borders, the exchange of prisoners of war and the payment of war reparations. The terms of the armistice were non-negotiable and included a provision that "The armed forces of Germany must not include any military or naval air forces."[1]

The Treaty of Peace set the parameters for Germany as a future military force. The new Germany in size and martial ability was, by the treaty, to be limited so that domination as a warring force would be restricted, if not totally compromised.[2]

The time, day, and month that brought the sunset on the First World War marked the sunrise of the Second World War. Into the cauldron of German politics and society, ready to be placed on a fire and stirred, were thrown the ingredients of retribution and revenge for the defeat of arms, the death of hungry civilians and the loss of territory. The times looked for and found someone who would rally the population, identify a political structure with promises of grandeur and salvation from past and future wrongs and the promise of continental domination, setting for all time a model of racial superiority, military might and social idealism.

Spelled out through the lens of his own personal, social and political struggles Adolf Hitler proclaimed in *Mein Kampf* [*My Vision*],

> What we must fight for is to safeguard the existence and reproduction of our race and our people, the sustenance of our children and the purity of our blood, the freedom and independence of the fatherland, so that our people may mature for the fulfillment of the mission allotted it by the creator of the universe.[3]

In 1922, Hermann Göring, an ace fighter pilot veteran of the First World War, visited with Eddie Rickenbacker who was in Berlin as a part of his honeymoon trip to Europe. The US aviator remembers that his rival in the skies during the war laid out his vision for the foundation of a new Germany with chilling specificity, clarity and foreshadowing—air power will be the mechanism by which the German empire will again rise and it will come about by teaching our youth gliding as a sport.[4]

"While the interwar years offered all nations ample opportunity to perfect the tactics and strategy for the military glider, only the Germans, constrained by the Versailles Treaty, had the motivation to capitalize on the opportunity."[5] Glider clubs flourished, attracting German youth who received instruction from

> ... ex-World War pilots ... instructing them in the elementary principles of flight ... Meteorologists in Germany saw gliding as a sport whose devotees could furnish them with information concerning weather conditions and wind currents; plane manufacturers saw an opportunity to learn new ideas in wing design. Even the heavy artillery division of the small German army began to see possibilities of obtaining from glider pilots a clearer picture of the wind currents and weather conditions through which gliders (and shells fired from heavy artillery) must travel.[6]

By the time Hitler came to power and the Luftwaffe was revealed to the rest of the world, the German army had been actively recruiting glider pilots from the nation's gliding clubs.

> I was always interested in flying and began building model airplanes when I was ten years old. When the Hitler Youth program came along it was an opportunity to learn to fly, fly gliders. The Hitler Youth program had three sections for boys to choose:

Above left: "Germany will either be a world power or there will be no Germany."

Above right: Building glider models, learning to soar in gliding clubs, recruitment by the Luftwaffe. *Bundesarchiv*

> flying, navy, army. I chose flying. It was free, we had uniforms as a part of Hitler Youth.
>
> In those years, everyone had to go into the service, so the Luftwaffe gave me the opportunity to fly and I signed up to go into the Luftwaffe. Flying was the most beautiful thing there was. Flying for hours at a time with the birds; it was quiet, peaceful.[7]
>
> Göring immediately issued to glider pilots the coveted uniforms of the Luftwaffe ... and eventually transformed them into military pilots. And, all over Germany, glider clubs were drawn into the Nazi organizational scheme.[8]

Glider training became a requisite for Luftwaffe flight training and by 1935, in direct violation of the Treaty of Versailles, the German Air Force had a formidable accumulation of aircraft with design and production pushing forward without international threat or interference.

At the 1936 Olympic Games, the Berlin Games—the stiff armed salute and swastika were in evidence in all corners of this international athletic competition. Hitler attended the games attired in a military uniform and the skies on the day of the opening ceremonies were festooned with gliders for athletes and spectators alike to see.[9]

A year later Germany claimed to have 40,000 glider pilots and 10,000 to 12,000 gliders active throughout the country.[10] And in two years, two very short years, on 1 September 1939, the blitzkrieg of Poland by combined ground and air forces of Germany 'including gliders' pushed Europe to full-throated war.[11]

"... it was an opportunity to learn to fly, fly gliders." *Courtesy of Tonya Langehans Mitchell*

2

Pug Ugly and Deadly

They weren't pretty. They had no graceful lines. Looking at them from the front, or a three-quarters portrait view, the US glider had a pug nose and a sloping Neanderthal forehead. Its wings looked like the ears of a jackrabbit that had been heavily starched and placed at right angles on a canvas-covered frame. Twice the length of the body, these self-same wings of the most common glider of the United States Army Air Forces, the Waco CG-4A (C for cargo, G for glider), were nearly eighty-four feet in length, 70 per cent as long as the Wright brothers first powered flight at Kitty Hawk, North Carolina.

By comparison, the primary British combat glider, the Horsa, had a body that was sixty-eight feet in length and a wing span of eighty-eight feet.[1] The glider used by the Germans in airborne assaults, the DFS 230 (*Deutsches Forschungsinstitutt für Segelflug*—German Research Institute for Gliding Flight) had a wing span of seventy-two feet and a fuselage of thirty-seven feet. None of these aircraft could become airborne, let alone fly, unless towed into the air by an engine-powered aircraft.[2]

These were the combat gliders of the Second World War, aircraft constructed of plywood panels, with doped cotton canvas stretched over metal tubes and plywood framing. The US Waco and large numbers of the British Horsa were towed into action by US Army Air Forces' C-47s, the Skytrain, and the British equivalent, the Dakota, a military version of the two-engine commercial airliner, the DC-3. It was nicknamed by many for the most clumsy bird to inhabit the islands of the Pacific Ocean, the Gooney Bird. Others gave it a nickname with a similar lack of glamor, the Vomit Comet.

With malice a forethought gliders were called by some: flying coffins, death crates, Purple Heart boxes, tow targets and in the best of times, flimsy, unprotected, unarmed 48 foot contraptions. These crates of canvas, motor-less and armor-less, with some plywood here, some welded steel tubing there, towed on a one-inch-thick nylon rope, were little more than military passenger and cargo carrying kites. Landings were often no more than controlled crashes into fields, hedgerows and trees, both wings whacked off. Walter Cronkite, the American war correspondent who accompanied glider airborne troops to battle, said of these fragile aircraft, 'I'll tell you straight out: If you've got to go into combat, don't go by glider. Walk, crawl, parachute, swim, float—anything. But don't go by glider.'[3]

Following the successful use by Germany of combat gliders in the taking of the Belgium Fort Eben Emael in early May 1940, and in campaigns in Greece and Crete in 1941, consideration for the development of a glider force that could deliver both troops and equipment to the battle front quickly and silently began to emerge in both the United States and in Britain. Both countries were committed to the production of fighter planes and bombers as defensive and offensive weapons, making glider research and development the 'new kid on the block' and an ignored product by the major aircraft manufacturing companies.

In February 1941, General Henry H. (Hap) Arnold, head of the US Army Air Corps ordered that a study of glider development and deployment be undertaken with the intention of using gliders to deliver a self-contained combat team to seize specific objectives not normally reached by conventional ground units.[4] In little more than a year after Arnold's directive, the newly formed I Troop Carrier Command recommended the design and procurement of gliders, communication between the tow plane and the glider, aerial pickup (a technique to become known as the *snatch*), development of the glider as an extra fuel supply for the transport, and instrument flying in gliders. Missing from the recommendations of the Troop Carrier Command was Arnold's call for using the glider to carry combat troops, a tactical doctrine embraced by both the British and the Germans.[5]

A new doctrine of deployment of gliders evolved that brushed away the sole role of gliders as air trailers, their pilots little more than aerial truck drivers. Gliders would assume a dual combat role: 1) transporting personnel as an integral part of larger airborne operations to engage in combat and seize specific objectives such as crossroads and bridges and hold on to these gains until ground troops arrived to reinforce or to replace them; 2) carrying heavy equipment and supplies that combat troops could not carry themselves but would need to secure their positions and advance their lines.

The Waco CG-4A combat glider: "If you've got to go into combat, don't go by glider."

Eventually, doctrine led to practice with the development of a training manual by the US Army Air Forces for *Glider Tactics and Technique*.

> The military glider was primarily developed for the use of airborne troops on the premise that as a means of transportation it would greatly enhance the chances for success in vertical envelopment or in the creation of a flank above and beyond the enemy front lines ... In general, the missions in which gliders can be employed are:
>
> (1) Combat carrying of glider-borne and other troops to tactical operations.
> *(a)* Airborne invasion.
> *(b)* Land troops in the rear of enemy lines to assist a break-through, disrupt communications and block the movement of enemy reserves.
> *(c)* Land troops to seize and hold key terrain features or enemy installations, to block movement of enemy reserves, or to prevent an enemy withdrawal.
> *(d)* Support a break-through by landing troops behind weak sections in friendly lines.
> *(e)* Capture and hold airdromes within enemy territory.
> *(f)* Precede spearheads.
> *(g)* Establish a bridgehead or beachhead.
> *(h)* Assist ground forces in the reduction of enemy strong points.
> *(i)* Sabotage missions.
>
> (2) Combat carrying of supplies and equipment.
> *(a)* Supply and resupply to airborne units participating in an airborne invasion.
> *(b)* Supplying other ground units cut off from normal communication channels.
> *(c)* Landing supplies and equipment in locations where powered aircraft cannot land.
>
> (3) Evacuation of casualties and other personnel.
>
> (4) Supplementing the transportation services of other agencies. Organizations that normally require additional transport facilities for administrative moves can be made mobile if their assigned aircraft are capable of towing gliders and gliders are available to them for such movements.[6]
>
> And, as it seems, with every well thought out and well-meaning set of guidelines there are those factors which make implementation difficult or hazardous: Air superiority, availability of tow ships, availability of departure airdromes, weather, terrain, enemy air and ground opposition, aircraft vulnerability and the availability of fighter escort.[7]

With the evolution of doctrine and deployment for the use of combat gliders, the US Army Air Forces identified guidelines which manufacturers would need to follow in order to be awarded contracts for aircraft development, testing, and manufacturing. When the US Army Air Force issued specifications and requested proposals for a combat glider the submission by Francis Arcier, vice president and chief engineer of the Waco Aircraft Company of Troy, Ohio, was the design of choice.

The Waco CG-4A, known as the *Hadrian* by Britain's Royal Air Force, was a strut-based high wing monoplane with fixed-type landing gear and tail wheel with more than 70,000 individual parts. Constructed of framed plywood and welded steel tubing it was covered with a cotton canvas fabric stretched into place like wallpaper with every seam, hold, and edge covered with an adhesive dope resulting in an airtight structure wherever it was applied. The floor of the main cabin was constructed of a honeycomb plywood configuration covered with reinforced plywood giving it the ability to support cargo loads greater than the weight of the aircraft. The instrument panel was simplicity in design and function and included an air speed indicator, altimeter, rate of climb indicator, and a bank and turn indicator. Light switches, compass and a tow release lever were also located in cockpit.

The Waco CG-4A had a two man crew, pilot and co-pilot sitting in a side-by-side configuration and could carry 13 combat equipped infantry men, or a jeep and six men, a jeep trailer fully loaded with combat equipment and nine men, a 75 mm Howitzer artillery piece with five men and eighteen rounds of ammunition, an anti-tank gun with five men, or it could be configured to carry six litters for the evacuation of wounded troops. The nose was hinged at the top and could be elevated to facilitate the loading and unloading of vehicles and cargo including fuel, ammunition, rations, medical supplies, mail and vehicles.

Its overall length was 48 feet 3¾ inches, had a wingspan of 83 feet 8 inches, a height of 12 feet 7⁷⁄₁₆ inches, and a wing area of 851.5 square feet. Empty it weighed 3,790 pounds with a maximum design gross weight of 7,500 pounds. Its maximum tow speed was 150 mph with a 7,500 pound load. It had stall speeds of 41 mph with the design load of 5,000 pounds, 50 mph with 7,500 pound loads, or 55 mph with a 9,000 pound load. The Waco average glide speed was 65 mph indicated airspeed.[8]

> Note: The small size of the Clarkair Crawler Model CA-1 permitted airlift by gliders to locations where it could be used to construct landing strips or other facilities. As the dead weight of this piece of equipment was approximately 4,640 pounds and the design capacity of the CG-4A was 3,790 pounds, the carrying of a bulldozer created an automatic overload which caused a higher speed on approach and landing as well as a more difficult tow. As a result of this weight discrepancy, the blade of the bulldozer would be removed and flown in a separate glider.

A total of 13,909 CG-4A gliders were produced from 1942 until the end of the war in 1945 and during that time more than 7,000 modifications were made. With the exception of the Corey skid, the Griswold Nose and the deceleration

CG-4A Cockpit. *Author's collection*

Specially designed bulldozer for glider transport. *Author's collection*

parachute attached under the tail of the glider, none were a major change from the original design.

The Corey Skid, a simple wooden ski-like device attached to the underside of the cockpit, deflected much of the debris that would slice through the thin skin on the underside of the cockpit during a rough landing.

> Made of six-ply mahogany, the three skids are attached to a welded steel tubing subframe bolted to the glider nose superstructure. The skids keep the wings in near level flight attitude during a landing. When the nose hits, they force the tail down and put more lift into the wings. A cushion landing results, with the glider planning to a stop like a speed boat over rough water.[9]

The Griswold Nose was a device constructed of steel tubing that rose vertically from the external base of the cockpit to follow the curve to the top. The framework provided additional crash protection for the cockpit crew.

The ten foot diameter deceleration parachute was stored in a pack mounted on a duck-covered board. The board gave rigidity to the pack and also provided a means of attaching the assembly to the glider. Four grommets, one in each corner of the board, were provided for bolting the parachute assembly to the glider.

The rip-cord method of opening the parachute pack was utilized in this assembly. A single pin rip cord approximately 18 inches long, fabricated with a small loop on the

The Corey Skid—Restored CG-4A; Silent Wings Museum, Lubbock, Texas. *Author's collection*

The Griswold Nose—Restored CG-4A Cockpit Frame; Silent Wings Museum, Lubbock, Texas, *Author's collection*

free end, was used to free the parachute from its pack. When the assembly was attached to the glider the rip cord was attached to a cable leading to the cockpit. To deploy the parachute the pilot pulled a handle in the cockpit which activated the cable and pulled the pin from the pack opening the pack to permit parachute canopy inflation.

A training manual for the operation of the deceleration parachute, *Pilot's Flight Operating Instructions for Army Model CG-4A Glider*, dated 15 June 1944, informed pilots to use it to: dissipate altitude without increasing speed when a landing approach is too high; reduce speed when an approach is low but too fast and cautioned to never release the parachute when the glider was on tow.[10]

Two veteran CG-4A pilots remember:

> (I) ... received no training in the use of this device before (the) mission and was reluctant to use it until the last minute. (I) had the copilot deploy the parachute just as the glider brushed the tops of some small trees on (the) landing approach. The glider came to rest with its tail lodged in the trees and the deceleration parachute draped down behind it.

Another recalls:

> It worked like a charm. (I) had five training flights in England with the deceleration chute before the Normandy mission. (I) opened the parachute at cutoff ... used full spoilers ... and the glider floated right into the landing zone.[11]

The major airplane manufacturing companies in the United States during the Second World War were engaged in producing large quantities of powered aircraft, fighter planes, bombers, cargo and transport planes. As a result, 'the glider program had to turn to many small, untested companies. Many of these companies existed solely to gain military contracts with no prior experience in aviation, large scale production or aerodynamics.'[12] The list of companies that produced the CG-4A included the Gibson refrigerator manufacturer and a wooden furniture maker. Sub-contractors were also from diverse prewar industries—Steinway and Sons, a New York based piano manufacturer, contributed wings and tail surfaces, the H. J. Heinz pickle company supplied wings to the G and A Aircraft Company, a brewery made inboard wing panels for another prime contractor and Gardner Metal Products Company, a coffin making company, produced steel fittings that connected the wing struts to the fuselage.[13]

Envisioned as an economical method of sending troops to battle, the per unit cost of $20,000 set by the government was met by only two companies, the Ford Motor Company and Waco Aircraft Company. The Ford plant at Kingsford, Michigan transformed its assembly line machinery and experience in producing wood-sided station wagon cars to eventually produce 4,190 CG-4As by war's end at a cost of nearly $15,000 each. The Waco company built 1,075 of the gliders at just under $20,000.

Workers were employed for eight-hour shifts around the clock. These were planes that had to be constructed largely by practiced hands and newly designed tools, a problem that had to be dealt with early on in the production process. No one in the US had built a combat glider in the past and the learning curve started out low and slow. But at its peak workers at the Ford Plant in Kingsford turned out eight gliders per day.

Gliders, once constructed and inspected, had to be taken apart and crated for shipment to US bases for crew training or to sea ports for transportation to overseas bases. Ford solved this problem by cutting a 120-foot-wide clearing through a wooded area at the end of the assembly line to an airport runway a mile away where United States Army Air Force (USAAF) planes could tow them to training bases or to port destinations.[14]

The Robertson Aircraft Company of St. Louis, Missouri was one of the prime contractors awarded a contract by the War Department in 1942 for the construction of the CG-4A glider.

> Our organization is headed by a competent aeronautical engineering staff, and all departments are headed by experienced men. Our employees are skilled in both machine tools and assemblies. There is no shortage of labor in this area, and we maintain a qualified staff to train unskilled personnel at all times. At the present time, the Corporation employs approximately: 390 hourly employees, 60 salaried employees; 285 male employees, 165 female employees.
>
> In this area, we have a diversified group of sub-contracting facilities available who employ approximately seven hundred trained workers and are now engaged in fabricating parts and assemblies for us.[15]

Welded steel frames and honeycomb flooring, CG-4A. *Courtesy of the Silent Wings Museum*

While other US war planes could fly to their theaters of war, gliders had to be disassembled from the factory, crated, lifted aboard a ship, transported overseas, unloaded upon arrival at their destination, shipped to a base for reassembly and moved to an operational airfield for eventual deployment. The crates were more than big, they were massive. CG-4A glider parts were packed in five standard sized shipping boxes for rail and shipping transport. The crates varied in size, the smallest containing the glider's nose section was 8 feet, 8 inches long, 7 feet 2 inches wide, 5 feet 8 inches in height and weighed 1,800 pounds. The largest of the five shipping crates contained the inboard wing panels and spoilers and was 25 feet 5 inches long, 4 feet 4 inches wide, 11 feet 7 inches high and weighed 5,375 pounds.

Chances are that if you flew a CG-4A glider in the European Theater of War (ETO) during WW II it was assembled by a specialized unit of glider mechanics from the United States, the 26th Mobile Reclamation & Repair Squadron. They were activated on 10 November 1943 at Crookham Common, a former British golf course west of London in Berkshire. When they arrived they were greeted by row upon row of enormous wooden crates that had been arriving in England by ship since July 1943. One of the first priorities of the Commanding Officer (CO) was to design and set up a glider assembly line and start cranking out gliders. There was no technical data or precedent to draw on, so the mechanics had to improvise.

Within days the CO hit on the idea of converting the glider crates into makeshift barracks. Employing a little elbow grease and some good old American ingenuity, the empty containers were quickly converted into living quarters. Windows and doors were cut out, roofing applied, bunks moved in and a stove installed. A single CG-4A fuselage crate was large enough to provide adequate living space for four men. By the

Box No. 4: CG-43A wings with ailerons. *Courtesy of the Silent Wings Museum*

end of December 1943, 167 gliders had been assembled, despite inadequate tools and the foul English weather—rain, mud, cold, windstorms and fog so bad at times that work crews couldn't see the end of the wing of the glider they were working on.

In preparation for the upcoming Allied invasion of Normandy, the assembly of gliders was accelerated with a quota of 600 gliders set for April, more than all of those assembled in the previous three months. Working fifteen-hour-days, seven days a week the glider mechanics of the 26th not only met their quota but exceeded it by more than fifty percent. By month's end 961 gliders had been delivered.

In May, June and July 1944, 606 gliders were assembled and delivered. Griswold Nose Modification Kits were installed on 247 gliders during May. Shortly after D-Day a glider recovery team was sent to France to salvage gliders and glider parts from the Normandy invasion, often in fields that still contained antipersonnel mines.

In August 1944, in preparation for the invasion of Holland, 838 gliders were assembled, 700 of them within a sixteen day period. On 15 August a new record was established with the assembly of 100 gliders in a single day. In January 1945, six hundred gliders were ordered assembled including 13 of the large 43 place Waco CG-13A gliders. The last assembly of gliders in the ETO (European Theater of Operation) was April 1945.[16]

As the glider program began producing aircraft, training crews and developing combat doctrine and strategies, the folks at home were beginning to see evidence of this new tactic of carrying troops to battle. *Life* magazine devoted its 7 September 1942 cover to a military glider and added a six page article that provided an artist's rendition of how gliders would be involved in the newest attack strategy of *vertical envelopment*. Training bases were being built and with the recruitment of volunteers, according to *Life*, "as old as 35 are being accepted for training."

CG-4A glider assembly. *Courtesy of the Silent Wings Museum*

"Insert Flange A into Slot B. Where the hell is Flange A?" *Author's collection—artist unknown*

But not all of the public relations efforts were successful. On 1 August 1943 the mayor of St. Louis, a city that was home to two of the prime contractors for construction of the CG-4A, participated, with nine others, in a publicity demonstration ride from Lambert Field on the outskirts of the city. When asked by a reporter whether or not he was nervous about the ride-along, Mayor William Becker responded in a half-joking manner, 'Gentlemen, you can only die once, and we all must die sometime.'[17]

The glider, on its second demonstration flight of the day, became airborne behind a C-47 tow plane and released its tow at 2,000 feet. Within moments the right wing folded and broke away from the fuselage. The CG-4A plunged nose-first into the ground, with pieces of the aircraft trailing after the main body that "smashed like a strawberry box," and "bits of bodies and fuselage sprayed 50 feet up into the air."[18, 19] All aboard were killed instantly.

Army investigators determined that the cause of the accident that ripped off the starboard wing and pulled the roof from the passenger section of the glider was related to a failed fitting at the lower end of the starboard wing brace that held the wing struts to the fuselage. The investigators determined that the thickness of the plate that was attached to the inner wing strut did not meet the manufacturer's specifications. Instead of a required machined brace plate thickness of three eighths of an inch at the counter sink holes as specified by the manufacturer's drawings, the countersink holes of the failed brace had been bored to an excessive depth reducing the wall thickness where the wing brace attached to the fuselage to one sixteenth of an inch.[20] Investigators also found deep machine tool marks, chattering and gouging on the part that failed.[21]

The crashed CG-4A glider with the failed wing strut brace had been manufactured by Robertson Aircraft Company, the failed wing strut brace from a sub-contractor, Gardner Metal Products Company, a St. Louis casket maker.[22] There was plenty of blame to go around, but it seems that in the end a lack of product oversight management and quality control could be ranked at least as important as the metal failure of the wing parts. There had been a stunning lack of parts inspection by the primary contractor, the sub-contractor and personnel of the Army Air Force.

The crash of the St. Louis demonstration glider ride with the loss of life of so many civilian dignitaries was a wake-up call to the public. The realities of war, death and destruction happened on the home front as well as on the battlefield.

The call for America's support of this new component of the air war continued with advertisements that encouraged readers to support the troops at war with the message that what's good for the men at war was good for the folks at home.

America was putting into the air more than just any Joe Blow who could meet the qualifications to become a glider pilot. America was sending to war Winged Commandos, Knights of the Air, Swift Gliding Champions (who) will ride their glider steeds into the capitals of the enemy' protected by 'super tough plastic' cockpit enclosures.

Two additional combat gliders were included in the air arsenal of The United States Army Air Force, the CG-13A and the CG-15A. The CG-13A saw combat

Above left: The CG-4A plunged nose-first into the ground. *St. Louis Post-Dispatch Archive Photo*

Above right: Home Front magazine advertisement. *Author's collection; used with permission of Celanese Celluloid Corporation*

service in the Philippines but other uses of the aircraft were limited to supply missions. The design for this glider was markedly different from the CG-4A, the mainstay of the US glider force. This latter glider had a deeper and wider fuselage and a straight back behind a rounded nose with a pilot's door. It was equipped with a tricycle landing gear with double nose wheels, its wings set farther back on the fuselage with a tall fin and rudder at the rear.

The CG-13A carried a pilot and copilot and as many as 42 troops. It was 54 feet 4 inches in length and was 20 feet, 3 inches in height. The wing span was 85 feet 8 inches and had an empty weight of 8,700 pounds, with a load carrying capacity of 10,200 lbs.

By comparison, the CG-15A assumed the posture of a bloated CG-4A, with a less pronounced sloping cockpit and shorter wings. It had the same troop carrying and cargo capacity of the CG-4A but because of its more streamlined design it could fly faster, at 180 mph, than its predecessor.

The men who trained and were assigned to guide these aircraft into battle were said to be the only pilots of the US Army Air Forces who had no motors, no armament, no parachutes, and no second chances.

3

Gliders in the UK

It was conceived and delivered in ten months, a gestation period for the Horsa Mark I combat glider that moved from required design specifications of the Air Ministry and the War Office to prototype construction.[1] The first production model appeared in June 1942 and by war's end, its manufacturer, Airspeed Aviation Limited and subcontractors had built more than 3,500 Horsas, the principal glider of the UK glider force.[2]

Britain, like the United States, had watched and learned from the successes of the German army in its use of the combat glider. Prime Minister Winston Churchill, 'committed the British Army to develop an airborne force' that was to consist entirely of parachutists. However, an airlift shortage required a revision of that commitment to include a glider force that by spring 1941 would consist of 2,700 glider troops and 360 pilots. The British Glider Pilot Regiment was established on 24 February 1942 and, unlike the U.S. approach to the training of glider pilots, would draw its flight personnel from the army.[3]

> THE AIRBORNE FORCES OF THE BRITISH ARMY CONSIST OF PARACHUTE TROOPS AND GLIDER-BORNE TROOPS OF ALL ARMS OF THE SERVICE.
>
> Officers and men in any Regiment or Corps (except RAC, Royal Armoured Corps), who are medically fit, may apply for transfer to a parachute or glider-borne unit of the Airborne Forces ... A limited number of officers and other ranks are urgently required for training as glider pilots. Applications for transfer or further information should be made to unit headquarters.[4]

The Airspeed Horsa Mark I/II was a long cylindrical monoplane with high wings set almost half way back on the fuselage from the front of the aircraft. With a 'snub, bug-like nose' it reminded an American glider pilot of a flying cigar.[5,6] Constructed primarily of wood and considered disposable after landing, it could be produced without dipping into the valuable and limited resources needed for the manufacturing of powered aircraft. It had a tricycle landing gear that could be jettisoned and was

Airspeed Horsa DP726 under tow. The Horsa Mark I had a unique tow line in the shape of a "Y". DP 726 force landed at Arnhem during Operation Market Garden on 18 September 1944.

A AS.51 Horsa Mk I showing troops embarking. The Horsa could carry 25 fully loaded troops.

fitted with a landing skid to protect the fuselage when making belly landings. When the Horsa was configured to carry heavy arms such as a 75 mm Howitzer field gun, the undercarriage remained in place giving the pilot more control when landing.

A civilian worker remembers:

> I was conscripted into working on the glider wings from November 1941 until 1943. I had never been in a factory before, so it was quite an experience for me.
>
> It was there that I met Gwen Pearson in the training shop. From there we were sent into the main shop.
>
> While the men fitted the spars to the jig, Gwen and I collected the small parts from the stores. This consisted of ribs, plywood, angle pieces, glue, small nails and a hammer. A plywood angle was glued to each side of each end of a rib. When set each rib was then placed in position using the hammer, the angles were then nailed firmly into the spar.
>
> Gwen and I suffered from bruised fingers, as it was difficult to hammer in such a confined space. Ernie from another jig made us a pair of tweezers in the shape of women's legs (this caused quite a laugh). But they were a great help. When all the ribs were fitted a skin of plywood was glued to the top of the wing and left to set.
>
> Not until I became involved in the glider project did I realise the significance of the job we were doing during the war.[7]

Wooden benches to accommodate twenty-five troops with battle gear were fitted along the sides of the main interior of the fuselage, a bench at the rear could accommodate three additional troops; a pilot and co-pilot sat side-by-side in a roomy cockpit with greenhouse paned windows of Perspex (a clear plastic material manufactured in the US as Plexiglass.)

The Horsa Mark I had a unique tow line in the shape of a "Y". The bottom of the "Y" letter-shaped tow line was attached to the tug, the two arms of the letter attached under the port and starboard sides of the wings near the top of each landing gear. A later version of the Horsa, the Mark II, discarded this tow-line configuration in favor of a single line that included a radio communication line woven into the tow cable.

Passenger doors were on either side of the fuselage and staggered allowing for passengers on each side to exit at the same time without getting in one another's way. Doors at the exits opened by sliding them upwards inside fuselage. In addition, a large rectangular door, hinged at the bottom and just aft of the cockpit on the port side of the aircraft was used for loading heavy equipment. In order to avoid damaging the door during the loading of equipment, two separate loading channels were attached to the bottom of the door opening providing a bridge to span the gap between the ground and the floor of the glider.

The Mark II also featured two additional door configurations: a hinged-nose on the starboard side allowing for entrance and exit of equipment through the front of the aircraft. An earlier more suspect exit strategy was the placement of a ring of Cordex explosives around the rear bulkhead. When fired the explosives would neatly cut the tail of the glider away from the fuselage providing a large opening for quick exiting of troops and cargo. This method of removing the rear section of the glider from its fuselage was soon replaced in favor of a series of bolts placed around the tail section that could be loosened by spanners/crescent wrenches managed by the crew members or passengers. This latter method was less dangerous than the explosive charge which could be set off by enemy ground fire and the possibility that the explosions could damage cargo and personnel.

The safer of the two maneuvers to remove the tail section from the aircraft was not without its difficulties. The glider would have to land in a manner so that it was level to the ground. The crew wielding the spanners worked in tandem to release the bolts at the same time to facilitate the dropping away of the tail section cleanly on the ground rather than having it lodged at an angle. Onc Horsa pilot remembers that upon a *perfect* landing enemy gun fire whistled around them as he and his co-pilot struggled to loosen the bolts on the rear hatch, sweating like pigs, only to have the tail section not fall to the ground as designed. The portable loading trestle had been placed directly under the tail section by one of the paratrooper passengers blocking its free fall. Kicking the trestle away and shouldering the tail section aside the cargo of jeep and trailer were unloaded, the crew members scrambling for cover.[8]

Airspeed Horsa Mark I & II characteristics

The Horsa was 67 feet in length, 19 feet 6 inches in height, had a wingspan of 88 feet, with a wing area of 1,104 feet. It weighed 8,379 pounds empty, the Mark I, when loaded, weighed 15,500 pounds, the Mark II, 15,750 pounds. The maximum tow speed for the Horsa was 160 mph and 190 mph when diving. It had an average glide speed of 80 mph and with its flaps half down its speed would reach 110 mph or 100 mph with its flaps full down. Its flaps could be set for 45 degrees or 90 degrees which gave the Horsa its characteristic steep dive in landing. In addition to compressed air brakes on the wheels under the wings, the Horsa could be fitted with a pair of arrester parachutes and when deployed could bring the aircraft to a stop in less than 100 yards.

In lieu of a full passenger load, the Airspeed Horsa Mark I & II could accommodate a cargo load of two ¼ ton 4 × 4 trucks, (most often referred to by its more familiar name, *jeep.*) A jeep and its trailer fully loaded with equipment and supplies, a jeep and a US 75 mm Howitzer artillery piece plus ammunition and crew, or a combination of troops and equipment could also be accommodated so long that the load did not exceed 7,380 lbs.[*]

[*]Horsa data characteristics are adapted from several sources: Denis Edwards, *The Devil's Own Luck, Pegasus Bridge to the Baltic*; Alan Lloyd, *The Gliders; An Action Packed Story of the Wooden Chariots of World War II*; James E.

The Airspeed factory floor at Christchurch, Dorset.

The Airspeed factory at Christchurch, Dorset, overlooking the Solent and the western tip of the Isle of Wight, *c.* 1945.

Airspeed Horsa assault glider at Christchurch with a destroyed upside-down Horsa behind it.

An Airspeed Horsa destroyed on the ground at the Christchurch factory grounds, the victim of gale force winds.

Mrazek, *Fighting Gliders of World War II*; *Pilot's Notes; Horsa I Glider*; Claude Smith, *History of the Glider Pilot Regiment.*[9]

The UK produced and brought into use two additional gliders that played a significant role in the Allies' glider war. The Hotspur was the first glider designed and flown in response to the PMW (Prime Minister's Wishes) to develop an airborne force including glider borne troops.[10] In addition to the development, test flights, and deployment of the Hotspur and later the Horsa, Britain also moved forward in the development of a giant of a glider aircraft for carrying large cargo loads, the Hamilcar.

The design objective for the Hotspur was to carry eight fully armed troops, or the equivalent of 1,880 lbs of cargo, its two pilots sitting in tandem in the cockpit. The Hotspur, made of wood by the General Aircraft Company Ltd., was produced in three models, the Mark I, II and III, from outside appearances looking very much alike.

The Mark I had the appearance, from the side, of a tear drop, the fuselage a long narrow oval of 39 feet 3.5 inches. Its wings, set approximately mid-body and spanning 62 feet, were remindful of sailplane sport gliders. The canopy over the cockpit was hinged on the starboard side and passengers sat in the two sections behind the cockpit, one compartment in front of the wings, the second behind the wings. Upon landing, troops exited the aircraft by disengaging the roof from the fuselage, tossing it back and scrambling over the walls of the glider making themselves easy silhouetted targets for the enemy.

The Hotspur troop compartments were very cramped giving a person who might have had even the mildest sense of claustrophobia a measurable level of discomfort. With wings 62 feet in length, its long landing glide made the aircraft and the troops it carried exposed to enemy sharpshooters for a considerable period of time. When released from its tow at 20,000 feet, the Hotspur had a range of 83 miles.

The limited troop and cargo capacity of the glider put into question the practical use of the aircraft. Landing a large contingent of soldiers on the battlefield would require a large number of Hotspurs, or two pulled by a tow in tandem, as well as an equivalent number of tow aircraft, a necessity that would be both uneconomical and dangerous.[11]

The Mark II and Mark III variants included a larger cockpit canopy, and exit doors in both troop compartments, while an improvement over the latched roof of the Mark I, still made exiting the aircraft cumbersome. A braking parachute was added to the rear, and a shortened wingspan of 45 feet 10.75 inches thereby allowed for a steeper faster landing approach.

The Mark III, was an adaption of the Mark II that placed flight controls in the second cockpit seat for the use of a flight instructor. 'Despite numerous modifications ... the Hotspurs were never used in combat. Its relatively light cargo capacity and exit difficulties relegated the Hotspur to glider pilot training.'[12]

The giant of the British gliders of the Second World War, the Hamilcar, deserves a doff of the maroon beret by members of the Glider Pilot Regiment. [The Glider Pilot Regiment was established in late February 1942 and by June of the same year the distinctive maroon beret was authorized and distributed to its members.][13]

Was it truly possible to construct a glider to the specifications accepted by General Aircraft Ltd. in early 1941? Could their Railway Carriage & Wagon Company factory produce such an aircraft? Was the command structure mad to consider that an aircraft without its own engines could be lifted to fly with a compliment of forty fully armed soldiers, or a light tank, e.g. Tetrarch or the M22 Locust, or two Universal (Bren-gun) carriers, or a twenty-five pounder gun with its power transport? 'Yes and No.' 'Yes,' the massive result, a Hamilcar prototype put into the air in March of the following year.[14] And, 'no,' it seems as though they were not mad, but visionary enough and determined enough to commit to the production of this aircraft and to have it ready for the expected invasion of Europe, bringing to troops on the ground firepower, ammunition, troop reinforcements and large quantities of supplies to sustain and provide aggressive offensive movement.

The GAL 49 Hamilcar/Mark I was the largest glider built by the Allies during the Second World War, weighing 18,400 pounds empty and 36,000 pounds when loaded with cargo. There was nothing graceful in its appearance and looking at it from any angle begs the question of its ability to either become airborne or successfully glide in free flight.

The wings of this wood-constructed aircraft, set high and forward on the fuselage, spanned 110 feet and had a wing area of 1,657 square feet. The Hamilcar had large flaps that could be extended as needed to control glide path/descent angle and rate of speed thus putting the aircraft on the ground more quickly and reducing its vulnerability from enemy gun fire.

Hamilcar and Locust light tank, with the Locust disembarking. *Life*

A section of 'C' Squadron glider pilots with their RAF ground crew in front of a Hamilcar at Tarrant Rushton during the summer of 1944.

> With their enormous flaps ... they descended very steeply, so whilst the air speed remained constant, the ground speed could be as low as 30 mph, meaning that a very short landing run was needed ... and a large number of gliders could be landed in a very small field.[15]

The body was box-like with a curved roof and the cockpit sat forward of the leading edge of the wing at the top of the fuselage where the pilot and co-pilot sat in tandem at an astonishing 25 feet above the ground—more than the height of a two-story building (pilots of the Boeing 747 jet airliner sit approximately 29 above ground level.) The length of the Hamilcar was 68 feet, with an interior nearly 33 feet in length, 7 feet 10.5 inches in width and between 6 feet and 7 feet 7 inches in height. Although cavernous, the light tank and Bren-gun carriers were snug fits in the cargo compartment requiring that their crews ride in their vehicles for the entire length of the flight.

The pilots were in radio contact with both the glider's occupants and the crew of the tug aircraft. Crews of the tanks and Bren-gun carriers started the engines of their vehicles just prior to tow release, a special ducting system venting exhaust fumes. Upon landing the large nose of the Hamilcar was unlatched, swung to starboard and, by releasing hydraulic pressure from the wheel strut shock absorbers, the nose was lowered. The drivers of the tanks and weapons carriers pulled a lanyard that released the anchors that held their vehicles in place during flight and drove out of the glider without the use of a ramp. In the event that the nose became jammed during descent and landing the vehicles smashed through the nose of the glider and onto the field of battle.

Several problems surrounded its production, including the availability of materials, fabrication technicians, and locating an airfield with sufficient space for storage and takeoffs using its large tow airplane, most often the Handley Page Halifax bomber. But despite these problems eighty of these transport giants had been produced and were ready for participation in the Normandy invasion on 5/6 June 1944.

Hamilcar glider disgorging a Bren carrier. *Life*

4

German Gliders

It had clean sharp lines. It looked rugged. The swastika on the tail was hardly needed to identify it as a German warplane. This was the DFS 230 (*Deutschen Forschungsinstitut für Segelflug*—German Research Institute for Gliding Flight), a troop carrier/cast members transport for *Götterdämmerung*. Originally conceived as a high altitude meteorological research glider in the mid-1930s, Ernst Udet, Director of Research and Development for the new German air force, observed a test flight of the glider and mused about its use. With modifications could this be used as a troop carrier, an airborne *Trojan Horse*, an aircraft that could bring troops quietly and unnoticed behind enemy lines?

The first flight test, late 1937, was less than two years from the beginning of the war.[1] The Luftwaffe was no longer hidden from view and at the time of Hitler's ascension to power, Germany had 67,000 licensed glider pilots; eager young men who would be adopted by the military with open arms, pilots who could be trained to land this emerging aircraft of stealth onto a short landing spot and send its cargo of fully armed troops into battle.[2]

The DFS 230 was not a radical departure from conventional glider design. The high wing, supported by a single strut, was situated nearly at the half way mark of the fuselage that had at its base a central keel along its interior length. The frame, constructed of welded steel tubing was fabric covered, the wing, made of plywood and fabric, had narrow ailerons almost three quarters the length of the wing. The body was a narrow rectangle, like a child's pencil box set on edge. Equipped with a two-wheeled carriage that was jettisoned after takeoff the glider landed on a central main skid under the front portion of the fuselage. It was also equipped with a tail skid.

With a wing area of 445 square feet, its wingspan of 72 feet 1 inch was almost twice its length of 36 feet 11 inches. The DFS 230 was capable of carrying ten fully armed troops, including the pilot, six facing forward, four facing the rear of the glider, or the equivalent weight in cargo, 4,360 pounds. In addition to its passengers, the glider could also carry six hundred pounds of cargo, stored

German glider, DFS 230. *Courtesy of the Silent Wings Museum*

through a cargo door on the port side and in a smaller storage area under the wing on the starboard side.

Several variants of the DFS 230 emerged during the war. The primary production model, of which there were more than 1,600 built, was the DFS 230A-1, an A-2 version had dual controls. The B-1 and B-2 models were equipped with a braking parachute to assist in making steeper descents onto the landing zone of the battlefield and stopping in a shorter distance than their predecessors thus reducing the time it was vulnerable to enemy fire. The B-2 had the same alterations as the B-1 but was equipped with dual controls.

Both the B-1 and B-2 were equipped with a permanently fixed MG 15 machine gun behind the cockpit canopy that was hinged on the right side. Some of these later models of the DFS 230 also had machine guns mounted on the outboard side of the cockpit providing some level of protective firepower during landing.

Perhaps the most dramatic alteration to the DFS 230 was the addition of three braking rockets placed in a specially modified nose section of the aircraft. When diving for the landing area, the pilot released the braking parachute followed immediately by the firing of the rockets in rapid succession bringing the glider to a stop within 16 yards. It was this model, the DFS 230 C-1, that was used in the assault on Gran Sasso, the need for landing and braking in limited terrain essential to its mission.[3]

Other variant designs for the DFS were concerned with getting the glider airborne. The standard flexible tow cable of 131 feet was attached to the nose of the glider and the tail of the tug, most often a tri-motor Ju (Junkers) 52/3m cargo transport. In lieu of this flexible tow line, experiments were undertaken for a rigid tow attachment between the glider and the tow aircraft, a *starrschlepp*. This arrangement was favored for night and bad weather flying.

Cramped quarters for the nine passengers in the DFS 230. *Bundesarchiv*

Top and side-mounted machine gun, DFS 230. *Bundesarchiv*

Gotha Go 242 in free flight. *Courtesy of the Silent Wings Museum*

An even more radical experiment for getting the glider airborne included placing a single-engine powered plane on struts that attached to the top of the glider and the bottom of the powered plane. One such combination included attaching the DFS 230 with a wheeled undercarriage to a Bf (Messerschmitt) 109E-1, also referred to as the Me 109. The Bf/Me 109 was able to provide covering gun fire for the glider during its descent. Although successful through a series of test flights, this *huckepack*, "piggyback" combination was not widely adopted.

The DFS 230, a successful combat glider was limited in its ability to carry a large number of troops or a large amount of cargo. The call went out for something bigger and more capable of carrying heavier loads. The Gothaer Waggonfabrik company responded with a design that was singularly striking in appearance and in functionality—the Go (Gotha) 242. In its construction the Go 242 was not unlike other combat gliders flown during the war—a fuselage constructed of a combination of welded steel tubing over which fabric was attached, the wings, a mix of wood and fabric. Its most unusual characteristic was the twin tail booms extending from the top of each wing to a dual empennage and, what became the glider's appearance signature, a rear section of the fuselage that lifted upward for cargo.

The Go 242 had a number of variants for the undercarriage including skids under the midway portion of the fuselage and nose, a nose wheel and a pair of single wheeled landing gear just forward of the leading edge of the wings. The glider could also be fitted with snow skids place at the nose and in place of the wheeled landing gears.

Like most combat gliders employed by both the Allied forces and the Germans during the war, the Gotha Go 242 was configured in a number of variants. The Go 242 A-1 was a cargo carrying aircraft, the A-2 a troop carrying version added doors in the hinged rear fuselage and was configured for the addition of a braking parachute. Defensive muscle was also added with the ability to fit four 7.9 mm MG 15 machine guns—one on either side of the fuselage, one at the rear of the cargo area, and another mounted on the cockpit roof.[4]

Other variants were developed that included substituting the upward hinged rear door, with double rear doors. Improvements were made to the landing gear and the interior cargo area was modified to accommodate wounded soldiers who could be placed on stretchers attached to the sides of the fuselage.

The cockpit of the Go 242 A1 accommodated two pilots seated side-by-side and could carry 23 fully equipped soldiers, or nearly 8,500 lb of cargo. It had a wingspan of 60 feet 5 inches covering an area of 693 square feet. The overall length of the glider was 51 feet 10 inches, the cargo compartment between the twin tail booms was 20 feet in length, 7 feet wide and 6 feet in height, not providing a great deal of room for troops cramped inside.[5]

In the fall of 1940 the Führer's plan for the invasion of England was shelved, eventually to be completely discarded. The beaches at Brighton would not become the landing spot for the jackboots of the Wehrmacht. The white cliffs of Dover would not be scaled by Kommandoes of the German army. On the plains of Salisbury, the Home Guard would not see tanks disgorged nor 200 troops disembark from the Gigant, the massive glider ordered for the invasion of England, *"Operation Sealion" (Unternehmen Seelöwe.)*

It was massive. It was beyond massive. It was the largest glider ever built—its empty weight was close to 27,000 lb. A normal load was considered to be nearly 76,000 lb and it had a maximum overload of 86,860 lb. It is amazing that design engineers could find a way to create this wood, steel pipe, and fabric behemoth as a flying machine.

It seems quite improbable that a single crewman, the pilot, was assigned to fly the Me 321, but there was but a small single seat cockpit perched atop the fuselage at the leading edge of the wings of the Messerschmitt prototype that first took flight in early 1941. Although it was determined that a single pilot could handle the Gigant, it was physically demanding and it was recommended that for long flights the cockpit be redesigned to accommodate a co-pilot's position with full dual controls.

The cargo area was designed to be large enough to hold the contents of a standard railroad flat car. Clam shell doors at the nose were hinged at the sides of the fuselage and could only be opened from the inside revealing a cargo area of 1,100 square feet. With portable ramps leading to the inside, the Gigant could swallow a Panzer IV medium tank, a self-propelled assault gun with crew, ammunition and fuel or with the addition of a supplemental deck, 200 fully armed soldiers—a figure disputed by some.[6]

The Me (Messerschmitt) 321 Gigant—it was massive. *Courtesy of the Silent Wings Museum*

This high wing giant of a glider with a rectangular fuselage had a wing length of 180 feet 5 inches, sixty feet longer than the Wright brother's first powered flight. Takeoffs and landings were major problems for the Me 321, a process made dangerous because of its size and weight. The wheeled undercarriage was jettisoned once airborne and spring loaded skids attached to the forward section of the fuselage were used for landing. Up to eight rockets placed under the wings just outboard of the wing struts could be fitted for takeoff assistance and a braking parachute was available to facilitate deceleration.

Getting the aircraft airborne was a major problem as the glider required almost 4,000 feet of paved runway for itself and its tugs—a multiple towing procedure using three Bf 110C fighter planes. The triple-tow, *Troika-Schlepp,* required superb flying skills of the three pilots of the tow planes as well as the pilot of the glider. A single aircraft designed to replace the triple-tow plane configuration was a five-engine conversion of two He (Heinkel)111 Z bombers, the wings of each merged at the center with the addition of a fifth engine.[7]

Landing required 1,310 feet of uncluttered landscape—not often found near the front where the cargo of the Gigant was intended to be unloaded. In addition to the requirements for takeoff runways of considerable length, the Me 321 also needed special ground vehicles for maneuvering the aircraft on the ground and a storage area that could accommodate its size. The logistical requirements of the Me 321 made it of limited value to the German army although 200 were made, most serving on the eastern front resupplying soldiers with fuel, ammunition, food, and other supplies.

Messerschmitt Me 321 gliders on airfield *c.* 1942

5

Japan and the Soviet Union

In addition to the United States, England, and Germany each developing and using combat gliders of various types, both Japan and the Soviet Union also saw the value of glider aircraft as troop and cargo carriers. Perhaps the most striking of the small collection of gliders produced by both countries is the Kokusai, Ku-7, code-named by the Allies, *Buzzard*, and by the Japanese something a little more refined and reflective of the aircraft's gliding abilities, *Manazuru* (flying crane).[1]

The Ku-7 built by Kokusai Aircraft Company was a twin boom glider that in some respects resembled the German-made Gotha Go 242. The cargo compartment with a hinged door at the rear could accommodate a small tank or similar equipment or 30 troops including a pilot and co-pilot. Even though it was successful in test flights it was never used in any combat operations and only nine were built.[2]

A more conventional design was developed by the Kokusai Koku Aircraft Company for the Ku-8-II transport glider. The Ku-8-II was an adaptation of an engine powered transport airplane. The two engines and fuel tanks were removed, and a wheeled undercarriage that could be dropped after takeoff was added; skids attached to the bottom of the fuselage were used for landing. The most innovative operational characteristic of the Ku-8-II was the addition of spoilers, a separate set of four foot long wings at the trailing edge and above both the port and starboard wing panels. The spoilers could be turned to as much as a ninety degree angle from the horizontal to give additional lift or could be used to reduce lift and speed. Although spoilers were found on other gliders used in the war, the ones of the Ku-8-II were unique in their placement above the wing and the degree of angle that could be controlled.[3]

Designed to carry 18 fully-equipped troops it could also accept, through the hinged nose at the front, a small artillery piece or other wheeled equipment with a total weight of almost 4,000 lb. With a reported 700 built it was used in campaigns in the Phillipines.[4]

The Soviet Union's contribution to glider warfare included two combat-cargo gliders, the Antonov A-7, capable of carrying seven troops including the pilot, and

Kokusai Ku-8-II (*Gander*)—note the spoilers above the wings.

Kokusai Ku-7 Manazuru "Buzzard", heavy transport, capable of carrying 32 fully equipped troops.

the Gribovski G-11, with a passenger load of eleven troops including the pilot. With 400 to 500 produced during the war years, they were used to supply Soviet partisans, operating behind German lines disrupting enemy communications and transportation routes, with provisions, trained soldiers, and weapons.

The Antonov A-7, a high wing monoplane constructed mostly of plywood, had a wingspan of 59 feet, an overall length of 34 feet 7 inches and a cargo compartment that accommodated six passengers or a load of approximately 1,800 lb. Like the G-11, the A-7 had a landing gear that could be retracted by hand, the mechanism for raising it situated between two seats in the middle of the compartment. This aircraft had limited space for its occupants with two seats in the front, behind the cockpit, and two in the back of the passenger/cargo compartment facing each other and two in the middle, one facing forward, the other facing the rear. Cargo was loaded through two doors at the port side in front of the wings, and two at the rear of the fuselage on the starboard side.

The fuselage section of an Antonov A-7.

The Gribovski G-11, constructed primarily of plywood, was a high wing aircraft with a single pilot cockpit that had an upward hinged canopy. It had a fixed landing gear enabling it to come down on improved landing strips, or the gear could be folded manually giving it the advantage of being able to land using a skid underneath the fuselage on fields, with a shortened landing area. Empty it weighed 2,640 lb, and could carry the same total weight in cargo. The G-11 had a wingspan of 59 feet and could accommodate ten troops sitting on folding benches in the cargo compartment.

6

Tugs and Tows

Before it became the primary utility plane of the Second World War, it enjoyed commercial success as a passenger airliner, the DC-3. Then when war came, like other civilians, it was drafted into military service and became known by its GI name, the C-47, the Skytrain and by the British as the Dakota.

In its conversion from peace-time passenger plane it would continue this role by carrying service personnel to all theaters of operation during the war in two rows of metal "bucket seats" that lined either side of the inside of the fuselage. It would be adapted to carry paratroopers and tow gliders in Europe, the Mediterranean combat areas, the Pacific and in the China-Burma-India (CBI) theaters.

There were 10,692 C-47s produced during the war at a cost of $88,574 each.[1] They were powered by two 1,200 horsepower Pratt and Whitney engines with three bladed propellers, had a wing span of 95 feet, and a cruising speed of 185 mph with a maximum speed of 230 mph at 8,500 feet. With a maximum loaded weight of 26,000 pounds, a ceiling of 23,200 feet and a long distance range of 1,500 miles it was dubbed the flying truck.[2] General Dwight Eisenhower noted in his personal account of the war that most senior officers felt that the C-47 was one of the four machines that was responsible for winning the Second World War—the other three included the two-and-a-half-ton truck, the bulldozer, and the jeep, none of which were designed for war-time use.[3]

But this unassuming legend of air transport of the war had its flaws, even 'fatal flaws.'[4] It was unarmed, unarmored and, arguably worst of all, it did not have self-sealing gas tanks. But for these flaws, it could take a pounding by flak and shell and still be airworthy.

In the CBI, a modified version, the C-47B, was fitted with extra fuel tanks and engine blowers for high altitude making it possible to fly the *Hump* over the Himalayas from India to China 'carrying a total of 650,000 tons of supplies in all. These flights were often difficult due to severe winds, weather, and deep cold temperatures, not to mention enemy action.'[5]

Its wide double doors on the left rear side of the fuselage made loading personnel and materiel easier and it could be converted to serve as an airborne ambulance accommodating 21 litter patients.[6] The C-53 version was a paratrooper only adaptation and lacked the large cargo doors and strengthened floor of the C-47.

The C-47 Skytrain/Dakota.

"It could take a pounding." *Courtesy of Clyde Martin Litton*

Inexperience among some of the transport pilots, combined with the sheer terror of flying a lumbering transport plane into combat, sometimes at night, in bad weather, with poor navigational aids and confined to radio silence, contributed to the 'every man for himself' syndrome. It took a special kind of hero to tow a fully loaded glider to the proper release point while enemy flak was indiscriminately violating the structural integrity of your plane, and machine gun bullets tore through your fuel tanks and hydraulic lines. When you consider that transport planes sometimes had wounded on board, were on fire, had engine trouble, and wing tips shot off, it is no wonder that confusion sometimes reigned supreme in airborne operations. If that is not enough there were the sights, smells, and sounds of battle to contend with.

In one particular well-documented incident, a glider pilot advised the C-47 pilot that the starboard engine was on fire and spreading over the wing of his plane and working its way down the fuselage. Rather than think of himself the C-47 pilot remembered his mission and had his entire crew bail out while he stayed at the controls and delivered the glider he was towing to the proper release point.

Early in the war the British favored using armed bombers for transporting paratroopers and towing gliders. Even after the American-built C-47, known in the RAF as the Dakota, came into widespread service in 1942, the British continued to use bombers to tow gliders in airborne operations.[7]

British Horsa and Hamilcar gliders were towed by a variety of tug aircraft, all armed bombers—the twin-engined Armstrong Whitworth Albemarle and the larger four-engined bombers, the Short Stirling, the Avro Lancaster and the Handley Page Halifax. The largest, the Avro Lancaster was used primarily as a tug for the large tank carrying glider, the Hamilcar.

For the glider troops who rode to war behind a C-47, their experience was no less frightening nor dangerous than the transport's crew who had the mission of getting them to their LZ (landing zone), at the right place and on-time. One glider infantryman remembered:

... (W)e were ready to go. This was it. The weather was perfect ... The gliders were stacked up end-to-end on the cement runways and alongside of them on the grass were the big C-47 Dakotas ...

"Hook your safety belts, the Nylon tow line is fastened, they're taking up the slack . . . hold on!"

Then with a lurch the tail comes up, the nose goes down, the plywood creeks, (*sic*) and we are barreling down the runway. Long before the tow plane leaves the ground the speed sends the flimsy glider skyward. Then the C-47 comes up under us and we're off for the rendezvous area. Gliders ride higher than their tow planes, and we can see the sky full of planes and gliders, including our own tow plane below us, roaring out to get into our respective position in the four column line.

First, over the English countryside with its tiny checker box fields, and then out toward Blitz Creek (the North Sea). Some of us would never see England again. We all had a lot of thinking to do. A thousand times we'd been over the plan of what to do, when, and where. Would this be a milk-run, a suicide, or neither? Once the initial takeoff and thinking spell

Above left: Armstrong Whitworth Albemarle.

Above right: Handley Page Halifax.

were over, we settled back for a 275 mile, three hour journey. Some combat veterans actually went to sleep, while others read, thought, prayed and watched the scenery. I just got sick. After the first fifteen minutes, I had already been sick for thirteen. Flashing my hash was but a momentary pleasure among the agonizing minutes between flashes. Seventeen times I tried to throw up the lining of my gizzard and sixteen times it said, "NO, I like it here!"

Out over the North Sea we could see a steady stream of traffic all around us and an occasional Corvette cutting the water below. Thunderbolt fighters would flash momentarily in the sun above us while from some other English field groups of six C-47s without gliders but with their cargos of paratroopers caught up and crossed our path at an angle. To our left and above there was a stream of British Horsa (Flying Boxcar) gliders with their Lancaster bomber tow planes. This was it, "the biggest air show on earth."

Huge four-engined Forts (B-17 Flying Fortresses) their silver bodies and high tails shining cross overhead on their way to pulverize Germany. And always the Spitfires, Thunderbolts, and Mustangs, so small yet so deadly, darting under, over, criss-crossing through the otherwise helpless air convoy they were protecting.

Occasionally a glider or a tow plane struck by flak or mechanical difficulties would be seen in the sea. I spotted two Horsas, one C-47, and one American CG-4A down which is a remarkably small percentage when you consider we were in on the greatest air invasion to date. On the wing of the American glider stood two lone figures. Were the others drowned or was it a cargo glider with only two aboard?"

As we roar over "flak island," that big mass of land in the Zuider Zee, the smoke puffs that denote ack-ack start to rise, but always the fighter planes harassing their accuracy. One burning C-47 is seen crashed in a field, but the chutes on the ground indicate all the paratroopers and crew had bailed out in time.

Most of Zeeland had been flooded in an earlier attempt by our Air Corps to bomb the dikes and keep the Germans bottled up. On one high spot stood a Dutch house, three trees and a glider which had made a perfect forced landing on the only available ground.

As we made our air trek inland, the flak grew heavier and the land grew drier. In between watching flak bursts, we could see the Dutch people in their Sunday-goin'-ta-meetin' clothes out in the streets of their villages and hamlets waving us on joyously with both arms. For them, after 5 years, it must have been a truly astonishing and inspiring sight. Soon we saw some of the parachute planes coming back on the sky road to England. They gave us the "W.C. Fields" nose light greeting. For them, it was the last lap of a run well won, for us, a reassurance for the tense climax ahead.'[8]

It would make little difference whether the tug was an American C-47, a British Short Stirling, or a German Ju 88, the pairing of glider and tow plane had to be a team effort from the loading, to the taxi and takeoff, to the release point. A directive from the United States Army Air Corps (later to be changed to the United States Army Air Force) spelled out what the SOP (Standard Operating Procedure) would be when operating as a glider tow, its first operational procedure emphasizing this point: "The tow ship and glider crews will be formed as a team and will function together at all times when practicable."[9]

PART II

The Men and their Training

7

The Men

Who were the men who flew the gliders of war? Where did they come from? What did they say about themselves, what did others say about them. Why did they decide to fly gliders? What were they like as men, men who flew in aircraft that others thought were of questionable worth? Or, as a chaplain of the British airborne described gliders as being, 'distinctly unsafe.'[1] *Oh, glider pilots; aren't they the guys who had more balls than brains?* Maybe so, but it was the "G" on their pilot's wings that proclaimed to all, *The "G" stands for guts.*

In their own words, here is who they were, and for those who survived the war, this is who they still are today.[2]

> Glider pilots were made up of lawyers, husbands, bankers, borrowers, students, professors, doctors, salesmen, storekeepers and professional soldiers. They were an aggregation that could turn into a group of suave cosmopolitans in London at the Ritz Bar or be at home in Sloppy Joe's in Fort Wayne, Indiana.
>
> We were the bastards of the air corps, an uninhibited breed of our own, brash high spirited pilots (who) were not a bit bashful about letting everyone know what the "G" stood for on the silver wings they proudly wore.

Glider pilots of the Second World War had never been seen before:

> they were a hybrid like jackasses with no need to reproduce themselves; definitely one of a kind understood only by themselves and some completely beyond understanding.
>
> They call the fellows all kinds of great names, GP, Good Pilot, Glamour Pilot, even Piss Ants by commercial pilots etc. But no matter what these men were called, G.P. was the short for GLIDER PILOT, or as some of us said, "Guts and Glory Boys."

It has been said that those who signed up were recklessly brave, or bored with their desk jobs, or were those who couldn't pass the physical requirements of the

United States Army Airforce glider pilot's wings: "The "G" stands for guts."

air corps. These were the fellows who wanted to avoid rain-filled foxholes and the trudging of the infantry. As a result, they rode in aircraft that lost crucial parts in flight and sometimes came back to earth like a wingless crowbar dropped from a thousand feet. They were seduced by Lady Danger and like their brethren on the other side of the Atlantic had one thing in common—the desire to fly.[3]

> We were the crazy ones ... we were all just eager to fly, and learn. Glider pilots were distinct individuals with upbeat attitudes.
>
> Ted could bitch more than any man I've known. Schapiro played the sax, and was quite a lady's man, but he still could blush easily! Scheck was a strong slow moving thinking fellow, who would do anything in the world for a friend. John was quite a character. Steim was a quiet person, never bothered anyone. Bob had worked on the railroad back in Pennsylvania, and seemed to want to be drunk as much as possible. He sure could make quite an ass out of himself in a group.
>
> Whether they entered the troop carrier commands because they dropped out of other programs, were turned away from fighters because men were needed to fly transports and gliders, or because they were crazy enough to volunteer, they all came because they wanted to be military combat aviators.

The toast offered at the annual reunion of the National World War Two Glider Pilots Association, reflects who they thought they were in the past and how today they remember themselves:

To the Glider Pilots—conceived in error,
suffering a long and painful
period of gestation,
and finally delivered
at the wrong place
at the wrong time.

To some extent American glider pilots were a rough crowd who loved pulling off pranks and living up the swashbuckling image of being part aviator and part commando:

> The most pervasive memory I have of Louisville was the addictive, highly charged 'aura' which took over when the sun went down. Every evening 3,000 well-paid glider pilots would head for the city in search of liquor and female companionship. The Seelbach Hotel was 'headquarters' for these prowling, carousing commandos. The overriding emotional attitude of all the GPs (glider pilots) was to live-it-up, NOW, for there might never be another tomorrow. As a result, most the GPs spent everything they could beg, borrow, or steal to have a good time.

But like all such revelry, it was difficult to keep these experiences for *satisfaction and enjoyment* within the limits of the city. As these new commandos of the air were finishing their training one base commanding officer expressed rather vividly his outrage over the boys' accomplishments:

> I called you out here to tell you how 'wonderful' you are. Obviously none of you ever go to church, less than 5% of you are buying War Bonds, I have over $5,000 dollars in 'bounced' checks on my desk, and you have filled nearly three wards in my hospital with venereal disease. This is not my definition of what a 'gentleman's' code of behavior should be. You are a raunchy bunch of humans, and a disgrace to the rank of officer. If I could, I would court martial each and every one of you. Since I cannot, I am placing Louisville 'Off Limits' to all glider pilots, until you finish your training and get the 'Hell-out-of-here.' Dismissed."

When men volunteered to become glider pilots they had to face a reality other aviators did not:

> Combat glider operations represented the most dangerous aviation pursuit of the entire war. Every time an Allied glider pilot soared into the air, attached to his tow plane by a 300 foot nylon rope, he defied gravity in a way that no other combat aviator did. They were unique because they were highly skilled aviators who intentionally crash-landed their aircraft behind enemy lines, where they remained in combat and fought like infantry until it was safe to get extracted.

> I was no different than other young boys. I wanted to be a cowboy, a fireman, a policeman, a major league ball player, and finally a pilot—and just about in that order. I was one of the thousands of Depression children and in my town, family, church and school were given top priority. A handshake was as good as a contract.
>
> I had taken a pilot's license while in Billings, 1939–41, and flew acrobatics, etc. I heard an advertisement on the radio about the army's need for glider pilots. The ad (advertisement) said that they needed 6,000 pilots and I was patriotic and wanted to do my patriotic duty so I decided that's what I wanted to do. I didn't want to fly fighters—those were throttle jockeys—they had 3,000 hp engines and all they did was push the throttle back and forth. In a glider you really had to know how to fly the plane.
>
> I was 18 and living in the small town in Oklahoma when Pearl Harbor was bombed. Thirty days later about 200 men of military age out of a population of 2,500 were in some branch of the armed services.

The US Army Air Forces campaigned to entice young Americans to 'Soar to Victory as a Glider Pilot.' A recruitment brochure offered: NEW Flying Opportunities—for men between the ages of 18 and 35 who want to serve their country in the air. When you complete your training, you'll KNOW your GLIDERS and your AIRPLANES! Let the enemy find out for himself, the hard way, when the gliders arrive! This is a real flying job, and requires REAL FLYING ABILITY![4]

> I came to the program after being washed out of aviation cadet training. I was a cadet in the navigation school when the glider pilot recruiters came to visit us. They had a razzle-dazzle recruiting program that was designed to appeal to the people who were pretty reckless. We were told that as soon as we signed up we would become staff sergeants and after six weeks of training would be second lieutenants. Then we would go on a secret mission from which many of us wouldn't return. But, those who did would be majors within a year. Well, you can imagine how exciting that sounded to a bunch of young cadets, so we told lies and busted our fannies to get in.

It was not long before reality set in; training became intense and sleeping in tents on canvas cots did not seem the way to attain the glory, much less the rank and the pay envisioned by the recruiters. What the recruiters did not mention, and did not know in the early days of the war, was what the combat experience would be like:

> Imagine flying a flimsy, unarmed, fabric-covered CG-4A glider loaded with infantrymen, cartons of highly explosive ammunition, gasoline and TNT at tree-top level, through a murderous barrage of heavy flak to crash land in a tiny field surrounded by 80 foot trees, planted with big anti-glider poles and deadly land mines and sometimes flooded. Then as you crawl out of the wreckage of your glider you

> are charged by big tanks and hostile enemy forces tossing hand grenades and firing small arms, mortar and machine gun fire at you. It was like flying a stick of dynamite through the gates of Hell.

For glider guiders and glider riders their experiences together were put in song by an unknown member of the 82nd Airborne Division and was sung to the tune of the "The Daring Young Man on the Flying Trapeze":

One day I answered the popular call
And got in the Army to be on the ball
An infantry outfit, foot soldier and all
Is where they put me to train
They gave me my basic at Camp Claiborne
Till one day they split us and made us Airborne.
And the pay is exactly the same.

Oh, once I was happy and now I'm Airborne
Riding in gliders all tattered and torn
The pilots are daring all caution they scorn

We glide through the air in our flying caboose
Its motion is graceful—just like a big goose
We hike on the pavement till our joints have come loose
And the pay is exactly the same.

Once I was a bastard and now I'm a dope
Riding in gliders attached to a rope
Safety in landing is only a hope
And the pay is exactly the same.

We fight in O.D.s (Olive Drabs) not fancy jump suits
No bright leather jackets, no polished jump boots
We crash land by gliders without parachutes
And the pay is exactly the same.

We glide through the air with Joannie the Jeep
Held in our laps unable to leap
If she breaks loose our widows will weep
And the pay is exactly the same.

We hike and we sweat and we load and we lash
We tie it down well, just in case of a crash

And if it cuts loose there's no chance of a dash
And the pay is exactly the same.

We glide through the air with the greatest of ease
We do a good job and try hard to please
The Finance Department to pester and tease
AND THE PAY IS EXACTLY THE SAME.[5]

And then there was the fellow who grew up different from the rest, a child movie star who wanted more than anything to be like everyone else and do his duty for his country. Jackie Coogan volunteered like those before him not only to fly gliders but fly them in India on a night raid behind enemy lines. "Flying gliders in the war was the only thing dad considered worthwhile in all of his life."[6]

He returned home and was discharged from the service in 1945, to be burdened forever with memories that would wake him up in the middle of the night, shouting, 'They're coming over the hill!'[7]

In the UK, one young man:

> joined the army as war clouds gathered—you could smell it coming. I joined the war to cover myself with glory, and medals, and free beer for the duration, surrounded by adoring females.

Spoken like a true patriot.

> I left school at age of 14 and was apprenticed to a company manufacturing equipment for dental surgeries. On my 18th birthday I took the King's Shilling given to volunteers for the armed forces and after going through primary infantry training, was posted to

Jackie Coogan, front row, far right. *Courtesy of Anthony Coogan*

> the RME (Royal Electrical and Mechanical Engineers) with the rank of Craftsman. Later an appeal was made calling for volunteers to join the Glider Pilot Regiment with the warning that "This might be hazardous." With two friends, I put my name down and we were sent to the RAF to see if we had "flying aptitude." I was accepted.

Like those who volunteered for glider pilot duty in the United States, those who answered the call in Britain came from a wide range of backgrounds.

The son of a pilot of the British GPR (Glider Pilot Regiment) remembers:

> I don't know why dad joined up, he had to lie about his age by putting a false birth date on his joining up papers. It appealed to him, his friends were joining and he enjoyed sports and being outside. He first joined the Gloucestershire Regiment and later volunteered for the gliders. He always wanted to fly and whilst on leave here and when overseas he and his mates did many wild things because they did not think that they would survive the war, which is not surprising as I believe that the Glider Regiment had some of the highest casualties of the UK armed services.
>
> They didn't pick fights with Americans but there was some friction and even some envy at how well supplied the US troops were. He enjoyed a beer and the company of his friends from the Regiment and was very proud to be part of an elite group and to wear the red (maroon) beret.

This son's father may have had a touch of envy with the US troops about how well outfitted they were, but another pilot remembers that when he and his mates descended upon Salisbury during breaks in their training, they would pick fights with the US troops who also hit town at about the same time looking for a little rest and recreation. They would drink the town dry but only if they had their jam jars well stuffed under their tunics with a string that went around their necks and around the lips of the jars. Glassware during the war was a scare commodity in many pubs and if you didn't bring your own drinking glass you were out of luck. When imbibing the string was tied around the wrist in order to keep the jar close at hand, from falling to the floor, or getting lost when you were drunk.

The son continues telling about his dad's days as a glider pilot:

> When not training it could be very boring and dad described some wild drinking sessions in local towns and sometimes having to 'borrow' transport home including a Canadian army jeep one night because they had missed the last transport back to camp. In North Africa it was probably worse as they were miles from anywhere with little to do. I believe that dropping empty bottles from training flights onto local Arab camps was a sport they all enjoyed.

Whilst some may have been in a position to invade the local pubs and raise a little hell, there were others who weren't quite so lucky.

> We were always training, physically or flying. The physical part was a daily run-march in battle order, with a weapon, ammunition and everything one would carry when going into battle; four miles to be covered in one hour.

England became the gathering point for the build-up of Allied forces and materials for the invasion of the continent from the north. For some of the US forces it was difficult for them to remember that they were coming to a land that had been at war since September of 1939. They were not familiar with British customs, the differences in language, or the everyday living conditions the English were experiencing as their cities were bombed—rationing of food, clothing and other necessities of life.

The US War Department issued a small handbook, *Instructions for American Servicemen in Britain*, in an effort to educate the men about the differences and the similarities of the two countries.

> Remember there's a war on ... the British people are anxious to have you know that you are not seeing their country at its best ... The houses haven't been painted because factories are not making paint—they're making airplanes. The famous English gardens and parks are either unkept (*sic*) because there are no men to take care of them, or they are being used to grow needed vegetables. British taxicabs look antique because Britain makes tanks for herself and Russia and hasn't time to make new cars ... The British people (want) you to know that in normal times Britain looks much prettier, cleaner, neater.

And about a serviceman's behavior:

> The British dislike bragging and showing off. American wages and American soldier's pay are the highest in the world. When pay day comes it would be sound practice to learn to spend your money according to British standards. They consider you highly paid. They won't think any better of you for throwing money around; they are more likely to feel that you haven't learned the common-sense virtues of thrift. The British "Tommy" is apt to be specially touchy about the difference between his wages and yours. Keep this in mind. Use common sense and don't rub him the wrong way.

Don't forget:

> Sixty thousand British civilians—men, women, and children—have died under bombs, and yet the morale of the British is unbreakable and high. A nation doesn't come through that, if it doesn't have plain, common guts. The British are (a) tough, strong people, and good allies.'[8]

A US glider pilot became friends with a family near his base and wrote about them to his wife back in the States. When his wife responded to a letter from one of the adult women of the family, she asked if there wasn't something that she could send to the young woman knowing of the lack of goods available to English citizens. The return letter to the glider pilot's wife tells about life in those war years and what the family had experienced:

> I cannot thank you enough for thinking of me in asking if there is anything you could send me. Dorothy, you could never realize what it is like here in the way of clothes rationing and cosmetics, and anything you send me I can assure you would be more than appreciated.
>
> I would like some stockings, if possible. I take a 4½ shoes and if you could send me some step-ins (aka knickers/wide leg panties), I take an ordinary woman's small size, and well Dorothy, just anything.
>
> Did I tell you I work in an aircraft factory, 12 hours per day, 5½ days per week, so you can guess Dorothy I get very little time off myself. My sister, Ivy, 21 years of age, and my brother Robert, age 17 years both work in the aircraft factory. Bob and myself both are machine operators and make various parts of planes, but my sister works in the office.
>
> My father is in the Navy and came home about the end of May and that was the first time we had seen him for almost five years. His ship had been torpedoed four times and he was injured very much, but he is now better and on a ship in Portsmouth.
>
> The war news is great now isn't it? I think the war will be over soon, don't you? Won't it be just lovely to get back to normal again.
>
> Mummy says if you come to England you are to come and spend your holidays with us. We should like to have you.
>
> One day we hope to visit America and find out all about this lovely place Jack's always talking about. I'm sure it must be a lovely place to live in.
>
> Yes England is a very lovely place, but of course lots of it has been spoiled with the continuous bombing, but we really are very proud of our England.
>
> I guess this is all for now ... so I must close, hoping you will answer my letter soon.
>
> Sincerely yours,
> Jackie

But, it was the men, those who flew the gliders, those who raged through the terror of combat that tell the story that culminated in victory. Inscribed on the chapel doors at the American cemetery in Luxemburg, the eight virtues associated with being a good soldier serve as a reminder of the character of those who volunteered to serve.

Physical Fitness	Fidelity
Proficiency	Sacrifice
Valor	Family Ties
Fortitude	Faith[9]

The boys who became men in plywood and canvas planes were a different breed of cat from other airmen, those who flew powered aircraft. In addition to the eight virtues of any good soldier, seaman, or airman, glider pilots had to have nerves of steel, a personality of solid brass, courage beyond the norm, ice in their veins, tenacity and be risk takers at a moment's notice. A former member of the British Glider Pilot Regiment summed the experience of being a glider pilot with words fit for all who flew these fragile aircraft:

> It's not easy to make generalizations about the glider pilots that I knew and respected, because they were all individualists, sometimes to the point of eccentricity. When asked "how" and "why" they joined the regiment, boredom with what they were doing previously and the desire for action and excitement rated high on the list. Educational levels were higher than average, though some of us came from quite low on the totem pole socially.
>
> I've never met a glider pilot who did not feel that he was a member of something special. Glider pilots were frequently engaged in acts of extraordinary initiative and daring in response to dangerous situations.
>
> I was fortunate enough to become a member of a group of people who, like myself, were very ordinary guys, serving maybe in obscure stations, but who lived through not so ordinary experiences. To me they were special and still are. I was very fortunate.[10]

8

Training: Washed Out—RTU—LMF

The USAAF was specific about its expectations for the outcome of training of its glider pilots:

> Glider missions require precision flying under all conditions—in formation flying, minimum altitude flying and in flying with full loads. Glider pilots must be able to fly under nearly all conditions of visibility and enemy action and must be able to land safely at a given place at the proper time.
>
> In summary, training for all glider pilots will include:
>
> (1) Flight training
> (a) Landings: minimum speed landing, spot landings in restricted areas, landing over obstacles in limited areas, landings from various approaches, 90°, 180°, 270°, etc., minimum altitude approaches, high night approaches.
> (b) Familiarization with all types of landing gears and skids.
> (c) Knowledge of various formation, both en route and for release.
> (d) Proper technique for free flight, proper glide angle and gliding speed.
> (e) Proper technique in employing flaps, spoilers, tail parachute, and such other equipment as may be available to assist in short landings in restricted areas.
> (f) Proper technique in flying auto-tow equipment under all conditions: day, night and instrument.
> (g) Proper employment of pick-up device and glider handling during pick-up.
>
> (2) Combat training
> All glider pilots should be given intensive combat training consisting of basic infantry drill, infantry tactics, and the use of infantry weapons. The nature of their employment necessitates this training.

One veteran glider pilot expressed the importance of this training requirement:

> When you landed behind enemy lines you never knew what to expect. When we landed we were expected to go with the guys into combat until we could make our way back to an assembly point for the return trip home. Some pilots wouldn't be seen after landing for a couple of weeks or so; they weren't too anxious to return because they had been shacking-up with French or German girls and didn't want to give that up.[1]
>
> Glider pilots should not be considered as single-mission men, for the time required to train them to be pilots and the cost of that training do not warrant such employment. As soon as practicable, glider pilots should be evacuated for subsequent operations.

In Britain in early 1943,

> I was like millions of other young men. I had changed overnight from being a carefree seventeen-year-old to being an eighteen-year-old guardian of King and country. Like most of my fellow conscripts, I had only a hazy idea of what the future had in store, but sitting on a 40 mm Bofors gun (an anti-aircraft cannon in common use during the war) didn't seem to be it. Our sergeant an ex-coal miner from Tyneside was a tough, broad chested well-muscled man, but generous and fair minded, with a somewhat robust sense of humour.
>
> I was bored most of the time and one day read on a bulletin board at headquarters a notice asking for volunteers for a newly formed regiment of glider pilots. Although I had only a vague idea of what a glider pilot did, I volunteered immediately. I was given a pass to go down to London to attend some kind of selection board. We took various tests for agility, co-ordination, hearing, eyesight, colour blindness and a few I.Q. tests. When word came that I had passed the tests and was to report for training at Fargo, a camp on the Salisbury Plain, my sergeant's farewell, with a broad grin, was "Next time we see a glider, Martin, we'll shoot the fucker down."

It was at Fargo that the winnowing process began, where the raw recruits to the regiment were assigned to a team of instructors who did all they could to try to break them or toughen them to the hazards and dangers of flying gliders.

> We were subjected to a systematic regimen of what can only be described as mindless bullshit. We spent most of our time polishing boots or brass work, cleaning rifles in preparation for endless inspections and drill parades or blancoing web equipment (blanco was a compound of either powder or soap-cake like form used to colour various webbed equipment parts to a specific color often related to a specific branch of the military, e.g. the RAF Blue—the Royal Air Force). We were continually subjected to shouted commands, to be instantly complied with.

Failure to obey to any of the commands or expectations to the instructor's satisfaction resulted in being sent back to one's parent unit with notations on personnel files of, RTU (Return to Unit) and LMF (Lack of Moral Fibre), notations that were to carry no stigma attached to the individual. "No stigma attached." Not bloody likely!

> The company Sergeant Major from the Scots' Guards, reputed to be almost human when sitting over a pint in the Sergeants' Mess, was six foot two, ramrod straight, with fierce blue eyes and a pointed waxed moustache, and with a broad Scottish accent, could strike terror on the parade ground. Most of us, I believe, would have been far more willing to face the enemy in battle that to face his scornful invective on the parade ground.

Another glider pilot from England remembers his training at Fargo where:

> a team of instructors did all they could to try to break you so that you would ask for RTU. This breaking process had two parts, physical and mental.
>
> Each morning reveille would be at 0600hrs—be on parade at 0630hrs in battle order for a run-march of four miles to be completed in one hour, five minutes marching, five minutes running. That was followed by breakfast, but should the one hour time limit be exceeded, it was "Let's go round again."
>
> The mental side of our training was more devious. We slept on steel beds on which were three pads called 'biscuits.' These, laid end-to-end, formed a mattress. Each morning, after breakfast, every item of ones kit was to be laid out for inspection, in a specified order, on top of these stacked biscuits. Some would fail that inspection. Something was always "not good enough." Trousers had to be well pressed, though they could have been soaked the previous day and boots had to be polished to a high shine. Those still there at the end of this six week process were promoted to the rank of corporal and could, for the first time, enter the corporals' mess to be greeted by a painting on the door of a hideous grinning devil; beneath this were the words: "So you want to be a glider pilot." From that day on, nobody requested an RTU.

In the United States, training was no less demanding:

> Training officers from Fort Benning, Georgia were assigned to teach us mental toughness. One of their favorite activities was to make us stand at attention until someone in the ranks passed out.
>
> Boy, was I a really hot rock! Me, in the Air Corps, and going to fly way the hell above the heads of the Coast Artillery where I had come from.

Transformations were occurring. Civilian clothes were put away. Uniforms were issued. Brass was polished, boots were shined and beds had to be made so that a coin could bounce off the top; that was the 'Army way.' Boys became men. Men became soldiers and in time, soldiers would become pilots and pilots would become glider pilots.

They learned a new language. Mess kit—a combined metal kit consisting of a plate, cover, knife, fork and spoon for use in the field or in combat conditions; canteen—portable water container with attached cup; lister bag—36 gallon canvas bag for storing water; KP—kitchen patrol to include everything from washing dishes to peeling potatoes.

On the second day, I made my first military mistake. While getting water out of a lister bag, I laid my mess kit on a ledge by the lister bag. The Mess Officer asked who it belonged to. As a good recruit, I said, "It belongs to me, sir." He said it was my first cardinal sin, and he personally took me to a large grease trap and told me to clean it out. Never again did I lay my mess kit down.

Additional words and phrases made their way into a glider pilots vocabulary:

Air knocker: Aeronica three-place glider.

Bird brains: what it takes to be a good glider pilot—the ability to feel air currents and trace blind sky trails by instinct.

Braid the rope: Occurs when gliders swing in toward each other on the tow, causing the rope to bend and stiffen. (Too many braids and you're washed out.)

Deadleg: Pilot's leg when he's on the right or left side of a three-glider tow and must hold full right or left rudder to prevent collision.

Flying freight car: Big troop-carrying glider.

Gravy slot: Center position in a three-glider tow where the pilot can relax and enjoy the scenery.

Kangaroo landing: Landing in which a student bounces the glider along the runway.

Riding the prop wash: When the glider gets too low and falls into the wash from the tow plane's propeller, causing the glider to bounce roughly.

Sweat out a thermal: Try to find a rising current of warm air so the glider will soar.

Thread/Joy string: Rope/cable to tow gliders.

Thread the needle: Several gliders trying to land at the same time'.[2]

The goal was to make them tough, to instill in them the need to follow orders, to recognize that there would come a time when you reacted to an order when

Glider missions require precision flying under all conditions.

someone said, 'Give me more flaps; give me more spoilers.' You pushed the flaps down, you pushed the spoilers up because somewhere, sometime in the past a burly infantry sergeant had bellowed at you:

> If I come out here with one ear missing, you fall-in out here with one ear missing.

One training objective for glider pilots was to make them a contributing part of the fighting force they were carrying in behind enemy lines. As a result, the War Department:

> ... decided it would be appropriate for us to be equally useful in the pursuant battles. Our specific task here at Bowman Field for the next five months was to take "Commando" training and become proficient in all the phases of combat. We were trained in the various martial arts jiu jitsu and judo in the day time and then go to Louisville and practice on the "tank jockeys" from Fort Knox in the evenings.
>
> Once a glider pilot who had been an All-American football player in college and weighed 185 pounds of steel was challenged by a trooper in the NCO Club (Non-Commissioned Officer). The glider pilot told the trooper that he wouldn't fight him, but would fight the biggest and meanest son-of-a-bitch the troopers had. In about ten minutes the biggest meanest trooper I had ever seen walked in, the heavy-weight champion of the division boxing team. The action started, and after these two bulls had pounded each other for a while, they stopped and asked each other, "What in the hell are we doing this for?" Everyone had a beer together and the glider pilots were accepted from that point on.
>
> A next training step was to master all the weapons the airborne would use in combat. It was only natural to start with the M-1 rifle and the 45 pistol (the M-1 rifle

was the standard rifle issue to U.S. infantry; the Colt 45 caliber pistol the side-arm weapon issued to officers).

We spent seventeen days at Fort Knox on the firing range—we would shoot one day, and pull targets the next. We ate from portable kitchens on the range and rode trucks back to Bowman Field. One day while shooting, a guy next to me accidentally fired his weapon. This resulted in a seven-mile hike from the gate of Fort Knox before we could load up and head back to Bowman Field.

Later in England, we spent two weeks on the firing range of the 82nd Airborne, at General Ridgeway's request, and were checked out on all airborne weapons that might be a part of our load on a glider. These included the Thompson sub-machine gun, the Browning rifle, the Bazooka, the 30 and 50 caliber machine gun, the M-3 Grease Gun, throwing hand grenades, and working with a crew on the 57 mm anti-tank gun. The airborne leadership wanted us to be able to fill in and support any airborne units.

One of the most difficult tasks encountered during our training was making forced marches, twenty-five miles per day, with full field pack, and only one canteen of water to last all day. It was hard to decide whether to drink the water or use it to bathe your feet. A marching band would join us for the last mile, and help us finish with a flourish, otherwise they would have had to jack up the seat of our pants to keep us from sweeping the streets.

Another equally difficult task was jumping from a forty foot tower into a swimming pool covered with burning oil (to simulate the "abandon ship" evacuation from a torpedoed troop ship.)

The British were also demanding in the process of turning each glider pilot into a 'complete soldier.'

The airfield at Denham lay beside a wood, and it was here that a certain Colonel assisted by an Irish captain had constructed a battle course. The captain, a parachutist, seemed to be in love with high explosives and gunfire, in that order, and had secreted charges of amatol (an explosive mixture of TNT and ammonium nitrate) at various points along the course, timed to explode just before or just after we hit that part of the course. The captain contributed to the course by screaming invective and firing live ammunition over our heads, as we scrambled our way through the course. At the end of it we were supposed to crawl through a ditch, and under a low plank bridge, holding our jungle rifles above shoulder level to keep them dry. However, thanks to the captain's liberal use of the amatol, the ditch had become flooded with thick oozing mud, leaving very little air space under the bridge. Consequently, it became impossible to keep our rifles uncontaminated with mud. Emerging from the ditch, we were supposed to charge down the last stretch with fixed bayonets, firing live ammunition. Unfortunately, thanks to the captain's efforts, all our rifles had become liberally smeared with wet mud, and refused to fire. Panting, mud bespattered and exhausted, we lined up before the colonel. Wearing his best uniform and his WWI medal ribbons, his leather riding boots shining like mirrors, he gazed down as us in extreme distaste. "Only one rifle fit to fire" he said. "Dismissed!"

Only Sissies Need Engines

Now only sissies need engines
A real man needs only the air
Soaring on high like an eagle
We glide with never a care.
You can have your high-powered 'Cyclones'
And your liquid-cooled 'Allisons' too
Give me a handful of thermals
And a quick thunderstorm or two.

A bomber needs two miles to land in
A glider needs sixty-five feet
A fighting plane lands at two hundred
A glider lands slowly and sweet.

Now I've got no use for a motor
A true one may seldom be found
They're temperamental and vicious
They love to let you down.

Oh, give me a fast-flying glider
With wings long and graceful and thin
Set me loose in the air over Dover
And we'll win in the streets of Berlin.

We'll go on some dark, moonless evening
With five jeeps and a six-by-six truck
Close in with sixty commandos
Aided by God and by luck.

Now after we capture Herr Hitler
An have Göring sewed in a sack
There's only one question unanswered
Just how are we going to get back?

By Cornelius J. Dwyer

The tests of coordination, strength, and vision were passed, the medical examinations taken again, and yet again. Finally it came time to put the basic indoctrination and inoculations behind and begin what they had all volunteered for—flying. From the beginning, it was clear that there was a lot to learn but one basic and potentially life-saving lesson had to be learned and learned well:

> We were assigned a Flight Instructor, six students per instructor. In the orientation before the first flight our instructor said that he wanted us to have an understanding before we had a misunderstanding. We were to know at all times what was in front of us, what was behind us, what was to each side of us and what was above us, and he said I want to see your eyeballs moving at all times ... "AND GENTLEMEN, HAVE I MADE MYSELF CLEAR?" (To this day I have a consciousness of what is going on around me at all times.
>
> Flight school turned out to be a pre-glider exercise using small, single-engined aircraft. We would take off from a large grassy field and gain whatever practice altitude was specified for that day. The engine would then be turned off making a forced landing necessary. After gliding back to the field for a practice landing, the engine would be started by a ground crew person pulling the propeller (by hand) through its rotation so another flight could be made. These 'deadstick' landings simulated 'no-engine' glider flight and were designed to provide us with experience and confidence in our ability to establish a viable flight pattern and pinpoint a landing upon some targeted landing spot. The spot landings were practiced during the day time and also at night.
>
> After the first few landings and takeoffs like these you kept your eyeballs peeled and your head on a swivel... If you let the daytime deadstick landings make you nervous, you were bound to become absolutely paranoid over the same training at night.
>
> The constant thought of moving on to the next phase of our training encouraged us and everyone was relieved when the pre-glider course was completed and we boarded a troop train heading to California for the next phase of our training—flying sailplanes at Twentynine Palms.

Twentynine Palms, on the 'high' desert of southern California, must have seemed like the end of the earth and civilization for those were part of the 1,600 glider pilots trained at this facility. But as an historical marker on the now abandoned site reads:

> Condor Field had the primary mission of training glider pilots for airborne operations during World War II. To accomplish this the Army Air Corps established 29 Palms Air Academy. This area provided reliable winds and thermal air currents to keep the gliders aloft.

The marker fails to acknowledge that day time temperatures in excess of 100 degrees Fahrenheit at Condor Field are the norm.

> We flew Switzer sailplanes and the TG-5A, a modified Aeronica. Training in these aircraft was predicated on the number of landings you made and not flying hours. In flying the small sailplane you learn that there are always down-drafts on the leeward side of a mountain range or large hills because the prevailing wind in normally from the southwest. Also, flying over cement or black top roads on a very hot day would cause you to experience up-drafts.

They would continue to fly the (modified Aeronica) 'Streamlined Bath-Tubs,' with nicknames like Hopeless, Sweet Potato, Red, Bug Eyes, Sharkey, Magillicuddy, and Downwind, and would become what their song proclaimed them to be:

US Army Air Corps Glider Song

On wings of Silence fly the Glider men,
The truest airmen of them all.
There is no roar of an engine, no whine of a prop.
But when the fight is over Glider men will be on top.
And when you see them soaring in the blue,
You'll know the job is being done.
We fly to free our country's liberty,
The Nation's battle must be won.
We are Commandos of the sky.
On wings of silence as the night
We'll give our all to do or die
To keep the light of freedom burning bright.*

[*The lyrics for the U.S. Army Air Corps Glider Song were written by aviation students 42-11 (the 11th class of 1942). Provided courtesy of the George Boyle private collection.]

In the next phase of training one of those who pursued the dream to become a 'commando of the sky' remembers something quite different from the glorious lyrics of the song they sang:

> Once again a troop train carried us back across the southern deserts to Fort Sumner, New Mexico. The town's only claim to fame was the tombstone of an outlaw who was buried there—Billy the Kid.
>
> Trucks took us far from town to a flat, mesquite covered expanse of nothingness, where two air strips were being graded for use. We were housed in four-man tents,

each with a wood burning stove to burn the mesquite roots being removed from the airstrips. Gravel pathways led to the latrine. We ate from mess kits and pulled our share of Kitchen Patrol (KP) and Guard Duty. Cold water showers were available for the hale and hearty and clean sheets were exchanged the first of each month.

Roll call at 6.00 a.m. in class "A" uniforms, started each day, followed by double time and close order drill. Our officers were "A-holes" and took great delight in making our lives miserable: "If someone falls down, run over them."

To celebrate my eventual promotion to staff sergeant I was 'invited' to pull KP for the Thanksgiving Day dinner. My job was to keep the trash cans full of boiling water to wash pots and pans. Eating the holiday meal from a mess kit was quite an experience. I found the pumpkin pie fits best on top of the mashed potatoes and gravy. Hot soapy water in trash cans cools when pots and pans are submersed and results in a residual greasy, soapy film (G.I. soap) that does not wash away completely during the rinse cycle and continually gets worse. The end result—equal expectancy for all, diarrhea.

In Britain similar training sequences were put in place for those who desperately wanted to walk under the sign of the Corporals' Mess that questioned a person's sanity with the exclamation about one's desire to be a glider pilot.

I think it's safe to say that with few exceptions, our main motivation was not patriotism, idealism or even male aggression, but simply the youthful desire for challenge, adventure and excitement.

While Condor Field at Twentynine Palms, California might have been described as the end of the world, a hot arid landscape filled with mesquite and rattlesnakes, it was the progenitor of training fields that were developed across the United States. America could provide wide-open spaces for flight training and still have the availability of supply and civilized social contacts within a relatively short distance from a training base.

The bucolic setting for Britain's first glider training base could not have been more different from the open spaces of the southern California desert than the small aerodrome in Haddenham, Buckinghamshire, to become known as RAF Detachment Thame. But questions arose across a broad range of concerns including the length of the runway at Thame and the colossal problems related to finding available airspace in the Midlands for training.[3] Eventually, training bases were developed and the work initiated at Haddenham blossomed to include other fields, notably at Booker Airfield, also in Buckinghamshire.

I was posted to a place called Booker, a small airfield in Buckinghamshire. This was one of several places designated as an EFTS, or Elementary Flying Training School. At this point we were all relieved and delighted to be issued with the proud maroon beret of the Airborne Forces, plus two stripes as trainee pilots.

It was at Booker that I learned to fly the de Havilland Tiger Moth, a biplane only a small step away from the fighter planes of the First World War. It was a most forgiving plane, versatile and maneuverable and you could do almost anything in it.

Like the famous flyers of earlier years, we wore leather flying helmets, goggles, flying suits and wool lined flying boots. Day after day we struggled slowly through take offs and landings, stalls, stall turns, spins and even an occasional loop.

The average instruction time before being allowed to go solo was, I believe, between six and ten hours. The famous Baron von Richthofen, who was not a naturally gifted flyer, took over twenty-five hours to solo. I was very pleased with myself when I was given permission to solo after eight hours.

After EFTS. I was posted to Stoke Orchard. At last, a glider. The Hotspur looked something like a large cigar with wings, with the pilot's cabin on top, one pilot behind the other. It could carry eight passengers and had little round port holes down the fuselage. It was not difficult to fly, but I would not have wanted to be a passenger in the back.

It was here that we learned the important difference between powered and non-powered flight. The most demanding part of flying is the approach to a landing. Should it go wrong for any reason, an approach that is too high, or too low, the landing run is obstructed or for any other reason, the pilot of a powered aircraft can open the throttle, climb and go round again for another approach. A glider does not have a throttle to open, so every approach to a landing must be right the first time. There are no second chances.

The nylon tow rope, about a 100 metres long, was attached to the nose of the glider by a sort of clamp, which was released by the pilot at the appropriate moment. On takeoff, the glider usually became airborne before the towing plane. We would cruise to about 2000 feet and pull off the rope just before approaching the runway. On very hot days it was possible for the Hotspur to maintain height or even gain a little height by gliding over the hot tarmac of the perimeter, but military gliders, even trainers like the Hotspur, were not built for sport, or free flights of long duration.

I doubt if I flew more than 20 hours on Hotspurs before being posted to another airfield to a Heavy Glider Conversion Unit, where we entered the final stage of training. Here we were introduced to the Airspeed Horsa and the Hamilcar, the two operational gliders. The Horsa was a large somewhat grotesque creation reminding me of a big black crow, yet it had remarkable flight qualities. The Hamilcar was even bigger and carried an enormous load. From the ground seen in flight, these gliders appeared to be very silent, but inside it was quite noisy. We did circuits, cross country, occasional mass landings, stall turns, and a somewhat hair raising type of landing in the Horsa which we called a "slash." This consisted of gliding over the near end of the runway at about two thousand feet, and then going into an almost vertical dive with full flap on, and landing in a remarkably short distance. Because of the width of those flaps the Horsa did not build up to a dangerous speed, even in a steep dive. I doubt if this maneuver was ever used on an actual operation, but it was interesting to know that the aircraft could do it all.

Not all who served in the pursuit of glider warfare during the Second World War were combat pilots and their lament of being bound to another job in the war effort, that of training the pilots for combat, is acknowledged by one of their own:

The Flying Instructor's Lament

"What did you do in the War, Daddy?
How did you help us to win?"
"Circuits and bumps and turns, Laddie,
And how to get out of spin."

"Woe and alack and misery me!
I trundle around in the sky.
And instead of shooting down Nazis
"I'm teaching young hopefuls to fly!"

Thus is my service rewarded,
My years of experience paid,
Never a Hun have I followed right down
Nor ever gone out on a raid."

"They don't even let us go crazy,
We have to be safe and sedate.
So it's nix on inverted approaches,
They stir up the C.F.I.'s hate."

"For it's oh such a naughty example
And what will the A.O.C. think!
But we never get posted to fighters
We just get a spell in the Link!"

"So it's circuits and bumps from morning 'til noon
And instrument flying 'til tea—
'Hold her off! Give her bank! Put your undercart down!
You're skidding, you're slipping'—that's me!"

"As soon as you've finished with one course,
Like a flash up another one bobs,
And there's four more to show round the cockpit
And four more to try out the knobs."
But sometimes we read in the papers
Of the deeds that old pupils have done,

And we're proud to have seen their beginnings
And shown them the way out of the sun:

So if you find the money and turn out the planes
We'll give all we know to the men
'Till they cluster the sky with their triumphs
And burn out the Beast from his den.

"What did you do in the War, Daddy?
How did you help us win?
Circuits and bumps and turns, Laddie,
And how to get out of spin!"*

*Words to the lament are provided courtesy of Peter Chamberlain as noted from the logbook of George Cliff. An internet website posting attributes the lament to Owen Chave.
C.F.I.—Chief Flying Instructor; A.O.C.—Air Officer Commanding.

Upon having attained the necessary skills came promotion to senior NCO (non-commissioned officer), the award of our pilot's wings, posting to an operational squadron and pairing of two pilots to form a 'crew.' For operational reasons, every glider had to have two pilots. Should one be disabled in flight, there was another on the flight deck able to take control; and secondly, it would be too tiring for one man to be at the controls on a long flight as no auto-pilot was installed. When the pairing had been made, the members would live, fly, eat and train together until they both knew that each could depend on the other, come what may. I should mention that parachutes were not issued to the men in gliders. We were now members of the Glider Pilot Regiment whose motto was, "Nothing is Impossible."'

At this juncture, their training completed, their pilot's wings attained, and the pairing with a second pilot, they were members of the British Glider Pilot Regiment, they raised their voices and sang with gusto:

A crashed glider pilot lay dying
as on the tarmac he lay;
to his comrades around him crying,
these last passing words he did say.
'Take the main spar from out of my backbone,
take the rudder from out of my brain,
from the small of my back,
take the instruments back,
and assemble my glider again.'*

*The composer of the lyrics is unknown and are provided here through the memory of GPR veteran, Frank Ashleigh.

Fifteen hours of advanced glider pilot training for many in the United States was received at South Plains Army Air Field in Lubbock, Texas, one of forty glider training sites scattered throughout the country. The CG-4A gliders were often towed aloft by the twin engine C-60, the Lockheed Lodestar.

> During the 15 hours of flight training and landings at the Texas base, we learned a couple of exciting things to do with the CG-4A glider. One operation was known as the "British Blitz." The gliders were released from tow some distance downwind of the airport. The glider pilot pushed the control yoke forward putting the glider into a fast dive. He would recover from the dive at about 100 feet above ground level, then utilizing the greater speed, he would exert back pressure on the control yoke as he approached a tree, building or other obstacle in his path, hedgehopping all the way to the runway, hopefully.

In addition to learning the 'British Blitz' a variation on this landing technique amid obstacles was remembered by another U.S. glider pilot.

> It seems that tactical minds in our War Department decided the invasion of Europe would take place in France. Because of stone walls erected between vineyards the current technique of landing would not work. This method required us to dive into the landing area, dump the glider up on the nose skids, and skid to a stop. In France the stone walls would stop us too abruptly. The answer was to land very slowly.

A Waco CG-4A coming in to land.

> Our task was to learn how to "slow glide" into very "short" fields. We called this new technique "Colonel Curry's Death-Glide," as we would be flying only a few miles per hour above "stall" speed. Below that speed the flight terminated in a fatal crash landing.
>
> To simulate short field landings, the ground crew drilled large holes across the runway and placed rows of cut trees in the holes.
>
> This was a costly learning procedure. Looking back I am sure we lost more pilots in death glide training and in short field maneuvers than we ever did in combat.
>
> Spoilers built laterally into the top wing surface helped to steepen the glide path and when extended upright to a full 90° the airflow would create turbulence and destroy the wing's lift. Consequently, the glide path resembled the flight path of a hotel elevator. We didn't even break the glide angle to land; no transition into a smooth landing, only a sudden "thump" as contact was made with the ground. We just established a glide angle, using minimum air speed, and waited for the impact. If necessary we used brakes and nose skids to stop. If not, we would mow down a row of trees. Needless to say, we kept the ground crew busy cutting forests to replace our mistakes. Obviously, when the glider wouldn't stop, the pilot guided the cockpit between the tree trunks. This procedure saved pilots but kept the glider factories busy replacing wings.

Memories of the advanced flight training at Lubbock are notable for their range of topics:

> Learning the meaning of "thermal," the strong up and down drafts when flying in west Texas, the 180 degree wind shifts every day, drinking the gyp water of west Texas (bitter foul tasting mineralized naturally occurring water that would make your teeth turn brown), and less obnoxious, the importance of football to the people of west Texas.

Members of the training classes feasted on special occasions. The Thanksgiving day menu from South Plains is testimony that while food may have been rationed in the civilian world, at this air base, those stationed there did not want for the components of the traditional holiday meal.

The Americans' British counterparts remembered meals that were a good deal less lavish.

> Dad remembered that the food was not great and I think that corned beef (bully beef) was a staple for the troops. I know that his parents sent him food when he was in the UK. They could get meat, etc. as they lived in the country and had pigs, chickens and shot local game. Also my grandfather was a gardener for a big country house so they could grow a lot of food themselves. Rationing for the population was very tough.

As with the RAF (Royal Air Force), we were fed rather better than the average squaddy (a member of the British Army) and there was always a large bowl of raisins on the bar, unheard of in Civvy Street (a phrase used by members of the British military for civilians/civilian life). We also had access to fresh milk from the farm nearby, chocolate, oranges and other special rations. The powers that be seemed to think that raisins improved night vision as did carrots, at least that's what we were told. In the Sergeants' Mess, there was always plenty of drink, beer and spirits, with the possible exception of rum. The hours during which the mess was open conformed to the licensing hours everywhere in the UK, but any member of the mess could request and often was granted a one hour extension, unless we were in readiness for an operation, then the mess would be deserted.

A training accident ends the career of this Waco CG-4A troop glider, 1942-43.

9

The Devil is in the Details

There were specific risks that were a part of glider operations that indemnify failure of a flight if ignored or were out of the immediate control of the glider crew. Even when all of the risks of glider flying were addressed, there were no guarantees as to the probability of a successful flight and landing. The risks were numerous, the reward, the ability to walk away from a successful landing. What contributed to the risk in flying gliders?

- Broken tow line between tug and glider.
- Malfunctioning communication line between tug and glider.

> On our flight to Arnhem, the telephone gave an ear-splitting whistle. It was so bad we switched it off and communicated with the tug by Morse Code using a torch (flashlight).[1]

- Release from the tug too soon/before the landing zone objective.
- Unmarked Landing zone or marked incorrectly.
- Weather at landing zone—fog, clouds.
- Injured pilot or co-pilot.
- Landing zone obstacles—trees, rocks, ditches, hedgerows, fences.

> One of our landings was pretty rough. We were coming in pretty fast and I had to go between two trees to stop the aircraft—it tore off both wings, but we stopped.[2]

- Cargo breaking loose during flight or landing.
- Anti-aircraft/flak attack.
- Attack by enemy fighter planes.
- Attack by ground forces while airborne or upon landing.

One time we were fired on just as we were landing and exiting the glider and one of the boys was hit. His friends dragged him to cover beneath a tree. He looked up at me and said, "Take my rifle, I'm dying." I reached down and took his weapon and he slumped back and died. That was tough.[3]

Despite these risks to tactical glider operations, the USAAF Troup Carrier Command shed a more positive light on the benefits of such missions:

Nothing that flies would seem to be quite so vulnerable as a formation of large ships towing gliders, at, say, a lumbering 120 miles per hour over enemy lines by broad daylight. But there is an effective defense against both ack-ack and fighter interception, known as contour flying. This means flying so low that the craft practically strums power lines, caresses treetops, and sets weathercocks whirling in their slip streams. They roar between farmhouse and barn, lift over hillocks, bank around hills, hugging the earth, in a breath-taking ride as rough as a Coney Island roller coaster. Doing that in a formation is about the toughest kind of flying there is for a pilot. But it's relatively safe if they don't hit anything. To startled enemy troops on the ground the planes have come and gone from sight before there is time to train gun sights on them. To enemy planes aloft there are no silhouettes to spot, and the streaking drab green surfaces are practically indistinguishable from the landscape.

The critical moment of such a daylight glider flight over hostile territory comes not *en route* but as the planes near the objective of the surprise attack. Then they must gain a few hundred feet of altitude before the gliders cut loose. The glider pilots must choose the fields in which they will land in a predetermined area, rightly judge their rate of descent, and get to earth as quickly as possible. Gliders are expendable, and landing among trees that will rip off their wings or on rocks that will stove their bottoms is common practice. The package of men inside is protected against everything but head-on collision by a framework of steel tubing.

The other distinctive TCC (Troop Carrier Command) glider tactical method is the silent night landing. This works in the reverse of hedgehopping flights by daylight, and takes advantage of the glider's ability to soar at a ratio of normally about fifteen to one; i.e., for every foot of altitude lost it can travel fifteen feet forward, more or less, depending on load and wind currents. Thus theoretically, always depending upon variable factors, a glider cut loose a mile high can travel silently to an object about fifteen miles distant, without the giveaway sound of its tow plane to spoil the surprise.[4]

The success of any sortie was in direct proportion to the skill and knowledge the pilot had of his aircraft. He had to be able to identify component parts, and their functions and complete pre-flight, post-flight and other inspections of his aircraft. In the Waco CG-4A glider a reminder, an operational checklist, was made available for the pilot and co-pilot under the instrument panel near the floor. And, when all is in readiness, ground crew and flight crew needed to communicate directions and intentions.

Standard Signals for Glider Crews. *Author's collection*

With the hours of practice required for mastering the demand of flying gliders, from take-offs to landings, and when all of the classroom ground subjects had been completed, there was yet one more skill to develop—"The Snatch."[5]

In the spring of 1942 the USAAF arrived at the decision that the troop and cargo carrying gliders under development were too expensive to be abandoned after one combat mission. The terrain in which gliders landed was usually too small and uneven for a plane to land and retrieve a mission-completed glider. While aerial retrieval of ground based objects was not new—the Postal Service All-American Aviation had demonstrated its practicality in 1939—such a retrieval system designed to retrieve one plane from a field with another had not yet been tried.

In 1942 the All-American Aviation (AAA) company tested a "snatch" technique using a specially designed wench mounted in a Stinson high wing monoplane. The Stinson successfully snatched from the ground a Schweizer military training glider and a Piper Cub minus its propeller. Following these successful demonstrations, the USAAF let a contract to the AAA company to develop and provide pickup equipment for its gliders using the twin engine C-47, Skytrain as the retrieval aircraft.

The "snatch" technique using a C-47/Waco CG-4A glider combination consisted of a nylon tow rope 182 feet long made by the E. I. DuPont Company. Tow ropes of nylon fibers were elastic and would stretch 25 per cent to 30 per cent of their length and absorb much of the shock as the glider became airborne.

A cable ran from a winch with a braking system inside the pickup airplane through guides to an external boom mounted on the fuselage, then to a hook at the end of the boom. The pickup airplane would fly approximately 20 feet above the ground over the pickup station and hook a nylon loop stretched between two poles approximately 12 feet above the ground. Just as the hook snagged the loop the pilot would push the throttles forward for a surge of power and climb away at a steep angle.

The pickup mechanism, bolted to the floor on the left side of the cabin about six feet from the front of the aircraft bulkhead, consisted of a controllable, motor-driven, energy absorbing drum containing 1,000 feet of flexible ⅝″ steel cable, twin pulleys, a torque tube, hydraulic cylinder and explosive cable cutter controls. The reel was equipped with a friction clutch that could be adjusted for different glider weights and speeds. The steel cable from the energy absorbing drum was secured to a polished steel hook at the end of a twenty foot wooden arm that was mounted on the left side of the fuselage. The amount of cable played out was directly proportional to the weight of the glider and the nature of acceleration of the glider after pickup and was usually less than 600 feet.

CG-4A troop gliders awaiting snatch by low passing C-47 Skytrain, Wesel, 17 April 1945.

C-47 Skytrain with hook lowered preparing to snatch CG-4A glider.

Glider retrieval station—"The snatch."

The retrieval C-47 approached the pickup station with the tow line attached to the nose of the glider at an indicated air speed (IAS) of 135–145 miles per hour and at a 45 degree angle. At the moment the tow hook snagged the trailing hook the winch drum began to feed out cable rapidly, then slowed as the brake took effect. The glider was snatched into the air in as little as sixty feet and went from zero to an IAS in as little as six or seven seconds.[6]

One American glider pilot recalls that:

I could hear the aircraft coming in behind me and then there was a sudden surge. I kept my knees against the yoke because we went from a dead stop to 120 mph straight up. It scared the crap out of you.[7]

Thirteen CG-4As were snatched from Normandy following D-Day, the remainder of the 292 Wacos and all of the Horsas were either too damaged from the landing or enemy fire that they couldn't be retrieved. The snatch was tested again when the interior of a CG-4A was modified to accommodate litters for the removal of combat wounded following the battle for the bridge at Remagen.[8]

Flight nurse Suella Bernard volunteered to accompany and care for the wounded soldiers on the litters in the Waco as it was snatched from the front and flown to a military hospital in France.

Since the aircraft used for air evacuation also transported military supplies, they could not display the Red Cross. With no markings to indicate their non-combat status, evacuation flights were vulnerable to enemy attacks. For this reason flight nurses and medical technicians were volunteers.[9]

For her courage and caring for the wounded in this modified CG-4A, 2nd Lt. Suella Bernard was promoted to 1st Lt. and received the Air Medal:

A decoration awarded to any person serving in any capacity with the AF (Air Force) who distinguishes himself (herself) by meritorious achievement while participation in aerial flight.[10]

PART III

The Missions

(In Chronological Order)

10

"Far Away Places, with Strange Sounding Names"

Some went on first class cruise liners—the *Queen Mary* and *Queen Elizabeth*. The *Queen Mary* during the Second World War was reconfigured from her role as a luxury ocean liner to a troop ship and at one crossing from the United States to Britain carried a total of 16,082 American soldiers. Her greatest protection from lurking German U-boats was her speed. She could cruise at 28.5 knots (32.7 miles per hour) faster than enemy ships that lurked about the ocean in search of the Gray Ghost, and earning the Führer's reward of $250,000 and the Iron Cross to any U-boat captain that could sink her. Her sister ship, the larger *Queen Elizabeth*, was also refitted as a troop ship and by the end of the war had carried 750,000 troops, cruising at 29 knots per hour (33.3 mph) across the Atlantic Ocean.

Others going to war sailed overseas in less elegant vessels, that were, nevertheless, capable of carrying large numbers of passengers.

> This afternoon, after two days of additional processing, standing in lines, final physical check-ups and sloshing around in rain and mud, etc., we boarded a 17 car train at 1700hrs. They were positively the oldest cars we had ever see, but it mattered little because it was only about nine miles from Camp Patrick Henry to the docks in New Port News, Virginia. At the docks we boarded our ship. I didn't see a man hesitate in coming up the gang plank, and if, bitching in general is any indication, morale is very high. The actual loading was very orderly, no blaring bands, no milling masses of friends, relatives, etc., just a single file of uniforms proceeding up each of the three gang planks.
>
> Our ship, the *Gen. W. A. Mann*, looks damn nice. She is 682 feet long, turns two 6 ft. props 100 rpm (revolutions per minute) to obtain a cruising speed of 19.5 knots (22.4 mph). Crew and Marines number close to 500 and it is capable of transporting 5400 passengers. Armament for unescorted crossings consists of three 5 inch guns, four 1.1 pom-poms (40 mm anti-aircraft guns), and ten 20 mm automatic ack-ack guns. She is equipped with radar for detection of enemy craft on, above, and below the sea for a distance of 10 to 80 miles. According to a crew member it was

commissioned only five months ago. Ours is to be its 5th trip. There have been three to Casablanca and one to England.

We were told that we officers would be berthed four to a state room—as it is, there are over 100 of us in about the same floor space as a three-car garage. Berths are 4 deep, the bottom one being about eight inches off the floor and the other three are stacked so that when lying on your back, the canvas of the above berth is no more than three inches above your nose. We are wondering where our B-4 bags (a government issued canvas folding garment bag), rifles, helmets, packs, etc. are going to ride. It seems that every available bit of space is devoted to berths.

Everyone was so tired last night that we didn't mind sharing our bunks with rifles, helmets, etc. but this morning we really fell all over ourselves trying locate equipment.

In the chronicle of events that identify battle actions during the war, operational code-names and place names are often used to locate unit participation and involvement of specific individuals, groups, or battle fields and fronts. Napoleon's defeat at Waterloo specifies a person and a location, the Battle of the Coral Sea, identifies an ocean battle and again, location, and the Battle of Britain evokes an historical event or series of events that are forever tied to the many who owed so much to so few. It is in this same manner that names identify missions in which the combat glider of the Second World War played a major role. These missions,

"Our ship, the Gen. W. A. Mann, looks damn nice." The U.S. Navy transport USS *General W. A. Mann* (AP-112) in San Francisco Bay. The photograph was probably taken during or shortly after the Second World War as ship is painted in Camouflage Measure 22. *All Hands Navy magazine, August 1949*

as a chronology of events mark fields of combat, but only partially cite the use of the glider as a component of the arsenal of war used by both the Germans and the Allied powers. Scores of sorties were flown that have gone unrecognized by name or circumstance. These flights accounted for the resupply of troops in the field, the evacuation of the wounded, the ferrying of gliders, glider parts and personnel and training missions beyond number.

> At 1102hrs., we cast off and started down the Chesapeake headed for—according to rumor—Casablanca. We were surprised by the absence of an escort—maybe it will join us later. However, a seaman gunner has informed me that this ship has never traveled in convoy. It's supposed to be able to out run a German sub and do 38 knots.

(43.7 mph! This is perhaps a little braggadocio or wishful thinking on the part of the seaman. A current US Navy internet web site states that a nuclear powered submarine typically travels at 25 knots/29 mph.)

> The food on board is excellent! Breakfast consists of orange juice, coffee, toast, cold cereal and fried eggs. Supper consists of steak, mashed potatoes, succotash, etc.—all very excellent. There is one hitch, however, on board a troop ship—unless assigned to a special job, two meals per day is all you get. My schedule is at 0900hrs. and 1700hrs.
>
> All day the sea has been calm, the roll is gentle, and the sun shining brightly. Our course changes about 20 to 30 degrees every 10 to 15 minutes, but we are headed generally east to south-east.
>
> God! What a long trip Columbus must have had. Ocean going tourists don't realize what a big pond the Atlantic can be without the benefit of magazines, deck games, beach chairs, etc. Our sole entertainment is a single radio in the officer's lounge. Most of us had too much equipment to lug aboard without worrying about reading material. The few copies of *Reader's Digest* or *Coronet* and various pocket book editions are rapidly becoming well-worn and much in demand.
>
> The weather, so far, has been quite beautiful. We are not allowed on deck during the hours of sunrise and sunset, nor during hours of darkness so most of our day is spent mopping up sunshine.
>
> Daily life on board varies but little. We get up about 0700 hrs., shave, and make up our berths and still have time for a turn around the topside before breakfast at 0900hrs. At 1330hrs., each day, we have a General Quarters drill which means going below to quarters while the ship's gunners get ready to swing into action. Below, we don helmets, rifle belts with canteens, and in general prepare to abandon ship.
>
> At 1700 hrs. we eat our second and final meal of the day, following which there is time for another hour topside. When the command "prepare to darken ship" comes over the PA system, we climb into the births. Any delay means getting undressed in the dark which is quite a job in our limited quarters. Lights out is at 1822 hrs.

There has been very little sea-sickness on board. Most of it has been among those who are low in the forward hold. None of the GPs (glider pilots) have been sick so far as I know. Robert Weller put it well when he said that "anybody who has flown the CG-4A in those Goddamn thermals of Texas hasn't any business puking on these decks." Guess he's right, the *Gen. W. A. Mann* is smoother than any glider I've ever been in.

There was a little excitement during the early morning which none of us knew about until later. As a sailor told it to me, at about 0135 hrs radar picked up an unidentified ship some distance off to port, making course so as to intercept us. He went on to say that we "poured the coal on," took off to the starboard, and outran whoever or whatever was after us. For two hours, we raced along at 28 knots (about 32 mph) until finally the other craft turned back. We, in our hold compartment, had no idea what was going on. Some of us woke up noted the rough ride which we credited to a rough sea.

We were awakened a little earlier today to prepare to leave the ship. The morning was very cloudy and the sea calm. At approximately 0930hrs we got our first glimpse of land. Out of the bright mist in the east rose Casablanca, almost ghostly, so brilliant were the white buildings. The size of the city amazed all of us. It is a very large and quite modern city. Except for several ships sunk in the harbor, there was no reminder of our grim purpose in being here.

There appears to be three classes of people in town—the rich are French landowners, born in France and now own large farm tracts in the surrounding area. The poor are the native Arabs, dirty, syphilitic, and crippled. The middle class, some quite prosperous, are refugee prostitutes, women from France mostly, but others from Belgium, Holland, and Spain. Men in uniform, particularly Air Corps, are continually being approached by little Arab kids with "sucky-fucky 1000 francs." Or, "fucky sister, 500 francs," etc. A franc is now worth about 2 cents American money. The size of the bills is from ½ the size of our dollar to "wallpaper," four times the size of our bills. Arab whores for the most part are so horrible that few American boys will touch them. The refugees are a different story. All you have to do is find an interpreter and state your business. The price is 500 to 800 francs but most of it can be had for 200 to 250 francs. Money, incidentally, is a poor medium of exchange. American cigarettes are the most valuable commodity, then "American bon-bons," and then chewing gun.

Tonight, we boarded a train in Casablanca—and what a train. It is about 35 cars long and is made up of three of the most outdated wooden coaches I've ever seen. They have wooden benches, a hole in the floor to use as a toilet, no stool, and only 4 wheels.[1]

One ocean and one outdated wooden railroad coach closer to the war.

11

Another Route to War, Another Destination to Combat

The troop ship voyage to Casablanca lasted a matter of days, boring days perhaps, but nonetheless, days. The trip to Britain on the *Queen Mary*, also a trip of days at sea, was somewhat hateful as the soldiers were hot-bunking with one group occupying the bunks for a period of time, followed immediately by another group and so on until the passenger manifest had rotated through the available bunks.

For those glider pilots who were sent in search of other combat zones, they boarded planes in Miami and flew towards what many described as the forgotten front—the China, Burma, India theater, the CBI. The Japanese had crushed through the jungles of the Far East swallowing up Singapore and Malaysia, Siam and Burma threatening to punch into India.

To help in the Allied efforts to stop them, gliders were to become a part of the equation to halt the enemy flow through the jungles and prevent an incursion into India, the bastion of the British Empire in Asia. Placing gliders, at five crates of body parts each aircraft, their pilots, mechanics and ground crews in useful position and bringing in the tow planes, their crews, equipment, ancillary support personnel, gasoline for the tugs and the planes flying the Hump across the Himalayas required a massive logistics effort that could become stymied by the monsoons of the jungles and the aggressive advances of the enemy. The gliders in their crates would have to be transported by ship, a trip from the west coast of the United States to Karachi, India, that would require weeks.

One glider pilot remembered his trip by air to the CBI theater of war destination of Asansol, India in a C-54 Skymaster, a larger and more luxurious troop plane than he had been used to. The trip was weeks in duration and the sights at locations along the way were replete with commentaries of life and the conditions of war far from the combat zones of either the Pacific, European theaters or the jungle dominated battles of the CBI.

> Arriving in Karachi was an overwhelming experience. Never before had I ever been exposed to so many people or so much poverty. It was a heart breaking initiation to a way of life we Americans cannot conceive in our wildest dreams.

RMS *Queen Mary* photographed from HMS *Revenge*, 1942, somewhere in the Indian Ocean. *Queen Mary* as a troopship carried up to 16,000 servicemen.

RMS *Queen Mary* in troopship livery, 1945, returning US forces to Manhattan.

On top of this we were obviously not welcome, or wanted, in India. Signs were posted everywhere, or painted on fences, that said, "Yankee Go Home."

We five glider pilots spent about three weeks in Karachi, essentially doing nothing. Replacement gliders had been unloaded from a ship and were being assembled in Karachi. After assembly we had to fly them to make sure everything worked as it should. I always insisted that the crew chief who put the glider together fly with me on my test flights. I figured this honor was a testimony to the quality of his work, and insurance on my part.

I hired a personal servant while in Karachi for 1 Rupee per day, about 32¢. He called himself the "Brooklyn Bum." He was one of the homeless street kids who learned to speak some English. He acted as my guide, as my interpreter, and as a protector for my highly polished boots. The street urchins would try to smear beetle nut juice on my boots. He would say, "This is my man—get away." I liked him because he was innovative. Most beggars chant "bakshees, bakshees, Sahib." His approach to me was, "Shoe shine, Sahib. No mama, no papa, no flight pay—bakshees."

During this stay in Karachi, I found it necessary to ride bicycles with hand operated brakes mounted on the handle bars, a first for me. On one of my rides I purchased a pet monkey, a male Rhesus monkey I named "Joe-Monk." He would fly co-pilot with me during the long glider flights across India. We would fly from Karachi to Agra and then on to Asansol (approximately 100 miles north of Calcutta.) Each leg of the journey would take about 7 hours of flight time behind a First Air Commando Group C-47 transport plane. Joe Monk didn't care much about gliders. By the time we reached home base he had turned a very, very airsick green.

On our last flight to Asansol from Karachi we learned that we were to be the replacement pilots for those who had lost their lives at Broadway during the first phase of *Operation Thursday*.[1]

12

Eben Emael: Old and Conventional *vs* New and Unconventional

It is a conflict as familiar as are the arguments put forward by young bloods eager to be heard, and the old pros who have been around the block once or twice and have the scars of experience to show for it. Old versus the new, the conventional versus the unconventional.

The Old and Conventional

The fort near the Belgian village of Eben Emael, could, in retrospect, appear as a relic of war from the past and sorely out of place at the beginning of the armed conflict of the Second World War. Fort Eben Emael, built after the First World War as a fortress on the eastern reaches of Belgium sat almost on the political border of Holland. The Maginot Line, starting at the French/Swiss/German border snaked its way along the common border of France and Germany, a line of fortifications and obstacles designed to stop an invasion force from Germany. Fort Eben Emael, although not a part of this massive French defensive system to repel intruders sat at some distance from its northern terminus. Described as a "superb" fort by the standards of the First World War, at the dawn of the Second World War, it was no more than a 'good' fort.[1]

Eben Emael, a diamond shaped fort with its northern tip pointed towards the Dutch town of Maastricht, measured, at ground level, 1,100 yards north to south and 800 yards at its widest point, was a reinforced artillery position that had a commanding view of the countryside. On its east side, the walls of the fortification dropped away to the surface of the Albert Canal and yards away on its western perimeter was the Geer River. For external defense, a water filled ditch/moat was constructed in the northwest section of the diamond and in the southeastern side of the perimeter a twenty-foot high anti-tank ditch was constructed.[2, 3] Anti-aircraft positions, machine gun emplacements and blockhouses completed the seemingly impregnable fortress.[4]

Armament of the fort was divided into two batteries, one with a non-retractable cupola sat-on a platform that revolved 360 degrees and housed two 120 mm guns with a 12 mile range. The battery also employed two 75 mm guns in cupolas that could also revolve 360 degrees and had a range of seven miles. These cupolas, covered with 12 inch thick steel domes, could be elevated up to four feet above the casemates (concrete reinforced gun emplacements) in which they sat. In addition the battery contained four casemates, each with three 75 mm guns with a firing range of five miles.

The second battery consisted of ten gun blocks with one or two 60 mm anti-tank guns, 30 caliber machine guns, searchlights, and a small observation cupola. On the top of the fort seven anti-aircraft machine guns were strategically mounted, along with three false cupolas, and three large cupolas that served as observation platforms for the forts in Liege. Machine gun emplacements were embedded in casemates of the northern perimeter in the sheer embankment overlooking the Albert Canal. From these posts the Belgians could destroy the bridges and locks of the canal with explosive charges controlled from the casemates.

The majority of the physical structure of the fort lay underground, a rabbit warren of tunnels seven miles in length connecting its various artillery positions, fire direction control center, ammunition storage areas and command centers. Other sections of the fort contained barracks, a hospital, electric generators for the heating and air conditioning systems, and a purification plant for water from its internal well. Fort Eben Emael was the impregnable key to the Belgian defense system and was considered one of the most powerful fortifications in Europe.[5, 6]

The mission of Fort Eben Emael: protect the roads, canals, locks, and bridges bordering Holland and the northern approaches through Belgium leading into France.

The New and Unconventional

It was clear that the route to northern France for the German army was through the Low Countries which meant that the Führer's troops would have to take control of the rivers, roads, bridges and canals of Holland and Belgium. But the steel and concrete underground fortress at the juncture of the Meuse River and the Albert Canal along the Dutch-Belgian border stood squarely in the path of Hitler's war machine. The German High Command advised Hitler that it would take six months and cost the lives of 6,000 soldiers to conquer the impregnable fortress at Eben Emael.[7]

It was the Führer himself who made the connection between the unconventional and the conventional, landing gliders in a surprise attack on top of Fort Eben Emael—an unconventional move against a conventional deterrent of frontal ground attack. In late October 1939 Hitler summoned his newly appointed commander of the 7th Airborne Division, Major General Kurt Student, to Berlin. He had a question that would test his general's concept of three dimensional warfare—inserting airborne troops behind enemy lines and with secrecy and speed and overtake the enemy where and when he least expected. Could a glider-borne force be landed on top of and secure Fort Eben Emael? The next day the Führer received the answer he had wanted. Yes, it was possible but under special circumstances. The attack had to occur at dawn or morning twilight, a time when the Belgian defenders would be at their most vulnerable—not quite awake, their alertness compromised.[8]

General Student was warned of the need for the utmost secrecy regarding this plan for there was yet one additional weapon besides the glider-borne troops that would be made available to Student. The characteristics of this weapon were of such a nature that only a select few in Germany knew of it: a one hundred ten pound explosive device that blew inward and not upward as in a conventional explosive charge, a *hohlladung*. Along with a twenty-five pound smaller vision, these explosive charges (hollow charges and known in the US as shaped charges) could tear a six inch hole through steel and concrete showering those below with molten metal and shards of concrete. The *hohlladung* was not shot from a cannon but put in place by two or three soldiers, fused and exploded on site.[9] The need for secrecy was obvious—no one must know of the development of a new plan of attack from the air and an explosive device that could topple even an underground fortress.

It was only a short period of time after Student received his orders from Hitler to take Fort Eben Emael that the responsibility for planning and executing the mission was assigned to an officer of one of his regiments, Captain S. A. Koch. Koch's choice for the on-the-ground leader of the operation to take the fort was a young engineer (pioneer) officer, Lieutenant Rudolf Witzig, who began at once putting into place planning and training that would in later years be the hallmark for operations known as "spec ops" (special operations). In order for a spec ops to be successful it must exemplify simplicity and have a limited number of objectives, a good stream of intelligence about the target and innovative and unconventional methods for successful completion of the mission. Additional components of a successful operation of this nature include: security about the plan of attack, practice of methods for taking the objective, surprise, and speed.[10]

Each of these components was set in place for *Operation Granite*, the codename given to the Fort Eben Emael spec ops. The other segments of the overall mission, taking intact the Vroenhoven, Veldwezelt, and Canne bridges, were codenamed *Concrete*, *Steel*, and *Iron*, respectively. The objectives were limited: take the fort and the river and canal bridges below.

Each member of the attacking force would have a specific objective—taking out a specific gun emplacement or other target assignment. Intelligence about the site was readily available with information provided by aerial photographs, blue prints of the fort from a German construction subcontractor, German workmen who had participated in the fort's construction, deserters and in the most unbelievable of places. Belgium had produced postcards and postage stamps that depicted the shape and dimensions of the fort.[11,12]

The time for the attack, as unconventional as the method, vertical assault with the use of the German DFS 230 gliders, was for an early morning landing while the dew of dawn would still be on the blades of the vegetation atop the fort and the defenders would likewise be in a half-state of wakefulness. Glider pilots practiced landing after landing so that they would be able to bring their aircraft to a stop within a twenty meter area, barbed-wire wrapped around the wooden landing skids at the bottom of the glider to assist in preventing skidding and slicing through the meadow-like top surface of the fort.

The new explosive device, its characteristics known only to Witzig, became a challenge in physical management with its bulk weight of one hundred ten pounds. But members of Witzig's platoon, each carrying a half of the charge, ran with it again and again, learning how to man-handle it and set the fuses so that the hollow bomb would explode as intended.

The assault on Fort Eben Emael started with the first of the Ju 52 tugs and gliders lifting off at 0325 hrs at airbases near Cologne; the last of the group, Witzig's glider, became airborne at 0335 hrs. It was a large assault group that approached the fort and bridge objectives—ninety-six troops were assigned the mission of capturing the Vroenhoven bridge and groups of ninety-two men were assigned to take the Veldwezelt bridge and the Canne bridge.[13]

At 0505hrs the gliders, heavily loaded with troops, guns, and explosives, cut away from their tow planes and descended to their objectives. At a distance of only four miles from Cologne, Witzig's glider was forced to land in order to avoid collision with other aircraft and would arrive at the target objective two hours past the planned landing time; another glider was forced to cut loose 25 miles east of the target. The others:

> ... despite taking anti-aircraft fire ... landed within yards of their targets at Fort Eben Emael.[14] In their eagerness to attack the casemates at Objective Granite, troops catapulted out the glider doors and even burst through the fabric sides of the aircraft. Within the first twenty minutes the decisive struggle was over. German sappers (combat engineers), with their hollow charges, systematically destroyed the Belgian casements, neutralizing the big guns ... and trapping the Belgian fort garrison of 650 inside.[15] Meanwhile, German pilots ... landed their gliders near the other objectives allowing the glider troops to capture two of the three targeted bridges intact. By 1300 hrs on 11 May 1940 ... Belgian (forces) defending the fort surrendered.
>
> The glider assault of Fort Eben Emael, in conjunction with widespread airborne operations in Holland and Belgium, opened the way for German armor to drive through the Low Countries into France.[16]

The battle of Dunkirk and the evacuation of British and Allied troops followed the fall of Fort Eben Emael a little more than two weeks later.

In London, Friday, 10 May 1940, the papers reported that Germany had invaded the Netherlands, Belgium and Luxembourg by land and air and had appealed to Britain and France for help. The attack on Fort Eben Emael was not reported; other news was more critical: The prime minister had resigned and advised the King to ask

"Meanwhile, German pilots . . . landed their gliders near the other objectives." Courtesy of Willi Gänzler (German glider pilot)

Winston Churchill to form a new government, an event that, in the end, would be the most important news of the day.[17] Two days later, the *Daily Mirror* with bold headlines reported that during the previous night the 'Abbey, Houses of Parliament Bombed.'[18]

In the United States, the war was distant and for some awareness was no more no less than what was available from the daily newspapers and radio broadcasts. The change of government in Britain, and the invasion of the Netherlands and Belgium by German forces shared newsprint space with information about the available movies for a night out: *His Girl Friday*, *The Grapes of Wrath*, *The Shop Around the Corner*, and *Rebecca*.

A post-war appraisal by German military leaders of glider tactics and the assault on Fort Eben Emael included an evaluation of the tactical advantages of combat gliders:

> A commitment of gliders has the great advantage that they land their whole load in one place. Since debarkation is a matter of seconds, the troops can bring their full fire and striking power to bear immediately after landing. The almost noiseless approach of the gliders, which have been released from the tow planes far from the objective, increases the element of surprise. Furthermore, diving gliders are able to make very accurate spot landings within a limited area. Glider troops are also able to open fire with aircraft armament upon an enemy ready to repulse them. While the glider offers pronounced advantages during the first attack on an objective which is defended, in the subsequent phases of the airborne operation its advantages over the use of parachutes lie in the fact that it can deliver substantially greater loads, such heavy weapons, guns, tanks, and trucks.[19, 20]

13

Unternehmen Merkur—*Operation Mercury*—Crete

The German airborne *Operation Mercury* was the classic struggle of one party wanting something someone else has. The British and Commonwealth forces held Crete, the German forces wanted it. The island, 160 miles in length, east to west, varies in width from 37 miles at its widest and 7.5 miles at its most narrow point. A significant feature of the island is the scoliosis spine of mountains that divides it into a northern and southern half. In the end, the Germans would take control of Crete but the cost to both sides of the ten day campaign would prove to be staggering.

There were 42,460 troops in the Allied forces. These were troops from Britain who had been garrisoned in Crete; those who had escaped from Greece over the bridge at the Corinth Canal when Germany came to the aid of Italy in its efforts to take over Greece, and ANZACS—soldiers from Australia and New Zealand. In addition there were Greeks and a large contingent of Cretan irregulars defending the island. Out of all of these 1,751 were killed or became missing in action; 1,738 were wounded and 12,254 were taken prisoners. The Royal Navy, in its dual role of defender from the sea of the island garrisons and transporter of troops that would eventually be retreated to Egypt, suffered casualties of 1,828 killed and 183 were wounded. Three cruisers and six destroyers were sunk and seventeen additional ships were damaged.[1]

German losses were as blunt as those of the island's defenders. A total of 22,040 airborne troops were landed including 8,060 brought to the fight by gliders or parachutes. Those killed or missing in action totaled 3,986, including 312 air crewmen; there were 2,594 wounded. All of the "70 odd gliders" were lost in the air or on landing.[2, 3]

* * *

In an after battle report of the loss of Crete, Londoners read in the 2 June 1941 edition of the *Daily Express* how British and Empire troops fought with

All of the 70 odd gliders were lost in the air or on landing. *Courtesy of Willi Gänzler*

"magnificent heroism" when paratroops and "glider troops" descended upon the airfield at Maleme. And as though written by Winston Churchill there followed, a description of the fight that went on day and night, without rest, at the airfields, on the beaches and in the hills.[4]

* * *

Much had happened prior to the 20 May 1941 launch of the offensive to capture Crete. German forces had moved with remarkable speed and success in gaining control of much of the continent of Europe. Blitzkrieg worked. For the supporters of the new war tactic of vertical envelopment, gliders worked, bringing a new dimension to warfare: stealth in numbers in a compact area.

Erwin Rommel and his Afrika Corps were in control of all of Libya, and Alexandria and Cairo were reasonable targets for attack. The Desert Fox reigned as the Prince of the Desert. Malta had been pummeled from the air by the Luftwaffe and Italian aircraft, and planning for the invasion of Russia was well underway. But it was the presence on Crete of airfields that could be used by the RAF to attack the flank of German controlled territory and the oil fields of Rumania that bothered the Luftwaffe high command. Generaloberst Kurt Student, commanding general of the expanded German airborne forces, convinced Göring that Crete could be taken in an airborne operation and although Hitler had misgivings about the proposal, he relented with the proviso that nothing was to stand in the way of the initiation of *Operation Barbarossa*, the invasion of Russia.

An attack plan against Crete was drawn up that was modeled after the successful taking of Fort Eben Emael: "... an initial attack by gliders followed up by mass parachute jumps."[5] In practice this formula characterized successful employment of German airborne assets—surprise, noiseless approach, accurate spot landings, delivery of substantial amounts of materiel and most important a unit, when landed, ready for combat wherever needed.

A plan is not, however, universally applicable. In each case methods have to be adapted to the situation, terrain, type of objective, and the amount of resistance to be expected from the enemy; the commander of the parachute troops has to make his decision within the framework of his mission.[6]

To make it work, planning was paramount and included locating an adequate of number of trained troops; supplying a sufficient number of gliders, tow planes and troop carrying aircraft; gathering intelligence of the enemy's position and native population, and having air superiority for protection of the invasion forces.

Planning for the engagement had to take into account significant facts about the terrain and enemy entrenchments. Fields were furrowed with gullies and pockmarked with rock-strewn fences around fields and the plains provided ample camouflage shadows from groves of olive and citrus trees.

The primary objective of the attack was the main airfield at Maleme on the northwest coast. Suda Bay, a harbor that could comfortably accommodate a fleet of ships-of-the-line, was on the eastern end of the north coast.

The operational plan divided the island into four drop zones: from west to east, Maleme, Canea, Rethymno (Retimo) and Heraklion. Because of a lack of sufficient transport aircraft the island would be attacked in two waves, one in the morning and one in the afternoon of May 20. The first wave would send DFS 230 gliders to land west of Maleme airfield and around Suda Bay to neutralize any AA guns that had survived earlier air attacks. The second wave would land at Rethymno and Canea/Suda, and another group would seize the airfield at Heraklion.

Bad luck dogged the Germans from the outset of the attack. The island's defenders knew in advance where landing zones and drop zones for the paratroopers were located. The Allies had been able to gain significant use of intelligence from the deciphered German Enigma code. One of the commanding German generalmajors was killed when his glider crashed on an island off the Greek mainland, another was critically wounded shortly after landing. The Germans also underestimated the physical difficulties of fighting in Crete and the size and determination of the garrison and the Cretan irregulars.

The gliders came in so low and slow that the British and Anzac defenders could fire right into them killing all of the occupants before they had even hit the ground. Those that survived were quickly taken down by fire from the defenders. Gliders that managed to land with soldiers still alive hit the rocky terraced terrain and broke up, killing or injuring the occupants.

After one day of fighting, the Germans had suffered a high number of casualties and none of their objectives had been achieved. During the night following the first day of battle the New Zealand infantry battalion defending the strategic Hill 107 which rose above the Maleme airfield, withdrew from its position as a result of miscommunication and the failure of Allied commanders to grasp the situation. Maleme airfield fell to the Germans the morning following the withdrawal, enabling them to fly in reinforcements that would in the next several days overwhelm the Allied forces. Eventually, over a four night period, 16,000 Allied troops would be evacuated to Egypt; 12,254 Commonwealth and 5,255 Greek soldiers would be captured by the German forces.'[7]

The German High Command had learned a valuable lesson in the use of gliders and airborne troops in *Operation Mercury*. Generalfeldmarschall (Field Marshal) Albert Kesselring offered his personal summary of the operation:

> The exceptionally unfavorable landing conditions should have induced them to land in a single area away from the occupied objectives with their effective defense fire, and then to capture the decisive points (airport and seaport) intact in a subsequent conventional infantry attack at the point of main effort. In doing this it would not have been necessary to abandon the use of surprise local glider landings directly into key points, the possession of which would have facilitated the main attack.[8]
>
> The airborne operation against Crete resulted in very serious losses which in percentage greatly exceeded those sustained by the Germans in previous World War II campaigns ... Hitler himself lost confidence in operations of this nature. He had come to the conclusion that only airborne operations which came as a complete surprise could lead to success ... The fact that the Cretan operations came so close to defeat strengthened his opinions.[9]

Of the 350 aircraft lost during *Operation Merkur*, half were Ju 52s, the aircraft used as tows for the gliders. They would be needed soon for the assault on Russia and the Luftwaffe could not afford further losses of this magnitude.[10] The loss of the glider force and the soldiers on board the DFS 230s shook Hitler's confidence in their future role in combat engagements. He ordered that from that point forward gliders, paratroopers, and airborne troops would no longer be used as in large numbers. Gliders would be used only for the transport of cargo and personnel.

Members of the British armed forces read of the loss of Crete from the London correspondent writing for the serviceman's publication, *Parade*:

> No words can express the pride with which Londoners followed the details of the fighting in which troops from Britain and the Empire fought side by side with the Greeks.[11]

No more combat assault missions

The order by Hitler for an airborne assault stand-down would last for a little more than three years. In late May of 1944 Germany launched 35 DFS 230 gliders in a surprise attack against the Yugoslavian resistance headquarters at Drvar with the intent of eliminating the partisans' leader, Josep Broz Tito. Although the attack "was successful ... Tito was able to escape."[12]

In July, 1944, forty DFS 230 gliders filled with 400 troops and five Gotha 242 transport gliders landed near the village of Vassieux-en-Vercors on the plateau of the Vercors Massif, a village described during the mission briefing as:

> ... the command post where there was amassed a considerable force. Coming from below the massif 15,000 from various units would move up the roads to the plateau in support of the glider borne troops who had orders to destroy all houses so that there will be no place of shelter for terrorists.
>
> Three targets had to be reached simultaneously, the village of Vassieux, and the hamlets of La Mure and Le Château. The landings, protected by Luftwaffe fighters, were precise. Two gliders crashed on landing, killing all on board.
>
> The reaction of the Resistance fighters was severe and the German losses were heavy, 25% on this first sortie, including two glider pilots. The second sortie of twenty DFS 230s and two Gotha 242s experienced a two day weather delay and took off on July 23rd, 1944. Three of the gliders did not reach the plateau—one cut loose unable to maintain position behind its tug and landed in a forest clearing and flipped over on its back, all of the troops scrambling to safety. The tow rope of another broke, the glider landing seven miles short of the objective. Its occupants survived the landing and joined the 15,000 ground troops making their way to the top of the massif. The wing of a third glider was torn off in flight by its tow rope, and crashed, killing all on board.
>
> The glider borne troops, combined with the ground troops who made their way to the top of the massif, engaged the French fighters but it was an unequal struggle and the order to disperse was given to all Resistance units in the massif. The repression was dreadful. The German troops followed scrupulously the instructions of General Pflaum before the operation: '... Find the bands of terrorists and exterminate completely ...' A total of 456 were killed in the massif, including 148 French victims in Vassieux itself.[13]

Resupply missions

Hitler's command that gliders be used to re-supply troops on the ground was carried out during the remainder of the war. The last seven of a reported 333 re-supply sorties, beginning in January 1942, was made to Berlin, a city in flames and under continuous bombardment by the Russians, in April of 1945, days before the end of hostilities in early May.[14]

> Whenever it was impossible for the Ju 52 transports to land in the pockets (where German troops were cut off from ground supply lines) or to do so only at the risk of high losses, the call went up for the transport gliders to be sent in. Even if they avoided being shot down on the way, once on the ground those pilots shared the fate of the other troops in the pocket i.e. they died fighting on the ground or went into an often year-long captivity unless the pocket was relieved.[15]

One German glider pilot remembers those resupply flights as demanding the best flying skills. On a resupply mission in the middle of March, 1945 to Breslau, Lower Silesia, Germany (now Wroclaw, Poland):

> I flew my DFS 230 from Czechoslovakia to Breslau where our troops were completely surrounded by the Russians. Gliders were the only way that they could be resupplied. We would have to do a steep dive and level out to land in the streets of Breslau. There was only a 30 meter space for landing.
>
> Three of us were assigned to the mission. Two made it in and one was shot down. The one that was shot down was tracked by search lights. Once you're spotted by search lights, phttt, it's all over, you're shot down. He landed outside the area controlled by the Germans and he was never seen again.[16]

V-E day was three days later.

14

Operation Freshman

In 1942, there were few in the world outside of a select number in secret laboratories who knew that it might be possible to harness nuclear power and do so in a way that it could be used as a weapon, an atomic bomb. Scientists in both the United States and in England were making progress in their research, but it was the Germans who were thought to have the lead in this endeavor. Churchill and Roosevelt were aware of the work going on to create the bomb and it was their fear that Germany might be so advanced in their research that they would have a workable bomb before the Allies, a fear that would have likely been intensified had the destructive nature of the bomb as was demonstrated in 1945 in Japan were known.

Of the components necessary to construct such a bomb, a term came to be recognized as one of the major ingredients of this destructive soup—*heavy water*, later described by Churchill as sounding eerie and unnatural.[1] Heavy water. Did it weigh more than ordinary water? How did it differ from tap water? Why was it so important in the research of the development of an atomic bomb?

Heavy water looks the same as ordinary water, it contains both elements, hydrogen and oxygen that we learned about in school, but it is the hydrogen element that is special, it has twice the weight of ordinary hydrogen giving it a ten percent increase in weight over ordinary water. The creation of heavy water, through electrolysis of ordinary water, and collected in large amounts, was essential for 'slowing down neutrons in a uranium pile.'[2] It was the process of electrolysis of ordinary water, that life-giving and life-saving requirement for life on the planet, that was of concern to both Germany and the Allies.

The process of making heavy water through electrolysis required a substantial amount of electric power, power that could be produced in few places.

The Norsk Hydro-Electric Company at Vermork, located in the mountainous regions near the village of Rjukan in southern Norway, was ideal for harnessing the power of the naturally occurring waterfalls roaring down the mountains. It was here that Norway made heavy water available as a commercial product used in the manufacturing of fertilizer.

Vermork Hydroelectric Plant. *By an unknown artist*

Prior to the war Germany had contracted with the Vermork company for its output of heavy water but was denied the amount requested. In early April 1940, the problem of securing large quantities of heavy water from the plant was resolved with the invasion and occupation of Norway by German military forces, an occupation that lasted until the end of the war in Europe on 8 May 1945. Within a month of occupation, Germany ordered that production of heavy water be increased to three thousand pounds a year with the goal of an output of ten thousand pounds by the end of 1941.[3]

The gauntlet had been thrown, the challenge accepted. The heavy water making capability at Vermork had to be eliminated and it was going to be in the hands of the British to find a way to destroy the plant, its stock pile of heavy water and the machinery used in its production.

Three methods of attack were proposed: aerial bombardment of the hydroelectric plant, the use of Norwegian saboteurs, and the use of airborne troops. The first plan was rejected because of difficulty in identifying the precise location of the plant among the mountains surrounding the site and the danger of killing large numbers of Norwegians who would be at the plant and the surrounding area. The use of Norwegian saboteurs was rejected because of the amount of explosives needed to effectively destroy the plant and the time needed to train the participants in the use of explosives. The third plan, the one that had potential for meeting the objective of destroying the Vermork plant, was the use airborne troops.

A number of methods of transporting airborne troops to the objective were considered—by flying boat to land on a lake near the plant, by parachute drop of troops, or with troops flown in by gliders. Upon evaluation of each method of bringing troops to the hydroelectric site, it was the use of glider-borne troops that carried the day.

A glider landing zone (LZ) for the attack, code named *Operation Freshman,* was identified and would be marked out by Norwegian agents. Five hours marching distance away, the Vermork plant was located in an isolated deep valley with thickly forested sides that rose almost vertically for 3,000 feet from the river bed.

The operation required a force of 12 to 16 men, all skilled engineers. Because of the hazardous nature of the task, and its importance, the attack force was duplicated.

Troop training was comprehensive and strenuous, both technically and physically. The members of the attacking force had to train so that they could make the trek from the landing zone to the plant, destroy it and afterwards make their way over the mountains to Sweden. An air-to-ground radio location device, *Rebecca-Eureka,* was to be used to locate the LZ and was smuggled into Norway prior to the initiation of the mission. Norwegian agents would act as guides throughout.

The meteorological forecast for the night of the 19 November 1942 was reasonable, though not ideal. Operating independently, two Halifax aircraft and their Horsa gliders took off at 1750 hrs and 1810 hrs. For many hours nothing was heard of either of them; then, at 2341 hrs a faint signal from the second aircraft asked for a course home. At 2355 hrs a signal was received from the first aircraft that their glider had been released. Only one aircraft returned; the fate of the other and of the two gliders was not known until after the war.

The first party had made an accurate landfall through patchy clouds, only to discover that the 'Rebecca' was unserviceable, and they had no alternative but to navigate their way through the mountains by map reading. This they succeeded in doing, and on the first run-in actually passed over the LZ and the waiting Norwegian agents. As they turned for a second run they flew into thick snow cloud where ice formed on the aircraft, and on the tow rope, which broke. Unable to do more, the Halifax returned to base. The glider crashed on to the mountainside. Of the 17 men in it, eight were killed at once and nine captured, four of whom were injured. On 18 January 1943 five were shot by the Gestapo while the four injured were killed by poison by a German doctor.

The second party also made a successful landfall; but, for reasons still unknown, the glider crash-landed in the mountains near Helleland and the aircraft flew into the next range, killing the crew. Three men in the glider were killed, the remainder captured and shot within a few hours. A directive from a general order issued by Hitler, the *Führerbefehl,* stipulated that captured commandos, whether or not in uniform and regardless of the method of insertion to the front, were to be "exterminated to the last man." The airborne troops who survived the crash of their glider were shot within hours of their capture.[4]

> Although *Operation Freshman* failed—largely through the breakdown of the vital homing beacon—the first British glider operation demonstrated the range, flexibility, and the potentialities, or airborne forces. The soldiers and airmen who died in the Norwegian mountains that November night had taken part in one of the most daring and gallant small operations of the war.[5]

15

Sicily—252[1]

"This was a bad time for the Regiment."[2]

The decision to launch an attack on European territory controlled by Axis forces in Sicily was made at the Casablanca Conference (14–24 January 1943) attended by President Franklin D. Roosevelt, the British Prime Minister, Winston Churchill and their chief military commanders. French Free Forces were represented by Generals Charles de Gaulle and Henri Giraud.

The hotel in French Morocco where discussions took place about the course of the war was a far cry from what those on the home front had come to recognize as Rick's Café Américain, the cinematic meeting place for those who professed to have business in Casablanca but whose motives were as questionable as the reputation of Humphrey Bogart's character in the Vichy-controlled Casablanca of 1941. The motives of the Allied leaders in attendance at the Casablanca Conference were more sharply defined and resulted in a statement by the President of what would determine the end of the war—Unconditional Surrender of the Axis powers.

By the time American forces landed in French North African in November of 1942, the North African campaign, a series of battles that stretched from Egypt west across the northern countries of Africa, had been in full rage for two and a half years. With the last of Rommel's desert soldiers routed and captured by the first week in May, 1943, the Allies moved ahead with the final preparations and training for the invasion of Sicily.

A logistical maze of men and materiel not before undertaken, it would be the largest amphibious operation ever mounted. The battle for Sicily would include an assault force numbering 2,590 naval ships carrying 115,000 British Empire and 66,000 American soldiers, 14,000 vehicles, 600 tanks, and 1,800 guns. In addition, elements of two airborne divisions would take part with paratrooper drops and the landing of glider borne troops.[3]

What the Allies would leave behind in the North African lands of sand, grit, camels and thieving natives as they prepared for the invasion of Sicily could hardly be compared to a Garden of Eden. In addition to the combat toll of soldiers and Army Air Force personnel killed and wounded, other scourges created havoc for the troops on the Saharan front.

> Typhus, diarrheal diseases, including typhoid and dysentery, smallpox and malaria were known to be endemic throughout French Morocco, Algeria, and Tunisia. In French Morocco, plague, yellow fever, malaria, relapsing fever, and typhus were a most serious menace. The poor sanitary environment plus the general low level of field training, threw a heavy load on medical officers who themselves lacked practical field experience in these matters.[4]

And, it would seem that a good many of these gastro-intestinal ailments could be traced back to not only a lack of practical field experience but also to a substantial lack of some of the basics of food preparation and preventative disease control efforts.

> For some units, the difficulties began early and lasted long; for others there were only brief periods of such hardship; still others underwent only a few of them. But all units felt the lack of suitable burners for heating mess kit water; all units felt (some acutely) the lack of apparently trivial, but actually important items as suitable can openers, and all units were handicapped by shortages of tools for kitchen stove repairs, of picks, shovels, nails, lumber, screening, insect guns, insecticide spray, and galvanized trash cans, aka 'GI' cans ('GI'—an American acronym for either a US soldier, 'government issue,' or in medical jargon, the 'GIs': the shits, diarrhea.)[5]

Operation Husky, the overall code-name selected for the invasion of Sicily by Allied forces, called for a combined seaborne and airborne assault that would include paratroop drops and troop and equipment flown into combat by gliders. It was because of their quiet approach to the combat area that gliders were included in the planning by General Bernard Montgomery, the British commander responsible for implementing the airborne component of the assault.

The glider portion of the operation was composed mostly of US built Waco (CG-4A) gliders, but because the British Horsa was larger than the Waco and could carry a larger number of troops and equipment, thirty were flown from England to Morocco and then on to airfields in Tunisia. Due to insufficient numbers of British transport aircraft to serve as glider tugs, and none that could serve as transport for the parachute drops, 331 American C-47 Dakotas would serve as glider tows and troop carrier transport for the parachute drops.[6]

To provide Horsas for Montgomery's planned assault it was necessary to ferry the larger British glider from England to North Africa. The flight would be hazardous at best, without a certainty that the Halifax bombers assigned to the operation could complete the trip, even with additional gas tanks fitted into the bomber's bomb bays.

Most of the ten hour first leg of the 1,300 mile flight to Morocco would be over water skirting the west coasts of France and Spain, known hunting grounds for the German fighter aircraft. The second leg of seven hours would be no less demanding as flying altitudes in excess of 9,000 feet would be required as the tug-glider combinations crossed over the Atlas Mountains in the northwest of Africa. Thermal updrafts from the stove-top heat of the desert made the trip from Morocco to Tunisia nearly as treacherous as the first leg.

Because of the length of the trip and the physical strain of piloting the Horsas, each carried three pilots, rotating at thirty minute intervals the responsibility of keeping the aircraft aloft. Despite being attacked by Ju 88 aircraft, ditching into the sea or mountains and premature releases over the desert, the operation code-named *Turkey Buzzard* was able to deliver 19 of the thirty gliders destined for Tunisia. The invasion by then was only 12 days away.[7,8]

The initial glider flights into Sicily received the code-name *Operation Ladbroke* and an additional flight of gliders to support British paratroop landings to secure the Ponte Primosole north of Syracuse was dubbed *Operation Fustian*.

The majority of the glider pilots for both operations would be British, the crews of their C-47 tug aircraft, American. As the pilots arrived from England by ship in North Africa in April, a scramble took place to have the best possible preparation of pilots, tug crews, and aircraft ready for the D-Day of Sicily. British glider pilots were unfamiliar with the American Waco glider and their training had not included night time flying or landing. *Operation Ladbroke* required both.

The Waco gliders, arriving by ship in May from America, their parts packed neatly in five different numbered crates, were unloaded and stored in a haphazard fashion for pickup by the assembly teams. By the middle of June, with personnel pulled from other projects, 346 gliders had been assembled, test flown and delivered to British and American airfields in Algeria and Tunisia.[9]

Although significant training time was lost in the assembly of gliders, large-scale tactical formations were flown 14 and 20 June by the pilots of the British Glider Pilot Regiment and the US crews of the C-47 tug aircraft fresh from their training bases in the States. As D-Day for the invasion neared, British glider pilots as a group had accumulated only an average of four and a half hours of flying time in the Waco, including 72 minutes of night flying. None had been a part of any exercise involving flying and release over water, either in the daytime or at night. Would it be enough? Their indomitable will was obvious. Their regimental motto would be tested: *Nihil est Impossibilis*, Nothing is Impossible.[10,11]

A map view of Sicily reveals an island roughly in the shape of an isosceles triangle kicked over on its side by the toe of the boot of Italy, its northeast point a mere two miles across the Straits of Messina to the Italian mainland. The villages on the southern side of the triangle, identified as the site for the seaborne landings, were filthy, gray, drab, with few trees and indistinguishable one from the other, the people impoverished like the land on which they lived.[12,13]

These villages in the south are separated from the northern coast by mountains that are snuggled close together with steep narrow valleys that straggle across the island in a somewhat west to easterly direction.[14] The historic and prominent

Mount Etna dominates the east coast, overlooking the deepwater seaports of Catania and Augusta.

The mission for the British 1 Air-Landing Brigade during the initial phase of the assault was capture of the road north of the beachhead leading to Syracuse, just a mile away. To accomplish this they had to take and hold the Ponte Grande bridge over the Anopo Canal. Once the bridge was secured, they were to take the port itself and a nearby coastal artillery battery.[15]

The schedule for the invasion launch had been set in Casablanca as 10 July 1943, between 12:31 a.m. and first light at 4:30 a.m. This time period would give paratroopers and pilots just enough moonlight to jump and bring in the gliders, but not enough to silhouette targets of the soldiers and their troop carriers as targets for the Italian defensive artillery.[16]

The British airborne operation of *Operation Husky* got underway first in the early evening of 9 July as 109 American C-47s (Dakotas/Gooney Birds) and 35 British Albemarles rose into the evening skies at 1842 hrs towing 144 Waco and Horsa gliders. The gliders carried 2,075 men of the British 1st Air Landing Brigade, seven jeeps, six pieces of artillery, and ten 3-inch mortars. The takeoffs were difficult as the preceding tug-glider combinations kicked up clouds of dust and sand making it difficult to see other combinations in the stream of takeoffs or even their own tug aircraft. The flight plan called for the tug-glider formations to fly due east from their takeoff fields in Tunisia for up to three hours and at Malta, turn north for a distance of approximately 100 miles to Cape Passero off southeast Sicily. From there they would be on a direct path to the Syracuse LZ (Landing Zone).[17]

At takeoff, the heat of the day had yet to dissipate, the interiors of the gliders were hot, an engine of a tug sputtered at takeoff, recovered and gained altitude to form up with the others, a jeep broke loose threatening to rip itself free of the glider's flimsy fuselage. Some gliders broke loose immediately, a tug's engine caught fire. Seven combinations failed to clear the North African coast.[18]

For days prior to the launch of the combined air and sea operations the weather had been hot and dry. On the eve of the assault the winds from the southeast increased to near gale force levels—the tramontana, the Italian version of the French mistral.[19]

> The British contingent made rendezvous over the Kuriate Islands and headed for Malta ... though the sun was setting as the planes neared Malta, the signal beacon on the island was plainly visible to all but a few aircraft at the end of the column.... As the aircraft made landfall at Cape Passero, the check point at the southeastern tip of Sicily, formations became badly mixed. Two pilots who had lost their way over the sea had turned back to North Africa. Two others returned after sighting Sicily because they could not orient themselves to the ground. A fifth accidentally released its glider over the water; a sixth glider had broken loose from its aircraft—both gliders dropped into the sea.

> The designated zig-zag course threw more pilots off course, and confusion set in. Many of the communication lines between tug and glider failed to work, land marks were blurred from the rising dust caused by the tramontana and by smoke from defensive flak guns.[20]

To avoid radar detection the aircraft combinations flew at wave-top levels, ocean spray brushing over the tugs.[21, 22] Italian search lights pierced the sky looking for the vulnerable tugs and gliders. Some of the combinations climbed, others descended, turned left, turned right. Another lit up the sky as the Bangalore torpedoes it carried exploded as the result of a direct hit by anti-aircraft fire.[23]

> Exactly how many gliders were turned loose in the proper area is impossible to say—perhaps about 115 carrying more than 1,200 men. Of these, only 54 gliders landed in Sicily, 12 on or near the correct landing zones.[24]

Unable to make the coast, sixty-five gliders that had cut loose too soon crashed into the sea, their 252 occupants drowned.[25] *Operation Ladbroke* flight paths were in utter chaos. Had anyone had the time to think about it, *Operation SNAFU* (Situation Normal, All Fucked Up) would have been a more fitting description of the glider assault on Sicily.

An American glider pilot who went along with his British counterparts remembered that:

> at last we got our signal from the tow ship to cast off. It was 22:20. Here it was, whatever faced us on the island. The flak was getting thicker and our course took us over one of the anti-aircraft guns. Fortunately none of the flak hit our glider. As we crossed the shoreline I could see a glider bouncing on the shore to my right. The moon was covered by haze and our visibility was poor. We had cut at 2,200 feet and now we were at 1,000 feet just over the shoreline. I could not make out my landing zone, so I had to glide straight ahead, hoping for the best. At 500 feet I could distinguish a certain field and I let down in a small field with trees in it. As we landed, we ran into a tree, but were fortunate to hit it with the wing stopping us abruptly. No one was injured on the landing.[26]

An American co-pilot recalled that:

> from the moment I cut loose, I knew that I would never make it to shore. As we descended through the darkness, we strained for a glimpse of the shoreline, but all we could see ahead were tracer bullets and exploding flak. We eventually ran out of sky, as my British pilot guided us to a smooth landing in the rolling sea. In a matter of seconds, we all clambered out and were sitting on the wings trying to determine how far we were from shore. One British soldier and I decided to try swimming ashore

while the rest remained with the slowly sinking glider. Exhausted and about a half an hour later, I came upon another partially submerged Waco and decided to wait it out for rescue.[27]

The memories of a member of the British Glider Pilot Regiment personalizes the attack on Sicily and his role in the battle of the Ponte Grand bridge.

We had to capture a bridge just south of the deep seaport of Syracuse. The bridge was over two water obstacles, a canal and a river, and was the only bridge for miles and miles. The plan was for us to capture it so that Montgomery's tanks could move over into Sicily.

We were to go at night and land about midnight, capture the bridge, the original plan being that we would then move off into Syracuse once the bridge had been taken.

The flight was about three and a half to four hours during which a strong wind had blown up and we actually had sea spray.

We had trouble in our glider because when it got dark the lights failed on the tug aircraft which was very dangerous if you couldn't see where it was. We had to hack a hole in the Perspex so that we could see the towrope better and we flew on staring at the rope for well over half the trip. The moon came out for a short while and we could see the coastline. Flak started to come up and we could see firing on the ground and then the moon went in.

I remember crossing the coast and seeing the sand from about 300 feet. Then it went pitch black—we hit a stone wall at about 85 mph and we were all knocked unconscious. One chap broke his leg and another wasn't too clever but the rest of the troops were alright. We moved off towards the objective, went around three pillboxes and dawn was breaking got sight of the bridge. A major of the Royal Engineers who was in a Horsa that landed within 20 yards of the bridge took the detonators out of the explosives that the enemy had laid around the bridge.

We split the area up around the bridge and I took the southern bank. The firing against us got progressively worse and we had a lot of trouble with machine gun and mortar fire.

By 3 o'clock we had ran out of ammunition and there were very few of us left so we decided to surrender as it was the only possible thing left to do. Officially 78 of the 1,500 reached the bridge and there were only nine of us left when we surrendered. The major was next to me when a burst of machine gun fire shot him through the head and caught a few others and made a hole in my red beret. We were marched away over a river where we suddenly met a British patrol and were freed. We went back down to the bridge and the 8th Army had got through. There was one 8th Army soldier dead on the bridge and I always think of him, because he shouldn't have been there. If we could have hung on for another quarter of an hour, but we couldn't so that was that. [28]

* * *

Three days later *Operation Fustian* suffered a similar fate as the glidermen in *Operation Ladbroke.* Eleven Horsas and eight Wacos not used in the Ladbroke fleet were towed by British Halifax and Albemarle tugs were loaded with personnel and anti-tank guns to support paratroopers whose mission was the capture of the Primosole Bridge north of Syracuse. The tug-glider formations were fired upon by Allied ships supporting the invasion thinking that they were being attacked by German aircraft. The naval gunners fired their guns at the roar of planes overhead without knowledge of whose aircraft they were shooting at. Ten paratrooper-filled Dakotas were shot down, 24 turned back with serious damage and three British tugs were felled. Although the bridge was taken, lost and retaken only four of the nineteen gliders that left North Africa on the mission landed accurately.

* * *

"Attack on Sicily—252 Glidermen Drown!" This is not a newspaper headline that readers on the home-front would have seen, nor would Allied service men have read in *The Stars and Stripes* or the *Union Jack*. Instead, they would have read headlines that reported, "Sicily Invasion—Paratroops in Action!" "From the air one could see smoke and flame up from the beachheads for a distance of ten miles."[29] One London daily reported that troops from gliders had landed to disrupt Axis forces meeting the invasion; a little more than an hour later paratroops dropped through the night sky to continue the work of the glidermen.[30]

16

Commando Skorzeny

It was the lunch hour of 23 July 1943 when he was summoned to Hitler's GHQ (General Headquarters.) The room into which he and five other officers had been ushered was large, perhaps twenty by thirty feet. A large sturdy table covered with maps was in the center, a smaller table with writing materials and a group of chairs stood in front of a large fireplace that dominated one of the walls in what was called the Tea House. Why had he, Captain Otto Skorzeny, commander of a newly formed SS commando unit, been summoned to General Headquarters? He and the others soon found the answer to this question that they all had harbored. They were about to be presented to the Führer.[1]

Hitler entered the room, approached each of the officers in line who provided the information they had been told to give the Leader—a brief description of their military service and answers to any questions that were put forward. When asked by the Führer to tell him what they thought of Italy, the other five responded in simplistic terms about that country's role in the Axis partnership. Skorzeny, replied only that he was Austrian, knowing that his commander in chief had affection for this country and was unhappy about the annexation of the South Tyrol by Italy as a consequence of the First World War. He gave no other response. In a matter of moments, Hitler excused the others and told Skorzeny to stay.

With a preamble rebuking the King of Italy and his new prime minister, Marshal Badoglio, Hitler told Skorzeny he feared that the new government would form an alliance with the Allies and that would mean that Mussolini, Il Duce, would be handed over to the enemy. The Führer told the captain of commandos that, on orders of the King, Mussolini had been arrested.

At this point Hitler came to the core of the discussion, he wanted Skorzeny to rescue his friend and loyal partner. It was more than an order, it was a request, perhaps even a plea. Skorzeny was to locate and rescue Mussolini before he could be turned over to the enemy, he was to *save* his friend.[2]

Skorzeny would be under the command of General Kurt Student, commander of the Luftwaffe's airborne forces, who would oversee the operation, eventually to be code-named, *Operation Oak* (*Unternehmen Eiche*). The Leader added, the mission must be cloaked in the utmost of secrecy, only a limited number would be knowledgeable about the intent of Skorzeny's action and lastly, he was to "avoid no risk" in bringing the mission to a successful conclusion.[3]

Student and Skorzeny met immediately following the audience with Hitler and were joined by Heinrich Himmler, Reichsführer of the SS (*Schutzstaffel*) who provided a briefing related to the lack of knowledge regarding Mussolini's whereabouts, a reiteration of the need for secrecy of the intent of the mission. After this half hour meeting, Skorzeny was at last free to contact his second in command and told him to have fifty of his best commandos make their way to Italy—details would follow.

A significant amount of time slipped through the fingers of Student and Skorzeny's team as they chased down leads about the location of Mussolini's site of protected custody. Faulty intelligence regarding sightings of the Duce, led to wasted time in planning a rescue from one place or another. It wasn't until 8 September that word reached Student that it was likely that Mussolini was held in the mountain-top ski resort hotel of Campo Imperatore on Gran Sasso, the highest peak in the Apennine mountains.

Skorzeny had been assigned the 'search' phase of the rescue mission and one of Student's airborne officers had been directed to plan for the snatch of the Italian dictator from the hands of his guards at the hotel. Skorzeny reminded Student of Hitler's imperative that it was he who was requested to rescue the Duce. Student relented and approved the inclusion of the commando leader and seventeen of his men to be a part of the rescue force.[4]

The site of the Duce's incarceration could only be reached by a funicular, one station at the base of the mountain on which the hotel was located, another on the grounds of the resort.

> No military map carried its location. Not even mountain climbers' charts identified the place. The only information that Skorzeny could get came from a German citizen living in Italy. He had once spent a holiday there, and he had a circular describing the hotel accommodations. This intelligence was hardly adequate for a military operation, so Skorzeny arranged to have a pilot fly him and his intelligence officer over the camp.
>
> Skorzeny located the Campo Imperatore from the air and noticed a small triangular green area behind the hotel that might serve for an air landing operation. He and his intelligence officer tried to take pictures, but the camera built into the plane froze at 15,000 feet, and it was only with great difficulty that they managed to take some photographs with a hand camera.[5]

Planning began in earnest with the information regarding a landing spot and the visual evaluation of the terrain made by Skorzeny. But because the planners of the abduction were not certain that Mussolini was in fact being held in the hotel, Skorzeny '... induced a German staff doctor to visit the lodge on the pretext that it might be suitable for use as a convalescent home for soldiers recuperating from malaria.'[6] The best the doctor was able to accomplish was to place a telephone call to the top of the mountain from the lower funicular station, a call that verified that the top station was being guarded by Italian troops.

Time became a major factor in putting the operation in motion. For every hour, every day the Italians held the Duce, the more likely they were to hand him over to the Allied forces, an eventuality that could not be tolerated. The Führer had forbidden it.

Planning went forward even with the uncertainty of Mussolini's presence at the hotel. Student's plan was to send a group of paratroopers into the valley to first attack and hold the lower funicular station, followed by a surprise attack with a company of glider borne troops landing at the top of the mountain on the grounds surrounding the resort. The general ordered twelve gliders from the south of France to be delivered to an airport in the Rome area, and established H-hour for the mission at 0600 hrs, 12 September 1943, with arrival at the hotel expected to be at 0700 hrs, a time of day when the air currents at the mountain top were weakest.[7]

The attack would follow standard glider tactics, sending four groups of three gliders each. The glider force would include a signals detachment, a two-man medical team, a machine-gun section, and a mortar section. Skorzeny's group of SS commandos would secure the landing zone, guard Italian prisoners and provide security for Mussolini until he was taken off the mountain. Other groups were to take and hold the upper funicular station, secure the area around the hotel and provide support in case of a battle with the guards.[8] Skorzeny's personal addition to the mix of soldiers, technicians, and commandos was a war correspondent and a photographer, suggesting that the commando leader had at least an equal interest in the public relations the rescue might engender.[9]

A delay in the arrival of the gliders extended the takeoff time to approximately 1200. The element of surprise by arriving in the early morning hours and overtaking a garrison barely awake was lost. It was during this delay that Skorzeny's second in command, as reported by one historian, following a 'fancy of his own' hurried into Rome to persuade an Italian general who had been favorable towards the Germans to accompany the expedition as possible insurance against a reluctant guard force letting their captor fall into the hands of the Germans.[10]

It was at the new takeoff time for the twelve gliders and their tow planes that the Allies chose to bomb the airfield that was the starting point of the airborne segment of the Mussolini rescue. Although none of the aircraft were damaged during the raid, a further delay put liftoff at 1300. Skorzeny, in the first glider group was unaware until they broke through the cloud cover that two gliders in his group had not been able to liftoff, victims of bomb holes in the runway.

The mission gliders seemed to magically appear out of the thin air of Gran Sasso, the Italian guards standing in awe of the flying spectacle before them. One glider group landed on the green triangular grassy area that Skorzeny had seen from his reconnaissance flight, others managed to find landing spots within sight of the hotel. They could not have believed their good fortune as three gliders came to a halt so close to the entrance of the hotel that they could have called for a bellman to take their equipment inside and meet the Germans at the reception desk.

Skorzeny's glider crashed to earth less than fifty yards from the hotel providing him and his commandos easy access to the ski lodge. The commandos' leader noticed a figure in a second story window that he quickly took to be that of his rescue target, Mussolini. After an abortive try to mount the hotel's exterior wall to the second story, Skorzeny rushed inside roughly brushing aside the Italian guards and burst into the room that he had gauged to be the one in which Mussolini had been observed. The rescuer had the Duce under his protection as Skorzeny's men rushed the room to overtake the Italian guards stationed there.[11]

The other gliders had made tolerable landings their passengers rushing to control their assigned sectors of the hotel and its surroundings. One glider crashed and splintered without any of its passengers immediately exiting.

Skorzeny demanded to see the commander of the Italian forces and advised him that he had one minute to surrender his forces. The Italian left the room, considered the demand for capitulation and returned with a flask of red wine to congratulate the winner of the brief and the almost non-existent struggle for control of the hotel and the rescue of their prisoner.

All that remained was the removal of the Duce from the grounds. The pilot of the light two-seater *Storch* aircraft that had been circling overhead as an observer of the mountaintop situation as it developed, was called and told to land in a clearing near the hotel.

Germans, Italians, even Mussolini helped to remove rocks and boulders from the proposed takeoff area, a distance that was just barely within the plane's

" . . . they could have called for a bellman to take their equipment inside and meet the Germans at the reception desk." *Bundesarchiv*

takeoff limits with two passengers, the pilot and Mussolini. But Skorzeny had decided that he would be a third passenger riding behind the Duce on the trip that would take them from the mountain top to airfields where the rescuer and his prize would eventually travel on to Germany and a meeting with Hitler. The pilot of the tiny aircraft:

> ... was far from pleased at the prospect of taking off from the mountain top with so precious a passenger. Skorzeny's insistence on accompanying Mussolini increased (the pilot's) takeoff problem by adding to the weight. Skorzeny reasoned that if the little plane failed to get off the ground, he would not be around to explain his failure to an enraged Führer.[12]

After mugging for photos with his rescuers Mussolini climbed into the *Storch*, Skorzeny squeezed into the space behind the dictator, the pilot at the controls.

> Paratroopers held the wings and tail of the plane as the pilot revved the engine. Then with much shaking and bounding, the plane made its short run, barely cleared the rim of the escarpment, and leveled off only after a breath-taking drop below the mountain top.[13]

The Storch aircraft ready to collect its precious cargo. *Bundesarchiv*

Mussolini mugging for photos with German and Italian troops. *Bundesarchiv*

Skorzeny is with binoculars at Mussolini's right side. *Bundesarchiv*

Operation Oak Scorecard:

German soldiers KIA (killed in action)	0
Italian soldiers KIA	0
Number of shots fired	0
(a few lone shots in the distance by Italian posts after the rescue had taken place)[14]	
Number of dictators rescued	1

Honors accorded:

Mussolini—installed as dictator of German supported puppet state in northern Italy, the Italian Social Republic; duration of rule: approximately 20 months.

Skorzeny—promotion to rank of major, the Knight's Cross from Hitler, the Air Force Medal in Gold from Göring, the Order of the Hundred Musketeers from Mussolini.

Student—Oak Leaves to his Knight's Cross

Other participants—promotions in rank, Knight's Crosses, Iron Crosses.[15]

Mussolini's rescue was addressed by the newspapers in London on 13 September 1943:

> Last night a special announcement from Hitler's HQ broadcast by Berlin radio stated: "German parachutists and men of the security service and the armed SS today carried out an operation for the liberation of Mussolini, who had been imprisoned by the clique of traitors. The coup succeeded. The Duce is at liberty. The handing over of the Duce to the Anglo-Americans, agreed to by the Badoglio Government, has thus been frustrated." This is the first definite news of Mussolini since he resigned on July 25th.[16]

17

Burma—*Operation Thursday/Project 9*

"Tonight you're going to find out if you have a soul."

In 1943, British Major General, Orde C. Wingate's Chindits, fighting forces composed of British soldiers, Nigerians, Chinese, Gurkhas and Burmese, and trained in guerrilla warfare, fought the enemy in Japanese held Burma. They were successful at attacking behind their lines of the Japanese forces cutting off their supply system, exhausting their resources and disrupting their advance toward India. His troops 'marched fast and struck hard.'[1]

> In 1944 General Wingate wished to lead another expedition into Burma on a larger scale. Previously he had had to leave some of his sick and wounded behind his swiftly moving columns, but in 1944 he wanted to fly all of them to safety.[2]

Following the Quebec Conference, a war strategy meeting between President Roosevelt, Prime Minister Winston Churchill and the Canadian host country's Prime Minister, Mackenzie King, Lord Louis Mountbatten, Supreme Allied Commander South East Asia Command, travelled to Washington, D.C. and met with General H. H. (Hap) Arnold, Commanding General of the U. S. Army Air Forces. In a letter to President Roosevelt in late March of 1944, Lord Mountbatten wrote that,

> It was when I was visiting Arnold in Washington after the Quebec Conference that I suggested to him the formation of an Air Commando (Force) to help Wingate.[3]

Arnold's response to Mountbatten and to Wingate was unequivocal:

> Large numbers of Allied ground troops would be conveyed by aircraft deep into Burma and, once there, they would be wholly supplied by air. Allied troops could defeat (the Japanese forces as jungle fighters) at their own game, provided they were mobile, in sufficient force and exploited the military value of surprise.[4]

All that was left for Arnold to do was find the men to plan and command the operation. They would have to be 'aggressive, imaginative, and endowed with organizational talent of a high order.'[5] He found his men who had proven leadership skills and combat daring in Colonel Philip C. Cochran and Lt. Col. John R. Alison.

Cochran had been a fighter pilot in North Africa and had shown 'remarkable leadership' heading up a unit of replacement pilots who soon found their way to the front. To the American people, though, he may have been better known as the model for the fictional Colonel Flip Corkin in the comic strip *Terry and the Pirates*, the group of airborne glider riders who found time for a little romance and a little adventure while fighting the enemy in southeast Asia.

Allison had an outstanding record as a fighter pilot with the US 14th Air Force in China and had combat experience against the enemy flying from England, Russia, and the Middle East.

General Arnold brought the two men he had selected to his office and gave them their orders—Dislodge the Japanese from Burma and reopen the Ledo Road to make it possible to resupply China overland from the Burmese town of Myitkyina.[6] He ended the meeting with, 'To hell with the paper work, go out and fight.'[7]

Cochran and Allison selected a variety of aircraft for the mission: 25 transports, 150 Waco CG-4A gliders to move troops, equipment and supplies, light liaison 'grasshopper-type' planes for reconnaissance and for evacuating the wounded and covering fighters and medium bombers. Arnold later reported to the American people that:

> the glider pilots were selected volunteers. Liaison-plane pilots were chosen for their ability to repair as well as fly their ships. An exhaustive training program was begun in America and concluded in India. Everything to be transported by glider was loaded and unloaded endlessly. Army pack mules became accustomed to bamboo stalls in the gliders.
>
> In India there were work-filled months of final preparations. Morale was high, and there was little paper work. The men said, simply, 'If Phil or John says we do it, then, by God, we do it!'[8]

Some glider riders found time for a little feminine distraction and a little adventure while fighting the enemy in southeast Asia.

There is an old adage that suggests that the worth of something can be determined through experience—the proof of the pudding is in the eating. Lord Louis Mountbatten's letter to the US President, Franklin Roosevelt, offered proof of the success of the jungle fly-in that became known as *Operation Thursday*:

> This new formation has proved the most unqualified success and has revolutionised jungle warfare. Colonel Cochran and his Second in Command, Lieutenant Colonel Alison, have made a really grand job of No. 1 Air Commando. I sent two military observers to witness the fly-in of Wingate's brigades. The British observer, Major Dunn was killed; the American observer, Lieutenant Colonel Bellah, survived and has written a most dramatic account of the fly-in, which I am taking the liberty of enclosing, as it seems to me such a very vivid account. I think it shows the splendid spirit which exists between Wingate's and Cochran's forces.
>
> I also enclose an extract from an account from Air Marshal Baldwin which gives a vivid idea of how excellently air control of this landing field was exercised by Alison.[9]

This is the dramatic account sent to the President for his review.[10]

> This is how Phil Cochran and his 1st Air Commando gang flew the vanguard of General Wingate's forces over the mountains in bright moonlight and put it down deep in the heart of Jap held Burma. This is how some men died, how others lived to strike a vital master stroke to save China and to help Stilwell and Wingate conquer Northern Burma.
>
> Seven months of back-breaking, mind-searing work ended abruptly that last morning. Only hours were left, slow hours until takeoff. Jerry Dunn, the British army observer flying with me, kept talking about death and I kept shutting him up. He'd smile and say: "If you talk about it, it won't happen."
>
> There were two open spaces on the map, both ringed with jungle and mountains, one called Fifth Avenue, the other Bond Street. (***Note:** It is unclear why these names are mentioned in the report. The names associated with the proposed landing places for the operation were known as Broadway and Piccadilly.*) Nobody had even been on the ground at either place, but there were photographs. The troop-carrying gliders would start down into those places shortly, and the first ones down would pop a red flare if they drew enemy fire; that would warn us and the succeeding waves to turn back—only that wasn't going to happen. Enemy fire or no enemy fire Broadway and Piccadilly had to be taken and held at all costs because the gliders couldn't go back. The two power ships, stripped bare to haul the heavy loads of gliders, had barely gas enough after release to get themselves back through the hostile night miles. So it was agreed, and so it was known by everyone. Nobody would fly the flare.
>
> They would hit the ground and go into action and behind them in wave after wave would come the American combat engineers and more British troops and bulldozers and graders and jeeps and mules to build an airport between dawn and dusk, so that the next night troop-carrying power planes could fly in and start landing the army.

In the vast glider park there were voices from Brooklyn and Carolina, London and the North Country, Liverpool, Texas and Nepal. But nobody seemed to have any nationality suddenly. Phil Cochran, American commanding officer of the operation closed the briefing with "Tonight you're going to find out if you've got a soul. Nothing you've ever done or nothing you are ever going to do counts now. Only the next few hours. Good luck."

Dunn and I lay down on the ground in the shade of a glider wing and while I loaded his Tommy-gun clips with tracers he talked about his wife in London. We were in the first wave and the time for loading up drew on. Dunn got up and slapped me lightly on the shoulder. "See you" he said and walked back to his glider. Chaplain Marlin F. Kerstetter came by and we talked for a minute. It was Sunday night. "As soon as you take off" he said, "I'm going back to hold my service, but I'll be in the second wave."

All the ranking officers, Slim, Stratemeyer, Baldwin, Old, Wingate, Cochran and Alison were in a huddle. It was coming up on time. Our troops were lined up to go aboard. Doc Tulloch, co-piloting with John Alison, Cochran's second in command, looked over his medical equipment when suddenly Cochran called a quick, emergency briefing.

"We've got late afternoon reconnaissance photos. It looks as if the Japs have obstructed Piccadilly, as if they were wise to our plan. So, we're all going to pile into Broadway. Alright, get going! And just remember the dope on Broadway, forget all the rest."

John Alison came over on the run. John was a fighter pilot but had checked out on gliders a few days before just to make this flight. As Cochran's second in command his job was to make an airport out a jungle clearing in twelve hours. He got in and Doc Tulloch crawled in beside him. I climbed in with a detachment from the King's Liverpool Regiment. Every one of us was in full field kits and armed to the teeth with carbines, Tommy guns, pistols, knives and grenades. We were a pirate crew, Wingate's army and Cochran's Air Commandos, wearing mottled camouflage suits, with broad brimmed rakish, paint daubed jungle hats and most with a growth of rank beard.

There was no excitement, no eager babbling to quiet screaming nerves, no bravado. This was an army, filling the gliders row on row behind us, a force in heavy strength with hundreds of miles of night flying ahead over trackless jungle and jagged mountains; night flying completely over a formidable Jap force to let down far behind it and to operate on an extensive scale in its rear. It was history in the making.

The gliders were towed in pairs on long ropes. The left glider in our tow carried Brigadier Mad Mike Calvert with most of the Brigade staff members on board. Ground crews rigged the ropes as our tow ship taxied out like a great waddling duck. We were being hooked in when the Doc touched me and pointed ahead, "First tow airborne!" There it was clear of the tree tops in the late afternoon sun with its two lumbering gliders weaving behind it.

The second tow soon roared down the strip raising an enormous dust cloud, struggling and howling for flying speed, bouncing slightly, straining, straining and then tearing free of the earth and its own cloud of yellow dust and coming into clear silhouette above the tree tops.

Our glider jerked and shuddered as our tow ship took up the slack on the ropes. Then we began to move down the strip into the dust. On both sides of the field long lines of troops were still filing in endlessly to the fill the other gliders behind us. Suddenly our tow ship came to full throttle everything blotted out in the dust, everything but John Allison at the controls and the faces of the men in the glider—a little bit drawn at the mouth, a little bit tightened around the eyes.

We raced to take off, bouncing slightly, straining on the end of the long tow rope to gain flying speed. Ahead of us the great tow ship was up and the glider to our left was up and so were we, with Allison bearing down heavily on his right rudder, sweating over it and shouting directions to Doc Tulloch to trim ship. We came up over the trees fighting for altitude and presently settled into the long, slow, grind of wide circling to get our height for the mountains ahead.

Everyone unclipped their safety belts and eased packs. The soldier beside me handed over his maps, "Will you circle Broadway with your pencil—we're the Piccadilly party." The Doc and I went into a huddle over the map and got Broadway lined in for everybody. Then we settled to the long flying hours ahead, long, cramped, smokeless hours with God knew what at the end of them.

We were alone now, the setting Assam sun flooding the glider and tinting the inside of its fabric with rose gold. It picked out the red in the stubby beards of our party and shone in high lights on rifle barrels and knife hilts. It was quite glorious for a few minutes as we climbed for the mountains, then it faded into the quick jungle purple below and all of our faces were gone in the shadows of evening.

Ahead, all we could see was the blue blob of exhaust from the tow ship's starboard motor. The ship itself was shrouded in haze. All we could feel was the breathing of tightly packed men on either side and the animal shudder of the glider as it swung into the prop wash and swung out again, weaving at many miles per hour on its long snaking tow rope. All we could hear was the thundering noise of our thrust through the air. Gliders are as noisy as power planes.

Doc Tulloch touched me, "Four thousand feet" and I looked at my watch. We had been off for some time, with still a very long time to go. The moon was high over the clouds now, a great three quarter moon with a light that brought the bearded faces out of the shadows and into pale life again.

"Seventy-one hundred feet" Doc grinned exultantly, "That clears the mountains!"

Then in a moment we hit turbulence and began to kick around and bounce like hell. The tow rope looped back toward us and eased over our port wing. We bumped up and swayed out to the right and the rope snaked off straight ahead again toward the flame of the tow ship's exhaust.

We were alone as far as we could see. But we knew that the rest of the wave was behind our spear-point and that succeeding waves would take off on schedule as their time came up, that the show was on and that it would go through.

We were at eighty-five hundred feet and in a few moments would cross the Burma frontier, the mountains behind us. There had been village lights dotting the way as we crossed Assam, but once in enemy held Burma, the ground was completely blacked out. The thought flashed through my mind that if the Japs had even one night fighter pilot half as good as Cats Eyes Cunningham, that we could all be done-in like sitting birds, for we were sneaking the invasion in without fighter cover and in unarmed ships, counting entirely on audacity and surprise.

* * *

Audacity: boldness, courage, balls, guts. Surprise: Sun Tzu, the author of *The Art of War*, declared "War is based on deception—occupy ground that is unexpected by the enemy."[11]

* * *

John turned his head and shouted "The Irrawaddy River!" We crossed it and passed within a few miles of a Jap airfield and for minutes afterwards all of us who could, plastered our faces to the windows watching for tracers or pursuit aviation. But they let us through that bottleneck. They must have thought us a night bombing mission in force.

There was a bright fire far off to the right of us on high ground and somebody passed the word that we were ahead of schedule. God bless tail winds on nights like this!

"Target in twenty minutes."

We broke from our tight-packed, cramp-locked huddles. Bolts snicked sharply as cartridges snapped into chambers. Hangers on pistols cracked back and slid home again. Men straightened and got their packs adjusted, heavy jungle packs that would carry us out the whole way on foot if needed to. The word passed for safety belts and the catches clicked.

Ahead, the tow ship banked lazily and suddenly John Alison and the Doc called out together, "Lights, they've got the smudges lit!" The first glider was already down and there was no red flare. Half way around in the bank, Alison hit the cut-off at a thousand feet and we were gliding free, coming in sharply for a landing in complete darkness. The glider on our left was free beside us and slightly ahead.

Here we go with no power but gravity to bring us in. Here we go into a blind clearing at better than a hundred miles an hour, howling down the night wind, deep in the heart of enemy territory, with a whole Jap army between us still and our following waves. Here we go with little John Allison fighting the controls and Doc Tullock calling out altitude and flying speed to him. "Trees" we're over them! "Lights", and they've shot past under us! A long flat shadow-land ahead and we flatten for it, level off, sink toward it, strike it and bounce. The skids tear into it and the dust blots us out, streaming behind us across the clearing like the tail of a meteor. Then suddenly we swing slightly right and stop. The doors fly open and the security party is off on the run fanning out on a perimeter of 360°—moving toward the jungle that is all around us and that may burst into shattering enemy fire at the next breath.

"Gliders!"

Another tow ship is over us with its gliders cut off. You can see them over the distant trees, losing altitude fast, diving towards us, helpless to turn back or to go on beyond their glide, howling down into the clearing with their heavy loads, one of them with death reaching for it. It banks slightly before it quite clears the trees and a split second later there is a splintering crushing thunderclap echoing across the night silences and the glider is gone.

We start a party toward the edge of the jungle, running toward the sound of the crash, passing the word back for the doctor. Paddy birds chirp sleepily in their nests and the moon is still high and white above. But in there, somewhere deep in the tangled growth, there is nothing but silence. We cut in part way and call, but no answers come back. We hear the roar of more motors overhead and the slicing sigh of two more gliders cut free, and again two more, until the air above seems full of them for a moment.

The word is passed that the bulldozers are not down yet. Plowed ground and buffalo wallows and a log or two have taken wheels off some of the landed gliders. All hands gather to manhandle them and clear the landing space for the gliders coming in. Everybody turns to on the disabled ships, horsing and tugging frantically to get them out of the way. But a glider with one wheel off is a helpless thing and a damned thing to move. "Turn her port wing to the north, and keep her red wing tip light on! Lay on the next one. Heave! Here comes another tow."

Fifty men strain at the wreck but she doesn't budge. The landing skids are dug in. "Haul up on the wing, hold her shoulder high. Move her tail around. Sweat, you bloaters, lay on!"

"Gliders!"

Two more are howling down over the trees, roaring toward the congestion. One of the two sees it in time, zooms over it with the last of its speed plows in safely just beyond. But the other crashes head on and welds two gliders into a ball of scrap.

Screams tear the night and the wrecker crew claws into the wreckage with hare hands to get at the injured. A British surgeon is already inside doing something under a flashlight, something quite frightful with his kukris after his morphine has stilled the screaming.

And there is a quiet North Country voice in there. "Don't move me. This is where I am hit, and this is where I die." And somebody's damned good sergeant goes out on the tide.

John Alison began changing the lights, re-rigging them to give the following gliders a better runway to come in on. Indefatigable John was tearing all over the lot on his short legs, no longer the fighter pilot or the glider pilot, but the airport manager sweating himself soggy.

Brigadier Calvert had his command post set up at the jungle edge and his security patrols spread out in all directions. Quiet Calvert, with a soft English voice masking the most civilized of killers. Stringy Shuttleworth deep in the Burma jungles, unshaven, but with his polished monocle stuck firmly in his left eye, a well-bred jungle stalker.

The first, short range ground patrols were back now—no enemy. There had been one distant shot but there was no enemy in force as yet. John Alison laid out new landing strips and re-rigged the lights so that the second wave of gliders could avoid those that had crashed in the first wave.

Doc Tulloch set up his dressing station and it began to fill up. Men hobbled in singly and between two pals. Men were carried in on stretchers. There was no sound from them. There seldom is after the first shocked screams. Across the field the British surgeon fought all night to save two men and lost with the dawn light. It angered him for he had fought well.

The breather was over and again the roar of tow ships filled the night skies, and again the gliders swooped in two by two. One with a bulldozer aboard missed the strip in the darkness and went headlong between two trees that barely cleared the fuselage. Both wings were cracked off as it howled onward into the clear. The murderous bulldozer tore loose inside and slammed forward, unhinging the nose and heaving pilot and co-pilot up into the air, as it crashed straight out under them and letting the two men drop back to the ground, unhurt!

There was now enough of a security party down to hold the clearing for thirteen daylight hours, the thirteen hours necessary for the Combat Engineers to make an airport for power ships. Alison got on the radio and stopped the final waves of gliders.

With first light the bulldozers began to growl and the Engineers were at it, grading and filling, leveling off hummocks, cutting the rank buffalo grass, hauling disabled gliders under the trees.

A British captain hobbled in on a broken foot. He had found his way in from a deep jungle crash with his sergeant weaving along behind him, both of them dazed. Two more men were alive in that crash they said, so Doc Tulloch got the position from the captain and with machete in hand and stretcher-bearers behind him started across the clearing to cut his way in to find them.

Word came over from the other clearing station that there would be a burial of English and Americans, shortly because the jackals were already howling. It was the first time

"Bulldozers and Engineers were at it, grading and filling."

I had heard them howl in daylight. There was a burial in one grave regardless of rank or nation, with John Michael Matthew, the little Burmese Chaplain from the Rangoon diocese attached to the King's, reading the service and everyone fervently followed with the Lord's Prayer. Motors high in the air could be heard but no one looked up or moved to take cover until the rough wooden cross had been planted and the last spade-full of earth was in; then there was a scattering in all directions. But it was our top cover, cruising far above, during the daylight hours, according to careful plan.

All through the forenoon the Engineers toiled in the gathering heat. Doc Tulloch came back from his jungle trek empty handed. The captain with the broken foot had been too dazed to keep his directions straight. Doc got another set of direction from the injured sergeant and went in again. But again the directions were wrong and again Tulloch came out empty handed and dead-beat with cutting through jungle growth for upward of ten miles.

Brigadier Calvert roughed in the casualty list as it was known to us and as we could guess it from known missing gliders. It was amazingly small for what it had purchased. In another six hours thousands of troops would pour in in power ships on this airport of ours, the airport that some of the first wave men had died to secure.

There was the hum of light motors in the sky and over the treetops came the tiny planes of Major Rebori, jaunty, frail and insolent in their perfect formation. They had come across the vast enemy-held terrain at tree-top level, with belly tanks to get them here.

We got one of them to cruise the jungle and he located the crash that Doc had tried so hard to find. The pilot brought back the exact bearing, we shot the azimuth and cut into the rank growth of jungle and after an hour found the crash. Two men had survived it and we got them out. Jerry Dunn was in there, to stay. So were the rest. He had been wrong "You mustn't talk about it, you mustn't think about it." When you have an appointment in Samara, you will keep it, whether you talk or not.

The American Engineers toiled on throughout the long, steaming afternoon, smoothing the strip for the power ships, lengthening it, making the airport. Their officer lay in there in that jungle crash with the rest of them, the third officer they had lost to date. "Every time we get a job in Burma we lose an officer." They stood around for a moment, helpless, bewildered, angry deep inside themselves, then young Brackett, the last lieutenant they had, said, "O.K. Two more hours of daylight. Let's get going!"

The Combat Engineers, shovels and machine guns in hand had the toughest jobs in war. But with the holy fires of something in their souls they carry on with it. It's something that only a Combat Engineer can understand, and nobody else need try to.

The sun was low, sinking to the tree tops and the shadows were pooling deep across the clearing, a clearing far in enemy territory so far that when you looked at it on a map you still couldn't quite believe that you were there. But you were and it was no longer enemy territory. It belonged to us! It was an airport, ringed now with enough men to hold it for the time that was left to wait. A wrecked glider was the control tower; John Alison was ready in it, with his control radio. As the sun went down the lights were tested to guide the troop-carrying power ships. And, the lights worked.

All that airstrip needed was a name. Then suddenly, it didn't need a name. It had many names, names from Brooklyn and Carolina, London and the North Country, Liverpool, Texas and Nepal, names of the men who had paid with their lives to make the airstrip. Men who were there with it deep in the Burma jungle and who would stay there with it forever, watching over it.

We heard a motor roar far up in the evening sky, the first of the troop ships. They came in and circled watching for Alison's green landing beam and got it, roaring down for landings, taxing off the strip to disgorge the army. They came in faster than they ever could at La Guardia, one after another, circling, cutting in their landing lights, roaring down on the lighted strip. You could count them for a while, then you lost count, and you asked someone and the figure was unbelievable.

General Wingate's Army! And Phil Cochran and his gang flew in over the mountains in the bright moonlight and put it down deep in the heart of Jap held Burma.

Acclaim by Air Marshal Baldwin for the smoothness of operation at the air field carved out of a jungle clearing in *Operation Thursday* was included in Mountbatten's letter to Roosevelt.

At General Wingate's advanced airfield (200 miles inside the Japanese lines) control was magnificent and it might have been a civil airport running under peacetime conditions. I first located the strip by an aircraft taking off and a second took off as we approached; we were given a green as we came into the circuit and landed straight away. The Captain was at once signaled by torches and led to his pen without any danger of collision from obstacles on the ground, or other aircraft. As he moved in, the prior occupant was moved out; we turned round within seven minutes then held up while three aircraft came straight in without having to orbit and all were led to their pens with equal efficiency. As we cleared the flare-path taking off, another aircraft was accepted and was already committed to its final approach.

I cannot speak too highly of the drill and organization displayed at this airport. Guides had been selected and trained from the personnel of the Regiment who had arrived in the initial glider landing.

I feel that this control, both at the home and advanced bases, is, the major issue when conducting any future operations of this nature.

With regard to the control at the home base, the Commanding Officer had got this worked out to the most minute detail. His system of dividing the strip into two equal halves so that aircraft took off alternatively, first north then south, worked without a hitch and certainly got rid of the dust bogey. By so doing, the runway north was completely clear for No. 3 to take off by the time No. 2 had departed south.

His organization of the pens and his system of numbering was such that he could immediately substitute an aircraft to take the place of any one that went unserviceable or was delayed due to difficulty with its cargo. I think I am right, however, in saying that last night only in one case was an aircraft prevented from taking off due to cargo difficulties. In this case it was yet again a mule which broke away on the ramp and insisted on jumping on the aileron.

Our Transport Squadrons put up a first class show and I think this is true of both British and American. Our crews were in exceptionally good heart, although last night was the fourth night for all and in certain cases the fifth night of operations. Everybody last night did two trips bar the few who went unserviceable.[12]

Not Lords of the realm, not air marshals, not presidents, nor generals became the enduring symbols of *Operation Thursday*. It was the ordinary men of the war who flew the canvas covered box cars towed by unarmed overburdened transport planes, the Combat Engineers and the British Tommy of the Chindits who made an impossible mission, possible. They had taken the enemy by surprise, 200 miles behind the front.

An American observer flying in with the first wave of gliders supplied the low-keyed, yet monumental description of these men:

You don't have heroes in armies any more. You just have men.[13]

One of those men, a glider pilot, one of those non-heroes, flew re-supply missions to the jungle airstrips laid down during *Operation Thursday*. He remembered that to pass the time he sang,

Oh the moon shines bright on the Irrawaddy,
They'll find my body in the Irrawaddy.

(sung to the tune of Red Wing—'Now the moon shines tonight on pretty Red Wind …' Repeated as often as desired.)

I had taken out a $10,000 life insurance policy when I went overseas and my kid brother was the beneficiary. I figured that if I got killed, there would be money for him to go to college.

The non-hero continued his reflections:

Landing on that strip wasn't hard, the bulldozers and the Engineers had done a good job. The enemy still was in the vicinity though. One time, I was riding in a jeep with a British soldier who had just picked me up from where my glider had come to a stop when we heard a shot and a bullet whizzed by us. The Brit said, "I say, someone is having a pop at us." He stopped the jeep, grabbed a rifle and went into the jungle. A few minutes later I could hear gun shots and the Brit came out of the jungle carrying a Japanese good luck flag. I had been looking for a Japanese carbine as a souvenir, but the Brit gave me the flag for a carton of cigarettes. The flag wasn't very lucky for the Japanese soldier.

> In one stretch of ten days, 3,000 Japanese were killed around the base. There were so many dead Japanese laying around that the stench was awful and the bodies drew flies. The guys bulldozed them into a pile and covered them with dirt to keep the smell down and the flies away. The flies were still around though.

The glider pilot, soon to become a veteran of eleven flights into the Burmese jungle, remembered with some humor, the men with whom he fought and with whom he survived.

> The Brits had large gunny sacks of tea, and powdered milk to go in it (Klim). I never saw a Japanese soldier without a gas mask and I never saw a British soldier without a tea cup tied to his belt. One of the jobs I had was teaching the Brits how to fly gliders. When we would be up in the air if the British soldier I was giving a flying lesson to spotted the tea truck coming around, he would dive the glider and land for his tea. During the day, we would drink tea with the Brits and at night around a campfire we would drink hot cocoa. It was during these times, around the campfires, that you would find out who you were fighting with.[14]

Reprise: '*You don't have heroes in armies any more. You just have men,*' some of whom wore the A-2 airman's jacket with his name and what he was doing in the jungles of Burma.[15]

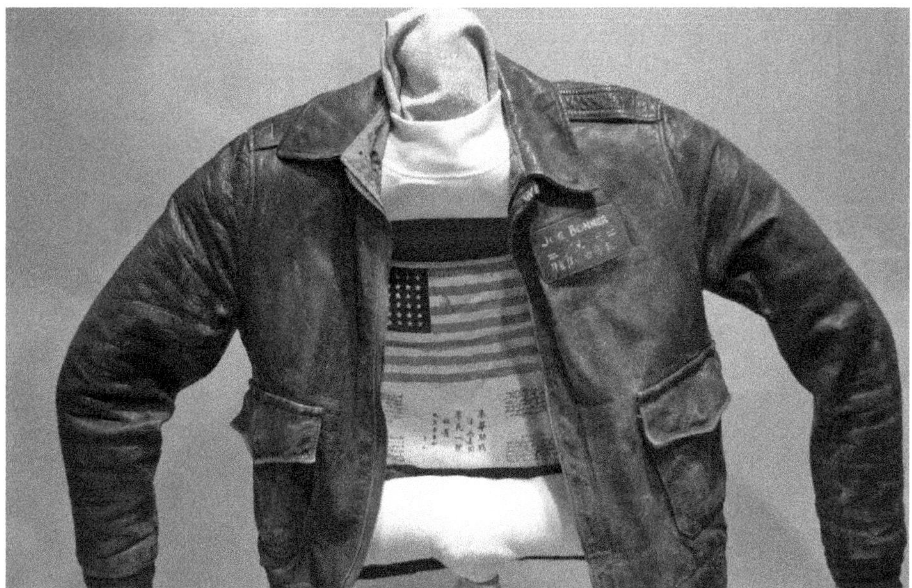

Below the glider pilot's name on the left chest panel: "This foreigner (American) is here to aid the war effort, to save and protect the military and civilians alike. The Aviation Committee." *Author's collection (Silent Wings Museum); translation of Chinese script, courtesy of Janet Hall*

18

D-Day—*Operation Overlord* Voices from Normandy

The history of the invasion of Normandy has been widely documented with details of how various individuals, groups, companies, battalions, squadrons, divisions, regiments and armies participated in the advances and set-backs experienced on that fateful day, 6 June 1944. In the United States the day of invasion of northern Europe has been portrayed through television programs, the miniseries, *Band of Brothers*, the movie, *Saving Private Ryan*, and the adaptation for film of the book by the same name, *The Longest Day*.

What follows here are collected *voices* of those glider men who participated in the Normandy invasion. In order to provide a sense of historical sequence and so as not to accentuate or diminish any one individual or group, the names of the participants who recalled their involvement in the events collectively known as D-Day and the identification of the military units to which they were assigned, with few exceptions, have been omitted. The memories that are included as a part of these *voices* have been adapted, edited, and combined from memoirs, letters, diaries, and discussions shared with the author as well as from archival files and published accounts.[1]

> About 30 days before the invasion, we were sent to southern England to fire all weapons the airborne used if it became necessary for us to fill in on a gun crew. We finished the exercises with a shoot-out with the airborne. Surprisingly, the glider pilots had the four highest scores.
>
> Later, I was thankful for those exercises because when I landed in Normandy, my first two days were spent carrying bazooka ammunition for two bazooka teams that were to stop any German tanks from crossing two bridges seven miles from the beach where the Allied troops were to land. There were two tanks at each bridge that tried to cross, but we knocked the tracks off and no tanks got across.
>
> Our next training consisted of three weeks of learning French from records in order that we could communicate with the FFI (French Forces of the Interior/Forces *Françaises de L'Intériuer*—French resistance fighters.) We were also exposed to a

CG-4A and Horsa gliders at an English airfield preparing for the Normandy invasion, May 1944; note the application of invasion stripes still in-progress

C-47 Skytrains and Horsa gliders from the 438th Troop Carrier Group lined up at Greenham Common, Newbury, Berkshire, prior to D-Day.

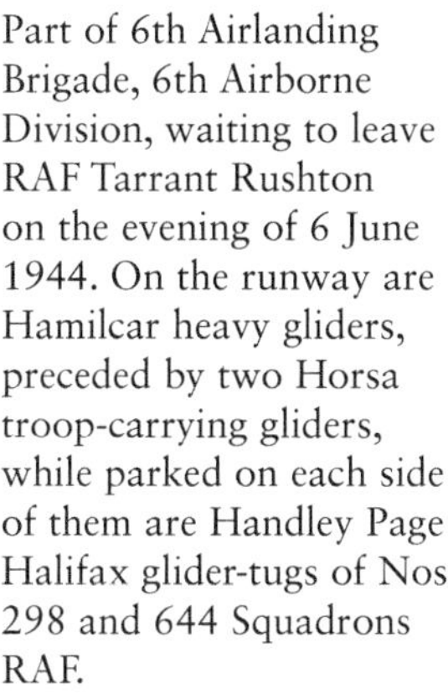

Part of 6th Airlanding Brigade, 6th Airborne Division, waiting to leave RAF Tarrant Rushton on the evening of 6 June 1944. On the runway are Hamilcar heavy gliders, preceded by two Horsa troop-carrying gliders, while parked on each side of them are Handley Page Halifax glider-tugs of Nos 298 and 644 Squadrons RAF.

A message to Adolf, 6 June 1944.

Waco CG-4A combat assault glider interior. The CG-4A could carry 13 fully- equipped troops plus a pilot and copilot. As a cargo carrier, its capacity was almost 4,000 pounds. Used late in the war, gliders were generally considered expendable in combat and few efforts were made to retrieve them.

Halifaxes towing Hamilcar gliders carrying 6th Airborne Division reinforcements to Normandy pass over the battleships HMS *Warspite* and HMS *Ramillies*, part of Bombarding Force 'D' off Le Havre, on the evening of 6 June 1944. The photo was taken from the frigate HMS *Holmes* which formed part of the escort group.

German record that would help us ask German POWs basic questions such as the names of the units, anything that would be helpful to G-2 (Military Intelligence.)

On the third of June at Aldermaston there was a high level of nervous excitement and tension was in the air. Airborne troops were moving onto the field in great numbers with much more equipment than could be used for a training flight. Military police were stationed at all the gates, and no one could get on or off the base.

In the afternoon of the 4th, all C-47 crews and glider pilots reported to the operations room for a briefing by the group intelligence officer. We all took our seats facing a small stage, and when we had all settled down he unveiled a map of France which showed our landing zone LZ on the Normandy peninsula. A low gasp and murmur went up from most of us as we realized that the time had finally come when we were to put our skills as glider pilots and tow pilots to the real test.

He continued, "The Germans within the last 24 hours have been studding the fields in the LZ area with poles and digging large ditches across other fields to prevent glider landings." That's when the eager, gung-ho looks on the faces of some of the glider pilots and tow plane crews in the audience started to change to looks of worry and anxiety, and the murmuring in the background ceased. Evidently the Germans knew we were coming and were preparing a lively reception for us.

His next announcement took us all by surprise. "Because of your excellent flying record and the expertise shown in glider training exercises, you will lead the glider phase of the D-Day invasion with fifty-two gliders carrying men and equipment of the 101st Airborne Division. Your code-name will be CHICAGO and your LZ will be five miles SE of Ste. Mère Eglise. Approximately five minutes later, a serial of fifty-two CG-4As, code-name, DETROIT, will depart Ramsbury with men of the 82nd Airborne Division. Their LZ will be five miles NW of Ste. Mère Eglise.

We were proud of the fact that we were to be the leaders of the glider phase, but some of us, I'm sure, secretly wished that we hadn't been so good on our training operations. Then the crap really hit the fan. We learned that we were going in at night because the paratroopers who had preceded us could not wait until dawn to get the anti-tank guns, ammunition, medics, jeeps and medical supplies which we would be carrying.

This was a tough nut to swallow. Most of our training in the States and in England had been for early dawn or full daylight landings, with very little night landing practice. The thought of a night landing in enemy territory, in strange fields with a heavily loaded glider, sounded like a recipe for disaster. The only good news was that the top brass had been convinced that casualties would be kept to a minimum if we flew the CG-4A rather than the English Horsa glider as planned.

In the afternoon of the 5th, I went down to the flight line to meet our passengers. We would be carrying supplies, ammunition, their 57 mm anti-tank gun, entrenching tools, a camouflage net and three boxes of rations.

On that same day we began the work of painting the "D" Day stripes on each wing and body of the planes and gliders. Some mark of identification was necessary for the fighters and anti-aircraft units had been given orders to shoot down any aircraft without identification. Many of us put our names on the nose of our glider: Dust Bowl, Black John, Deacon, Bulls Eye, Slim, Chief Lucky, Ape Tex, Curley and Red.

Takeoff was scheduled for approximately 12:10 a.m. on the morning of the 6th, with touch down in enemy territory at 0400 near Heisville. Our glider was 49th in the 52 ship formation. We (pilot and co-pilot) went to the mess hall for the proverbial last meal, and those of us who felt the need went to see the Chaplain. A lot of us hadn't been to church for quite some time.

The suspense was over, the waiting was over. The planes had been marshaled, gliders hooked on, equipment loaded, and the troops arrived from their waiting areas to the gliders. It was unbelievable to think that these troopers marching in the darkness, singing as they marched, would be behind enemy lines in France fighting for their lives, and that the glider pilots who had been with the squadron for over a year would be down on enemy soil with the airborne fighting with them until relieved. Not all would be coming back, but those who did would never forget those who did not.

Thirty minutes before takeoff, the engines of the tow ships began to start up. The muffled noise and throbbing from their engines spread around the field like a distant approaching thunder storm, and contributed to our uneasiness as we all climbed aboard the glider trying not to show our true feelings. My own perception, at the very moment, was that in roughly three and one half hours I might be dead. It was a very sobering thought and I wondered why I had been so foolish as to volunteer for this job. When I first went into the glider program early in 1942, the powers that be never explained to me exactly what gliders were going to be used for. At that time, I don't think they knew themselves.

At about 10 minutes past midnight our tow ship gunned its engines and started down the runway through a light rain shower into the black of night. As the wheels of our glider left the ground, someone in the back yelled, "Lookout Hitler here we come!" After that, no one said a word as I trimmed the glider for the long flight ahead.

For the next three and one half hours we would be alone with our thoughts and fears. It wasn't too bad for me because I was occupied flying the glider, but the men in the back must have been going through hell with their thoughts.

We settled down on tow, holding our position behind the C-47 by keeping the faint blue formation light on the top of his plane centered up in line between the faint glow from the tow plane's engine flame dampeners. This is not the easiest job in the world at night; the longer you stare at them, the more your eyes start to play tricks on you. I turned the controls over to the co-pilot occasionally so I could look away and get my eyes to refocus again. The added problem we faced was the extreme turbulence in the air from the prop-wash of the 48 planes ahead of us.

Shortly after we crossed the coast of France, small arms fire and heavier flak started coming up at the planes at the front of the formation, and intensified the closer we got to our LZ. It looked like fluid streams of tracers zigzagging and hosing across the sky, mixed in with the heavier explosions of flak; you wondered how anything could fly through that and come out in one piece. After the front of the formation had passed over the Kraut positions, we at the tail end of the line began to get hit by a heavier volume of small arms fire which sounded like corn popping, or typewriter keys banging on loose paper as it went through our glider. I tried to pull my head down into my chest to make myself as small as possible; I tucked my elbows in close to my body, pulled my knees together to protect the vital parts of my manhood and was even tempted to take my feet off the rudder pedals so they wouldn't stick out so far. By now, I was really starting to sweat it out.

A few minutes after we had crossed the coast, and before we reached our glider release point, the group ran into some low lying clouds and fog banks. All the planes in the formation started to spread out to avoid collisions, and this caused many of us to land wide, short and beyond our objective when we reached the cutoff point. In a very short time, too soon for me, the moment that I was dreading arrived. The green light came on in the astrodome of the tow plane, indicating that we were over the LZ and that it was time to cut off.

At that moment I had a very strong urge not to cut loose. I'm sure I wasn't the only one who felt that way on that night. It was dark, everything but the kitchen sink was coming up at us from the Germans below and that tow rope, as long as it was hooked up, was my umbilical cord. The steady pull from the tow plane signified safety, and a nice ride back to England out of this mess, if I hung on. I quickly put this thought out of my mind, and waited about ten seconds before I released the tow rope. It was a good thing I did, because I still landed about one half mile short of the LZ. If I had cut loose at the first signal from the tow plane, I would have landed in the area that been flooded by the Germans. Many paratroopers drowned in this swampy area that night.

As soon as the rope disconnected from our glider, I started a 360° turn to the left, feeling my way down into the darkness holding the glider as close to stalling speed as I could. It is almost impossible to describe one's feelings in a situation like this. You know the ground is down there, but can't see it; you don't know if you're going to hit trees, ditches, barns, houses or what, and all this time the flak and tracers are still coming up all around you. The only thing you know for sure is that the Krauts are shooting up at you and they are going to be right there waiting for you when you climb out of your glider. You hope you will wake up and discover you're having a bad dream. They say fear has no bounds, and at this point in time I was in full agreement. We still couldn't see a thing and I knew that we were about to run out of altitude.

Finally, out of the corner of my eye, I noticed a faint light patch that looked like an open field outlined by trees. It was. By now we were so low that we had no choice in the matter, there would be no chance for a go-around. With a prayer on my lips, and a very tight pucker string, I straightened out my glide path and headed in, the co-pilot holding on full spoilers. We flared out for a landing just above the stalling speed, and touched down as smooth as glass.

I couldn't believe it. How lucky can you get? But just when we thought we had it made, there was a tremendous bone jarring crash; we had hit one of those damn ditches that the Germans had dug across the fields. Their main purpose was to prevent gliders from landing in one piece, and it sure worked that way with us. We plunged down into the ditch and when the nose slammed into the other side, the glider's back broke as it slid up over the opposite bank. The floor split open, and we skidded to a halt in the field on the other side.

That ditch was ten to twelve feet across by five to six feet deep, with water in the bottom. For a split second we sat in stunned silence and I breathed a sigh of relief because none of us seemed to be injured. We bailed out fast because there was rifle and machine gun fire going off in the fields around us. Fortunately none seemed to be aimed at our field at the moment. It took us almost thirty minutes to dig the nose of the glider out of the dirt so we could open it up and roll out the anti-tank gun. When we were about half way through getting the gun out of the glider the Germans set off a flare right over our heads and lo and behold we saw the glider with the jeep that was supposed to tow the gun in our glider on the other side of the ditch, without a scratch on it. We now had to dig a ramp down into and out of the ditch to get the jeep over to us. While all this was going on the naval bombardment started on the invasion beaches and, even though it was five miles away, the ground shook under our feet and the noise was unbelievable. I think we all said a few prayers for the kids who would be storming ashore, and hoped they would be successful; our own lives would be at stake if they failed. We finally got the jeep across the ditch, and the gun hooked up. I left the group at Heisville, and the gun crew took off towing the gun to find their unit.

Elsewhere,

The tow plane blinked its lights and we cut loose—that was the miserable thing about the landing, it was night. You can't picture anything blacker than that night heading into Ste. Mère Eglise. I had on board a jeep, a trailer loaded with artillery ammo and nine men. We couldn't see anything and finally someone said to me, "Jim, turn on the damn landing lights." When I did, all I saw was the top story of a two-story stone house. We managed to pop over it and fell straight down over that damn thing into an orchard where we plowed our way between the trees, tearing off both wings and at last stopping.

In another field,

I landed fine and went out the window but what I hadn't counted on was landing in a fresh pile of cow dung. From that point on, my buddies never let me forget it. Another glider followed one of his buddies down into an open field when suddenly the lead glider touched down and exploded into a huge fireball. The following glider was forced to pull up to avoid going into an apparent mine field and flew into the tops of some nearby trees. Unfortunately, only a portion of the gliders that went into Normandy were equipped with the Griswold device that attached a metal birdcage structure over the nose of gliders to limit and prevent injuries during crashes.

Glider No. 1, carrying Brigadier General Pratt, the Assistant Division Commander of the 101st Airborne Division, crashed into a line of trees on the edge of a field, killing the co-pilot and the general. The pathfinder pilot on board the tow plane warned the glider pilot just before they reached the LZ that the wind had shifted. The glider pilot replied, "It's too late to change plans." The glider was overloaded and probably nose-heavy because of the steel plates that had been placed under the seats of the pilot, co-pilot and the general as protection from flak. The field was wet, and the down-wind landing no doubt increased their landing speed. It was this deadly combination that probably contributed to the crash.

After landing in an open field near St. Mère Eglise I went to inspect the condition of another glider that had crashed through the second floor of a large stone building. Unbelievably the crew and passengers were alive. The building was occupied by German soldiers who had slept through the noise of the early morning invasion. They were taken prisoners by the troops on board who went on to secure their objectives.

We had been given a device that sounded like a cricket when we snapped it. This is the way we signaled each other when approaching. As we were making our way to Ste. Mère Eglise, I saw a trooper hanging in a tree from his chute. He never had a chance to get down. When we arrived in the town I also saw another trooper hanging

Above left: Hamilcar gliders carrying Tetrarch tanks of the 6th Airborne Division's armoured reconnaissance regiment, coming in to land.

Above right: "*. . . and flew into the tops of some nearby trees.*"

Dead American glider troops next to their wrecked Horsa glider behind Utah Beach.

from a church steeple, still in his chute, playing possum—he survived while others didn't.

On my way through the hedgerows I stopped a jeep driven by a paratrooper who was headed in what we hoped was the right direction to the CP (Command Post). I hopped on the hood/bonnet, and we started up a narrow path between the hedgerows. About five minutes later, some Krauts opened up on us with machine pistol and rifle fire. I fell off the hood, and the jeep almost ran over me. That was enough. I got up and started off on my own again.

A short time later, while walking up this same narrow lane, I glanced to my left and saw a rectangular opening at about waist height; a rifle barrel was sticking out pointed right at me. I froze in mid-step, waiting for the bullet that I thought had my name on it. Nothing happened; the gun didn't move. By now I was curious. I crawled over the hedge and looked in; it was a complete German bunker, large enough for five or six soldiers. Its sole occupant was a dead German, his rifle was poking through the slot. Thank god for the paratroopers who had taken care of him earlier and probably left him in this position to scare some of their buddies. They succeeded; it scared the hell out of me and made me much more cautious. When I moved on I started to walk in a crouch and kept my head on a swivel.

The next German I saw was lying at a road junction in a pool of blood. He had just been hit by a mortar or shell fragment and was still alive. His gut was ripped wide open spilling his intestines out on to the road. I felt horrible while I stood there watching him die knowing there was nothing I could do for him. I still had not developed the hate for the enemy that came to me as the day progressed and I saw and heard of what they had done to some of our airborne men. This German, lying in front of me, was a young kid, and sure didn't look like a Nazi Superman.

A little later, I passed an opening in a hedgerow and looked through it and saw a paratrooper out in the center of a large meadow standing alone. Being a little on the lonesome side by now, and a little curious as to why he was out there by himself, I walked out to see what the scoop was. As I approached him, I noticed that he was wearing an Air Force flak vest. I introduced myself and he thanked me for coming out to help him, but suggested I go find a flak vest to wear. Being a little naïve, or just plain stupid, I asked him why, and he told me that there were German snipers in the woods on the edge of the field, and he was trying to draw their fire so his buddies could nail them. At this moment something went buzzing by my head, and I dropped to the ground. He remarked, while still standing straight up, "There's the son-of-a-bitch now." Needless to say I wished him luck, picked myself up and beat a hasty retreat in search of a flak vest. I couldn't find one in any of the wrecked gliders; the paratroopers had grabbed them for their own protection.

It dawned on me that by walking around alone, I was just asking to be knocked off by a sniper. At this point in time I still had not found the CP or seen any other glider pilots.

By late afternoon and after a few more encounters from sniper fire along the way, I arrived at the CP and was assigned with other glider pilots to guard the perimeter in case the Germans tried to infiltrate back into what we thought was a secure area. We didn't know it at the time, but they were all throughout the area playing possum. Some of the snipers were still in the trees around the area.

While resting in a courtyard in the town center, I heard and then saw a wagon coming down the lane being pulled by two paratroopers. In the wagon, lying on top of a load live German mines and ammo was what looked like the body of another paratrooper. He wasn't dead or wounded, just zonked out from exhaustion. He had picked a hell of a bed to take a nap on. One mortar shell or rifle round in that wagon and it would have blown all three of them to hell and back. By now we had all been awake for 36 hours or longer and the pep pills we had been taking to keep awake started to turn some of us into walking zombies. A few of the guys were out on their feet and nothing could wake them up.

I didn't see one soldier that wasn't scared, but when the area became solidified, I saw and heard something amazing from this group of tired and scared soldiers: a drag race. The fellows had captured two German three-wheeled motorcycles and decided to have a race raising. They covered the motorcycles with the U.S. insignia from the fabric of the gliders and were raising hell as though no war was going on.

Normally, our objective was to set up a perimeter guard around the CP and other supporting units in the area. On a few occasions we helped guard prisoners or take them out to bury their dead because the weather was warm and a body would start to decompose in a short time. The German soldiers had been indoctrinated to believe that if they were captured, they would be shot. It was sad when they would get down on their knees and beg. I had three watches put on my wrist because they thought I would shoot them.

At 8:30 on the 6th, some of us were asked to go back out into the fields to meet, and cover the landing of the second serial of gliders. A large group of Horsa gliders was expected to arrive at 9:00 p.m. They arrived right on time and then all hell broke loose.

The Germans in the fields around us who had been playing possum, opened up on them with everything they had. Their heavy AA (anti-aircraft) guns outside the perimeters were firing airbursts over and into the fields while the gliders were landing. The fields in this area around Heisville were much too small for these large British gliders and those that weren't shot down crashed head-on into the hedgerows. Some were fortunate and made it down in one piece, others came under heavy enemy small arms fire after they landed, and many of the glidermen and pilots were killed or captured while climbing out of their gliders. For an hour or so it was a god-awful mess, and the casualties in men and equipment were heavy before the situation stabilized.

After the gliders were unloaded and the casualties from the wrecks were taken care of, things settled down and I went back to the CP to dig in for the night in an apple orchard behind a stable. Fabric from our gliders was used to line our foxholes because when we dug about 18 inches into the ground, we would hit water; the glider fabric kept us dry and warm. While curled up in my foxhole trying to get some sleep, I recalled my boyhood days when I would get together with other kids in the neighborhood to play war. It was always the "Yanks" and the "Huns," and here I was in 1944, doing it for real, playing for keeps.

Shortly after dark, rumors started to spread between fox holes that there was a possibility that the Germans were going to drop their own paratroopers in on us. This did nothing for our morale, and for the rest of the night we were spooked at the slightest sound, especially when we heard some planes go over quite low. Any one that got out of his foxhole that night was taking his life in his own hands.

We got through the night and, in mid-morning of the next day, a call went out for volunteers to take over five hundred German prisoners down to the beach for transport to England. The airborne men had captured so many Germans that they were getting under foot and required too many people to guard them. Smart ass that I was, I asked the question, "Is the road to the beach open?" No one answered, so I volunteered anyway.

We lined the POWs up on the road and waited for the OK to take off. The Krauts were more anxious to get out than we were. The war was over for them and they wanted to get as far away from it as possible.

In the struggle to control Ste. Mere Eglise, which had been a rest center for German officers, the locals played a little game. Each time we gained control of the town, they would pull their Nazi flags in from the windows and hang French and American flags out. There was an exchange of control two or three times and whatever the situation called for, that's what they did.

Now as we passed through Ste. Mère Eglise we saw American flags hanging out the windows. A girl ran out and put a bottle of wine under my arm saying, "Vive

La Yankees!" It was gratifying to see their emotional freedom. As we made our way through town we also saw retaliation of those who had been collaborators—shaved heads.

As we marched the POWs toward the beach most of us had just about reached the limits of our endurance, so we gave the POWs most of our equipment to carry. One glider pilot was tempted to give them his Thompson sub-machine gun to carry, but on second thought decided it wouldn't look so good to the soldiers that we would pass coming up from Utah Beach.

On the march out, we kept going slower and slower and the POWs kept getting further ahead of us. Only by our making threats to shoot them did they slow down. The road to the beach was open and by the time we got there, our butts were really dragging. It felt like we had walked twenty-five miles rather than five.

We passed guys from the 4th Infantry on their way up from the beach. They couldn't figure us out because we were wearing a piece of camouflage parachute over our helmets with the first-aid kits tied on the back. We had a bayonet and knife strapped to each leg and two hand grenades hung from each suspender. I heard them talking among themselves asking each other, "Who in the hell are those guys?" One of them remarked that we must be some commandos on a special mission. Little did they know that we were a motley group of glider pilots doing our thing and looking forward to getting a hot meal after seven days of K-rations.

The sight on Utah Beach was beyond belief. As far as the eye could see, to the left and to the right, were men, trucks, tanks, vehicles of all types, and piles of equipment as high as houses. From the shore and out across the channel was an endless line merchant and war ships of all sizes. The Navy ships were shelling targets inland around the clock. The saddest part was the long lines of wounded and dead laid out in rows on the sand waiting to be loaded on ship.

The Navy Beach Master told us we would be going aboard an LST shortly and would be going back to England the following day. I immediately laid down in the sand and went sound asleep in spite of all the noise. That night German planes came in at low altitude and dropped mines around the ships just offshore. The next morning we boarded the LST but before any of the ships dared to pull up anchor, British mine sweepers came in close to sweep the area. One of them hit a mine less than forty feet away from our LST and sank within two minutes. The force from the explosion close alongside our ship scared hell out of us and made us think that we had been torpedoed. The only survivor from the mine sweeper was one of the stokers who was on deck getting some fresh air. He was blown overboard and picked up by the crew of our LST.

There ain't nothin' nor anybody that can put a scare into me after landing here (Normandy) in a glider.[2]

If newspapers had had an audible voice on 6 June 1944, the size of the font of the headlines of papers across the unoccupied lands of the Allied forces would have screamed so that all could hear: INVASION! In a smaller font but just under the history making headlines the first official communiqué of D-Day read:

> Communiqué No. 1. Tuesday, June 6, 1944: 'Under the command of General Eisenhower, Allied naval forces, supported by strong air forces, began landing Allied armies this morning on the northern coast of France.'

The D-Day invasion of France, *Operation Overlord*, will forever be remembered by the airborne participants, paratroopers and glider men, by the battles that engulfed them at Ste. Mère Eglise in the Cotentin Peninsula and just a scant few miles from the British beachheads of Juno and Sword.

> We began training at RAF Tarrant Rushton in Dorset for a secret mission. A few days before D-Day we were told our objectives—two Normandy bridges, the Bénouville Bridge that crossed the Caen Canal and the Ranville Bridge over the River Orne. Taking the two bridges, code-named *Operation Deadstick*, was needed to prevent the Germans from sending tanks to counter the landing of forces on the Normandy beaches and to provide a supply route for the invading allies.
>
> At 2245 hrs on 5 June 1944 six Horsa gliders towed by Halifax bombers left Tarrant Rushton for the target area. The attack force, under the command of Major John Howard, included members of the Oxfordshire and Buckinghamshire Light Infantry, (the Oxs and Bucks), a group of sappers (combat engineers with expertise in demolitions), and men of the Glider Pilot Regiment.
>
> I was the pilot of Horsa No 1 (nicknamed Lady Irene) and behind me and the co-pilot were 30 fighting men with blackened faces, including Major Howard—who encouraged the men to sing so that none got airsick. It was a midnight crossing in a rugby dressing-room atmosphere with songs and jokes.
>
> At 6,000 feet, when we heard "cast off" from the tug, the singing stopped and we began our descent. I could see it all, the river and the canal-like strips of silver in the moonlight, as we tiptoed quietly under the cover of darkness into two little fields in Normandy where we released 180 fighting men, and gave the German garrison the surprise of their lives.
>
> We hit the ground at 95 mph and ploughed through barbed wire defences before the cockpit collapsed and my co-pilot and I were thrown head-first, strapped to our seats, through the Perspex windscreen.
>
> The glider ended up on an embankment closer to the Caen bridge than we could have dreamed of. It was 20 minutes past midnight of 6 June, 1944, D-Day.
>
> Although often described as the first allied serviceman to set foot on French soil on D-Day when I was thrown through the windscreen, my head and knees were injured and in fact I became the first to hit French soil on my belly. I dragged my co-pilot from the wrecked cockpit and carried ammunition for the men of the Oxs & Bucks as they stormed the Caen bridge and captured it within minutes.[3]

"The glider ended up on an embankment closer to the Caen bridge than we could have dreamed of. It was 20 minutes past midnight of 6 June, 1944, D-Day."

Ford-built CG-4A glider sitting in a pasture, Normandy, France, June 1944.

A damaged US troop carrying Horsa sits amongst cattle in a Normandy field.

Nearby, one of the airborne infantrymen who had flown in one of the Horsas remembered:

> ... that whilst digging a trench at the Caen Bridge a German sniper shot at me. I was lucky because the bullet hit the shovel I was using and not my head. I couldn't see where the shot had been fired from but I lay down close to the ground until my breathing had slowed down and I was sure he had gone. The sniper was so close to hitting me he probably thought, that from his distant post he had shot me and not my shovel.
>
> While at the bridge my friend and I could see a figure wandering across on of the fields. On first glance the figure was British in appearance because he was sporting a Glider Pilot uniform. My friend was suspicious of the individual and so called out to him numerous times. When he failed to answer, my friend raised his gun and shot the man in the back of the head. It turned out that the man was a German soldier walking around with a Glider Pilot Regiment maroon beret on![4]

A reporter for the *Crusader, The British Forces' Weekly,* reported from behind enemy lines in Normandy that:

> ... at 3.20 every Allied paratrooper behind the Atlantic Wall breathed a sigh of relief as he heard the roar of bombers. Bombers coming in slow. Bombers towing gliders towards the dropping ground. We watched them in the pale moonlight and glare of flak, unhooking and then diving steeply for earth. We saw one, caught by ack-ack catch fire and fly around for three or four minutes, a ball of flame. We heard the crunch of breaking matchwood as gliders bounced on rocks and careened into undestroyed poles. But it was hard to restrain the impulse to cheer, for, out of every glider men were pouring and jeeps, and anti-tank guns.
>
> As dawn came I moved across country through German patrols to get nearer the coast. Wherever we moved there were traces of the airborne invasion. Emptied containers, still burning their signal lights, were scattered in fields and orchards. Wrecked gliders littered the ground some of them splintered to matchwood.[5]

A reporter from the *Union Jack, the newspaper for the British Fighting Forces*, reported that General Bernard Law Montgomery said of the invasion:

> The situation to-day is that these landings we have made on the coast of Normandy have all been joined up into a solid line—a continuous lodgement area. The troops have their tails very high up in the air. They are in tremendous form, full of beans. They are very confident and have already got the measure of the enemy.[8 6]

The injured glider pilot, Jim Wallwork, recalled that:

Montgomery inspects a Mk VII Tetrarch airborne/light tank secured inside a Hamilcar glider. The only use of the Tetrarch in its airborne role was with 20 tanks flown into Normandy on 6 June 1944. During the operation, one of the tanks was not properly secured, and fell out over the channel. As the crews had to remain in the tank during transport, the crew was lost along with it.

France was a very busy place that night. Our only claim to fame is not that we were the first to arrive, but that we were the first to fire a shot. By daylight my injuries got worse and my legs had seized but not before I helped liberate the first building in France, the local café, whose owner Georges Gondrée appeared with glasses of champagne.

The bridge was later renamed Pegasus in honour of the Glider Pilot Regiment, whose emblem was the mythological winged horse. The Ranville bridge over the River Orne was renamed the Horsa bridge in memory of the gliders built by Airspeed in Hampshire. Wallwork received the Distinguished Flying Medal for his participation in this the daring operation.[9][7]

Saluting the men and machines of the Pegasus and Horsa bridge battles, Air Chief Marshal Sir Trafford Leigh-Mallory rendered this salute to the men and machines of *Operation Deadstick*:

"It was one of the most outstanding flying achievements of the war."[8]

19

Southern France—*Operation Dragoon*

On 15 August 1944, forty-four American gliders from airfields near Rome and down the Italian coast struck in Argens River valley to isolate German units in the coastal area of Southern France.[1]

Operation Dragoon, the invasion of southern France, was a combined effort of airborne parachute troops, an amphibious assault by units of the US Seventh Army, and gliders bringing in infantry, howitzers, and ammunition.

Around August 1, I was assigned on detached duty to a troop carrier group in Italy for the invasion of southern France. We were flown from Ramsbury to Casablanca where we were billeted in the Italian Embassy. After a few days we were flown to Italy, about 100 miles north of Rome.

The use of airborne troops had proven so effective in the Normandy fighting, the commanding officer of "Dragoon" requested that airborne troops be assigned to this mission. They would be used in cutting off German highway communications from the interior to the beaches where our "seaborne" troops would be landing.

On the afternoon of 15 August 1944, at about 1530 hrs our glider tow began. I remember that in my glider I had four members of the famous 442 Anti-tank Battalion, a much decorated Japanese-American combat unit out of Hawaii. They received the Presidential Unit Citation eight times. Members of the 442nd trained for two weeks learning how to load a glider and to make sure that its contents were lashed down properly. The trailer the troopers in my glider had with them was covered with a tarp which had a big red cross across it; underneath, there were 700 pounds of Teller land mines.

The flight was uneventful, and there was very little anti-aircraft fire, but the landings were disastrous. About half of the gliders crashed into trees, ditches, road banks, telephone poles and lines, as well as anti-glider obstruction poles—Rommel's Asparagus. These poles, ten to fifteen feet in height, were about four or five inches in diameter and set out in fields with barbed wire and cables strung between them to wreck the gliders on landing. Some of them had Teller mines attached to them so that they blew up on impact.[2]

Another glider pilot on this mission remembers that he was:

... given a perfect tow at 500 feet over the center of the field that was the landing zone. There was no mistaking it. Hollywood never made a scene like this. We had a bird's-eye view of the burning planes, smashed gliders, collapsed parachutes, shell bursts, men running, dodging, dying.[3]

And from another glider cockpit:

"Red, Red, we aren't going to make it." Those were the last words that I spoke just before crashing in our glider in southern France 15 August 1944. There was no time to be scared; there were over a hundred gliders in the air and we needed eyes in the back of our head to see them in time not to run into any. What a damn mess that was.

Every time that Red would set his pattern for a half way decent, we would be cut out by someone with the same field in mind. It was either turn and make for another field, or take the chance that he may not see you and there would be a crash in mid-air. At about 300 feet Red spotted a small clear field, or so we both thought, and made for it. As we came in on the glide for a landing I could see that we were going to crash, but strange as it may seem, death was not in my thoughts.

Down, down, we went into what I knew would be hell. Red put the ship in a crab to wash out our landing gear and slow us up when we hit. Quick as a flash when we touched, the gear tore off. My feet went up on the cross bar above the rudder peddle as the bottom of the fuselage started to peel away. Still we were traveling across the ground as a fast clip when our crumbling glider hit a dip in the field. Darkness and the feeling of many objects hitting me made consciousness slip away for a fleeting moment.

Everything was quiet, green trees and beautiful skies were all that I could see when I opened my eyes. "Is this heaven?" My mind had almost made up that I was in heaven when the sight of my right leg brought me quickly back to earth. There it was sticking up in the air with nothing but blood and pieces of bone pointed at the sky. My leg was gone! No, I looked around and found my foot down by my knee, but still attached to my leg by the flesh.

My left arm pained me; I cried out for I could not move it. I had put two morphine shots in my money belt before the mission, just for an emergency such as this, I took them out and shot both of them into my good leg. Looking around at the glider, I saw a mess. The jeep that we were carrying was on me, and the four men that we had on board sitting in the vehicle with a wide grin spread all over their faces—they were very happy to be alive.

"Hell's bells, how about stopping my leg from bleeding, or I'll bleed to death." The men just sat there, I guess that the shock of the crash had not worn off yet. Finally after me hollering for a couple of minutes, they came over to me and one blonde kid took off his belt after I told him to and wrapped it around my leg, stopping the bleeding. He asked, "How am I going to keep my pants up?" I asked him if he would rather see me bleed to death so that he could have his belt and that shut him up.

The bottom of the glider and been torn off and the jeep that was in back of Red and me came forward in the crash and ran right over us. My pistol was torn off my hip, the sub-machine gun was broken in half and my M-1 rifle landed in the next field. What a lucky day it was that we were wearing our flak suits (steel plates covered by canvas from the neck down to the groin).

My body was all bruises and I would have had most of my bones broken by the glider's tubular frame, but the flak suit stopped any from entering my body. My head was all cuts from having it dragged across the ground. Red was nowhere to be seen. I called his name a few times and at last, he answered. He was over on the other side of the glider, where I could not see him. His leg had been cut and he was suffering from shock, but said that he was otherwise all right.

We had cut off our tow plane at 1909, landed at 1918 (my watch stopped) and the medics came down to us at 1930 which was very lucky for me as I had lost a lot of blood. The doctor and his aids carried me out through a window of the glider and the book that I was reading on the way in to the invasion, *The Robe*, kept getting caught. They had to take it out of my back pocket to finally get me out of the wreck. Someone found two boards to use as splints on my leg, and the doctor took my foot which was still down at my knee and straightened it out to where it should be. I held on to a medic's hand for dear life and cried out in pain. That was awful!

My arm was still useless and every time that it was moved, even a little bit, a gripping tearing pain caught me in the shoulder. The doctor said that my shoulder joint was smashed. As quick as they could the medics put me on a jeep and slowly went to the aid station. "Slowly," I said, for each bump would cause my arm to get that awful pain.

The first aid station was a large home with all the rooms full of wounded quiet men. The first thing that doctor did for me was to give me a transfusion to lessen the shock and replace some of the blood that I had lost.

All around on stretchers, cots and on the floor lay the slightly wounded and the dying. There were many there that never came from that room alive. Those that were slightly wounded gave the doctors more trouble by asking for morphine and wanting care than the gravely wounded who just lay there quietly as though they were waiting for their time of life to end.

Morphine is a wonderful thing for a person in pain, but you pay for it with the horrible dreams that flash through your brain every time that you close your eyes. All the rest of that day, the wounded poured in making very little room to walk around between the wounded. Through the window I could see Navy planes dive bombing the Germens in the surrounding hills, and could hear the putt-putt of our machine guns answering. Here we were in a valley cut off from our own forces, with the enemy just sitting in the hills around us, taking pot shots at us.

The night was very quiet except for occasional gun fire. Towards dawn, our planes from the 64th Troop Carrier flew over dropping ammo, medical supplies, whiskey and the Army newspaper, *Stars and Stripes*, telling us about our own invasion. What a write-up they gave us! The doctor came around giving all the wounded a paper, cheering up the morale. But best of all, we received a shot of good whiskey, the first I've had while overseas.[4]

From the pages of the *Stars and Stripes,* this story was filed:

WITH A TROOP CARRIER COMMAND, Aug. 16—The invasion extra of *Stars and Stripes* was delivered by parachute to Yank troops in southern France today through the cooperation of a Troop Carrier Command.

The delivery was made 12 hours later than originally planned but there was a good excuse for the delay. The first supply flight scheduled after the papers came off the press was canceled because things were going so well on the invasion front that supplies were not needed as soon as had been anticipated.

C-47s already have set up a shuttle service between southern France and bases in Italy and the papers went out with the first convoy this morning, along with tons of equipment. The planes swept unchallenged past the coast and into the interior where Allied troops were bivouacked.[5]

Anti-glider obstruction poles—Rommel's Asparagus.

20

Dingson 35A

The ten pilots of the Glider Pilot Regiment were told very little other than there was a special operation in the pipeline and that we were going to fly the Waco glider. 'Ours was not to reason why.' A few of the glider crews had flown the Waco in Sicily and all had flown them before. Nevertheless training commenced at once with up to six flights a day. By the time the operation got underway 84 training flight had been made.

In the morning of 4 August 1944, the Brigadier and ten jeeps crewed by French SAS (Special Air Service) drove into camp at Tarrant Rushton. These were Frenchmen who had escaped to England and had trained as special forces. Each jeep had a crew of three SAS parachutists and twin Vickers K machine guns, one mounted on the bonnet and another on the rear. They also carried explosives, sten guns and a PIAT anti-tank gun.

At the briefing the glider crews learnt that they were to fly the SAS into southern Brittany where they would cause disruption behind the German lines as the Americans, who were some 170 miles away, advanced up the peninsula. Take-off was 2000 hrs and the landing was to be at dusk on a small field surrounded by orchards at St. Helena, some ten miles or so from the town of Auray. During the mission briefing the glidermen were shown aerial photographs of the landing area and were told to watch for a small lake and then for a small fire which the Maquis (French Resistance) would light on or near the landing zone. They would escorted by 32 clipped wing Spitfires who shortly before reaching Brittany, would fly off to Brest where there was a squadron of Focke-Wolfe fighters to be kept on the ground.

Takeoff and the flight out over the Isle of Wight was uneventful. As the Channel Islands came into view the Spits arrived and took up position, circling 8 to port, 8 to starboard, 8 ahead and 8 above. The sky and sea were brilliant blue and they felt very secure and protected. As the coast of France appeared off the port wing, the tough looking SAS started to cheer and cry seeing their beloved homeland again.

They approached the coast of Brittany at 800 feet descended to 200 feet to avoid radar. At this point the Spits waggled their wings and left. They flew across Brittany over wooded countryside, fields and small villages but saw no signs of Jerry.

People in the villages were waving flags and towels as they passed overhead. As dusk came the gliders approached the LZ (landing zone); a farm building could be seen blazing fiercely at the edge of the field. It was learned later that the Gestapo had been there shortly before.[1,2]

One of the pilots remembers that after,

> ... a quick touch down in the gathering gloom and a cloud of dust, armed figures could be seen walking towards us from the hedgerows. They were the local Maquis and our welcoming party. After many French kisses and 'Vive l'Angleterres' the jeeps disembarked and our transport, two very old small trucks, drove into the field. Somewhere around 2300 hrs we set off in convoy along dusty lanes, through villages, avoiding main roads, with many stops at junctions where members of the Maquis were stationed. In the early hours we arrived at an inlet near the coast where the jeeps left us and drove off into the night.
>
> The tide was out and as our destination lay on the other side, we were taken into some nearby fishing cottages to await its return. Our hosts plied us with red wine and strong French cigarettes and eventually sleep overtook us. We were awakened at dawn to find the tide was high and the boats afloat.

> We were rowed across the water to some isolated farm building on the seashore, HQ of the local Maquis. Home was a loft of new hay. Meals consisted of rye bread, tinned fish from a nearby cannery, red wine and cider and an occasional egg. One morning a very skinny bullock was led into the farm yard, slaughtered by hitting it on the head with back of an axe and cutting its throat. Beef supplemented the meals from then on.
>
> During the days that followed the SAS in their jeeps came and went and were pleased to let us know that the Germans had put out posters offering 20,000 francs for our capture, dead or alive. One morning a member of the local Gestapo was brought in who, they said, had been responsible for atrocities in that area. That night he was stripped naked, hung upside down in a pigsty and for a time used as a punch bag before the hair on his testicles and body was burnt off with a cigarette lighter. A Frenchman with a sharp knife carved the cross of Loraine on his chest, cut him down and then took the skin off the bottom of his feet. The Gestapo man was then made to walk up and down the pigsty saluting a Maquis at each end until he collapsed, only to be revived by a boot. The following morning he was gone.
>
> Young French ladies who had been more than friendly with the Germans were brought in, sat on a chair in the farm yard and given back to front haircuts and shaved bald. Kept in the barn, we were asked to guard them but not to fraternize—as if we would.

News came in that the Americans had reached Auray and we drove over there to a right royal welcome from the French population as we were the only British in the area. Americans were everywhere and one, rather portly built, with no rank visible, asked where we had come from and what we were doing in his sector. His aid-de-camps seemed surprised that we did not recognize General Patton.

From there we went on to Vannes and spent the night with an American company. In the morning we helped to escort German prisoners to Rennes, where we found our way to the Hotel-de-Paris, British intelligence HQ. There we were given a slap-up meal in a dining room laid out as in peace time. An interesting night was spent in the town in a carnival atmosphere. On the next day we went to Rennes aerodrome and flew in a Dakota back to Netheravon—almost a non-event![3]

A glider co-pilot remembers that as he and his pilot approached the LZ,

... we saw the small lake that had been identified in the mission briefing and shortly afterward saw the fire, likely the same farm-building fire seen by others on the mission. It was a long narrow field slightly larger than a football field, with a tree, where several Wacos had already landed.

Unlike the Horsa, the Waco had no flaps but a lift spoiler, which, when operated from a lever in the pilot's cabin, would break the lifting surface of the upper wing, causing the aircraft to descend at a somewhat steeper angle, though maintaining the same gliding angle. As we came in I noticed several trees between us and the gliders which had already landed. As we made our final turn, Harry, the glider pilot, decided to land on the far side of the lone tree beyond the gliders. At the last minute he decided that we wouldn't quite make it and if we were going to land this side of the tree we would have to lose height very quickly which meant that we would have to use the spoiler.

Harry yelled, "Spoiler" and I pulled the lever back. Seconds later, Kapow!

I was knocked senseless as the aircraft, more or less, dove into the tree. When I regained consciousness, I found myself lying on my back, possibly on a makeshift stretcher of some kind with a bandage of some kind round my head. The moon was high in the sky and I heard muttered voices close by as I drifted in and out of consciousness.

After a while we were carried to a cottage near the field but someone decided that this house was unsafe because of the close proximity of German soldiers. I was carried to another cottage about a mile away where I was attended to by a woman and a seven year old daughter, both of whom were fearful of a German raid.

Any glider pilot who was captured could expect to be taken to a prisoner of war camp. On the other hand, as far as the Germans were concerned, anyone who aided or gave shelter to members of the Resistance or Maquisards, was a terrorist and a saboteur, who, under an order from General Von Falkenhorst, could expect to be shot immediately.

The Cross of Lorraine shoulder flashing/patch of the F.F.I. (French Forces of the Interior—*Forces Françaises de l'Intérieur*)

During the next two to three weeks, Harry and I were hidden in various places eventually ending up in a small hospital in the town of Auray on the coast of Brittany. The building that housed the hospital was actually a convent that had been converted to serve the wounded, all the nurses, nuns. Medical supplies and medications were scarce as the Germans had commandeered almost everything. The nuns were cheerful and solicitous, but I have no idea whether they had received any medical training.

One day, to our surprise, a young British officer, in the uniform of the British Parachute Regiment and wearing the maroon beret, came into our ward. He was surprised to find that two British glider pilots were so far behind enemy lines and promised to get us back to the UK.

The next day we were put in an ambulance and driven to the airport at Vannes, which was already under control by the Maquis, loaded onto a DC-3 and flown to Down Ampney.[4]

21

Operation Market Garden

It was bold and controversial, this plan championed by Field Marshal Bernard L. Montgomery. General Eisenhower, the Supreme Commander of the Allied Expeditionary Force in the ETO (European Theater of Operations) thought that it was risky. But Montgomery pursued approval of his plan from *Ike* allowing that its success would shorten the war by months and save thousands of lives by providing direct access to the German heartland. The plan was approved and *Operation Market Garden* was born.

There were several objectives identified for *Market Garden* that included maintaining the advantage over German forces retreating from Normandy where they had sustained heavy casualties, and freeing the Dutch from German control. And perhaps most importantly, the Allies wanted to capture a number of bridges to facilitate their march on Berlin.[1]

The Germans for their part planned to set up on the Maas River, the Waal Canal and the Rhine River three successive lines of defense where they would stand and fight. The American 101st Airborne Division was assigned the job of taking bridges on the route between Eindhoven and Grave. It was the mission of the American 82nd Airborne Division to seize the bridge over the Maas, north of Grave, and also the bridge over the Waal at Nijmegen. This would open the route to the main target, the bridge at Arnhem just 40 miles distant. The British 1st Airborne Division, along with Allied airborne forces, was designated as the attack force to take this last bridge in the chain of targets; a target referred to by some as 'a bridge too far.'[2]

* * *

US glider missions for *Market Garden* were flown on 17, 18, 19, and again on 23 September. It was a massive operation with a total of 1,899 gliders dispatched and 1,618 effective at reaching the target. Many were lost *en route* or over the target area and 163 sorties were aborted. Due to a shortage of pilots some of the gliders in the attacking force were flown without a co-pilot. The flights were costly—twelve pilots were killed, 37 were wounded or injured and 65 were reported as missing.

It has been impossible to determine how many of the missing pilots returned to their units, how many were killed, and how many taken prisoner.[3]

Airborne forces were heavily dependent upon the work of the pathfinders, teams of men who jumped into enemy territory ahead of the airborne assault force to set up a path to guide glider pilots and parachute troops to their respective landing zones and drop zones. Each team, consisting of one officer and eight enlisted men, began training together in secret in England beginning in March of 1944.

The mission of the pathfinders was to place seven colored lights and radar signal sending units to guide the gliders and pilots of the parachute jump planes to their LZs (landing zones) and DZs (drop zones). Glider LZs were marked with seven colored lights strung out in a line pointing downwind—first a red one followed by five amber lights and finally a green one. Drop zones for paratroopers were marked by five white lights placed to form a "T." Radar sending units, "Eurekas" sent signals to the "Rebecca" receiving units mounted in the nose of each tow plane or jump plane to guide them to their LZ or DZ.[4]

An American glider pilot assigned to bring in troops of the 82nd Airborne had worked for one of the US west coast daily newspapers prior to the war, the *Los Angeles Times*. He filed this report to the *Times* three days after having flown his CG-4A Waco glider into Holland during *Market Garden*.

England: Our troop carrier group participated in the airborne landings in the Groesbeek sector, just south of Nijmegen. I piloted the 11th glider to land on the second day.

Takeoff was routine. We left our base in England just as we have done in practice many times, but this time the CG-4A gliders were loaded with men and weapons instead of the sandbags we had carried in simulated missions. One by one the weather-beaten veteran C-47s of our group swept their gliders into the air and circled the field to get into formation.

At last the procession straightened out and in neat four-ship echelons headed for the coast. In my glider were 13 men with their equipment, some boxes of anti-tank mines and some mortar ammunition.

Six of the men had landed in Normandy with their airborne units on D-Day; the others had never been in a glider before. In the copilot's seat was Sgt. Michael A. Colella, the squad leader.[5]

* * *

A continued shortage of qualified glider pilots forced the Americans to "deputize" glider infantry troops as emergency co-pilots. These brave souls were given a five minute lecture on how to make an emergency landing in case the pilot was killed.[6]

* * *

Soon the sky was filled with other formations like ours; they were coming from airfields all over England to join the party. All met at the rendezvous, and a few minutes later the chalk cliffs were behind us and we were over the Strait of Dover.[7]

Up ahead a glider was in trouble, apparently out of control in the slipstream of the planes above it. It cut away from the formation and glided down. Immediately its tug ship dived down and started to fly in a circle close to the water. From the right an air-sea rescue boat streaked toward the spot.

A flight of Spitfires joined us, wheeling overhead in tight circles. There was the first signal—we were 20 minutes from the landing zone. The men behind me draped my flak suit over my shoulders, and just in time, for in a minute we emerged from a light rain squall to see the twinkle of smokeless flak right in the middle of the formation ahead.

The shells were bursting precisely at our altitude, but none of the planes or gliders went down. We flew straight ahead into the fire, and soon tracers were coming up on all sides and from all angles, and we could hear the pounding of the guns below as they pumped the stuff up at us.

The Germans had cut through the British corridor between Eindhoven and Grave, and were now busy giving us a little unexpected excitement. The fields below were covered with American gliders that had landed the day before.

I looked back at the men. They had no flak suits, but were sitting as they had been trained to do under fire—shoulders hunched, heads drawn down, knees together.

C-47 Skytrains towing Waco CG-4 gliders over Bergeijk, Holland *en route* to the *Operation Market Garden* landings near Eindhoven, 17 Sep 1944.

"The fields below were covered with American gliders that had landed the day before."

A squadron of Mustangs crossed our flight path just ahead and, one by one, the silver craft turned and flashed down to the attack. We were out of the fire in another moment, and co-pilot of my tug, called over the intercom, "Are you still with us?" Above us was a glider sailing along all by itself. Its tow plane was nowhere in sight.

There was the Maas, and beyond it the landing zone, and up ahead the gliders were peeling out of formation and going in. Then came my signal to release, and I made a 90-degree turn for the final approach. There was no sign of enemy resistance. I picked a spot between two gliders pulled up over a fence, and settled in on the springy turf of a cow pasture.

It was like landing on a feather bed. The glider rolled a few feet and stopped easily. The men jumped out quickly and looked around, but the only indication of action was the sound of distant artillery fire. All the heavy fighting in our immediate area had been done by the airborne forces that had landed the day before.

C-47s were coming in low, dropping supplies by parachute, and all the while more gliders were landing, in back yards, gardens and pastures. There was remarkably little damage to the ships and, in our squadron at least, not a scratch on a man or piece of airborne equipment except for one small flak wound. A cow that failed to get out of the way became the only serious casualty of our part of the operation.

Within five minutes after the last of our ships touched the ground, the troops were marching in orderly columns down the road to the battalion command post, carrying heavy loads of weapons and ammunition, while farmers and their families ran out from their spotless white houses, bringing apples, pears, peaches and pitchers of milk—the first fresh milk some of the men had tasted in two years or more. Many of the civilians volunteered to help with loads; most of them wore the orange armbands of the Dutch underground.

British paratroopers stood along the way, grinning happily and shouting their welcome. In front of a little inn an old Hollander in wooden shoes was leading the town folk in "Tipperary." Apparently he was the only one who knew the words, but the others carried the tune very well and as the column passed the GIs joined in. Dutch flags flew from upstairs window of every building we passed and the children waved little homemade American, British and French flags.

We marched until about 10:30 that night, when my group of glider pilots left the road to sleep in a wood about a mile and half from the German border.

In the morning we proceeded to the divisional command post, got on board two trucks about to go south.

A little way along the road we met the first Churchill tanks coming up to Grave after breaking the German roadblock at Uden a few hours before.

An endless column of British tanks, trucks, half-tracks, motorcycles and Bren gun carriers was racing northward; overhead a light observation plane kept watch, and for miles the fields on both sides of the road were covered with American gliders.

Also along the road were hundreds of thousands of felled trees that the Germans had cut to use in the fields to prevent the airborne landings. If our operation had been delayed a few days there might have been a different story to tell.

In one small field there were three C-47s. Two had made successful belly landings; the other had crashed and burned. Near Uden was the scattered wreckage of another that apparently had been shot down and exploded. Nearby was a new grave, piled high with fresh flowers. We rolled into the town where armed civilians were running from house to house, ferreting out the last of the Germans. Burning British and Nazi tanks stood in the ruined streets.

Bricks, mortar and glass were still falling from the shelled buildings in dusty avalanches. There was a bullet-riddled lorry lying on its side. Three dead British soldiers lay beside it. Rifles cracked in the side streets as we careened into the town square. Fifteen or twenty Sherman tanks stood there while their crews rested or made minor repairs.

Beyond the town we rode past the advancing British columns for mile after mile. The amount of equipment they were taking up the corridor was incredible. Portable trusses and pontoon bridges had been thrown across the canals and streams and traffic was flowing over them steadily.

Louvain (the French name for Leuven in the Flemish region of Belgium) is in ruins—shattered by our bombers—yet the people there seemed more overjoyed to see us than any we had passed. Their modern factories, railroad yards, find public buildings and homes are gone, but they loaded us down with peaches, apples, pears and even money, embraced us and posed with us for pictures.

On we went into Brussels, where we were welcomed in grand style. There had been few Americans in Brussels and I imagine we were something of a novelty as we went about the city, unshaven, dirty, in helmets and paratrooper clothing, submachine guns hanging from our shoulders. After a night's rest we went out to the airfield and caught a plane for England

* * *

A battle report, marked SECRET, was sent by the commanding officer of the 82nd Airborne Division, Brigadier General James M. Gavin, to Major General P. L. Williams of the IX Troop Carrier Command in which he notes his "reactions to the Troop Carrier-Airborne aspects of the present Operation."[8]

The mission required the Division to land and seize bridges over the WAAL River, the MAAS River, the WAAL-MAAS Canal and to seize, organize and hold the GROSBEEK-NIJMEGEN hill mass dominating those bridges. The area was occupied and well held by the Germans.

Glider landings followed the parachute landings on D Day exactly on schedule and as a result of the elimination of the ground flak crews by the landing parachutists gliders were landed under excellent conditions and there was little loss except that caused by terrain hazards.

Early on the morning of D plus 1 the Germans launched a strong attack in the REICHSWALD forest area. A message was sent back to the rear base in an effort to direct the pilots to land on the high ground along the western portions of the LZ which was free of enemy fire. It was considered too late at this time to attempt to brief the pilots on a new LZ, and if the message, as sent, had reached all the pilots, I believe it would have accomplished its purpose.

The tugs and gliders arrived during considerable flak and ground fire but landings on the west side of the LZs generally landed unscathed. Those that landed on the portion near the REICHSWALD Forest came down about five miles into Germany. Several hundred gliders landed on the proper LZ and the enemy fire from the REICHSWALD was very heavy.

Despite this, they continued beyond the LZ through the heaviest enemy fire and landed beyond, suffering, no doubt, considerable and unnecessary loss. The glider pilots stated that they were not given the green lights by the tugs and, despite the fact that many landings were taking place on what they estimated to be the proper LZ, they thought it more proper to wait until the tug gave them an indication to release.

Twelve gliders landed together three miles south of the LZ. To date seventeen glider loads from the D plus 1 Field Artillery landings are missing. All things considered, I would say that the D plus 1 glider landings were very successfully accomplished. There is obviously, however, considerable room for improvement; but the fact that so much was accomplished in the midst of a very intense ground fight on the edges of the landing zones speaks well for the training of the Troop Carrier pilots and the airborne personnel their lift.

On D plus 6, 43 glider landings were made on LZ "O". This area was free of all enemy small arms fire and comparatively free of flak. Several rounds of enemy artillery landed on the LZ during the landings. Troop Carrier serials arrived in compact formations with time intervals that permitted landings on the same general area without too great a possibility of collision.

Missing gliders landed all the way from the UK to BRUSSELS, to LZ "O". As well as can be determined landings were caused by tugs being shot down, gliders being shot loose, technical difficulties with tow ropes and flight equipment. All things considered, unit commanders participating in the D plus 6 flight feel that the flight was successfully accomplished.

One thing in most urgent need of correction, is the method of handling our glider pilots. I do not believe there is anyone in the combat area more eager and anxious to do the correct thing and yet so completely, individually and collectively, incapable of doing it than our glider pilots.

Despite their individual willingness to help, I feel that they were definitely a liability to me. Many of them arrived without blankets, some without rations and water, and a few improperly armed and equipped.

They lacked organization of their own because of, they stated, frequent transfer from one Troop Carrier Command unit to another.

Despite the instructions that were issued to them to move via command channels to Division Headquarters, they frequently became involved in small unit actions to the extent that satisfied their passing curiosity, or simply left to visit nearby towns.

* * *

One US glider pilot recalled that:

Some pilots wouldn't be seen after landing for a couple of weeks or so—they weren't too anxious to return because they had been shacking-up with French or German girls and didn't want to give that up.[9]

Another remembers that,

I got in the back of the jeep to go to an area that was to be an assembly point for glider pilots. I didn't work too hard at finding my way to the assembly point; it took a couple of days. Meanwhile I looked for the prettiest girl I could find—"they were very congenial."[10]

* * *

Gavin continued—

When the enemy action builds up and his attack increases in violence and intensity, the necessity for every man to be on the job at the right place, doing his assigned task, is imperative. At this time glider pilots without unit assignment and improperly trained, aimlessly wandering about cause confusion and generally get in the way and have to be taken care of.

In this division, glider pilots were used to control traffic, to recover supplies from the LZs, guard prisoners, and were assigned a defensive role with one of the regiments at a time when they were badly needed.[11]

* * *

Note: Because of fierce fighting in various locations, Gavin ordered several hundred of the glider pilots who had been serving as guards and performing less hazardous duties to take up positions and hold the line along the Reichswald Forest, thus freeing up a regimental combat team for an attack on the Nijmegen bridge. The glider pilot assigned to organize and lead this group in battle was Major Hugh Nevins.

After rounding up the glider pilots in the area, the major asked for volunteers from the exhausted group and despite the fact that every man was lightly armed with no more than .45 caliber pistols, M-1 rifles or some hand grenades, 295 glider pilots stepped forward to fight as infantry to prevent a German counterattack on Groesbeek Heights. They held their ground for thirty-six hours against small arms fire, German 88s, mortars and Nebelwerfers (Screaming Meemies) until they were relieved.

Two bazooka teams sent from battalion and division command posts destroyed three of eight German Tiger tanks that had arrived in broad daylight from the Reichswald Forest; the others turned around from the brazen conflict with the glider pilots and retreated back to the forest.

By the time they were relieved two glider pilots were killed in action and twelve were injured and wounded. It was the first time in military history that a group of aviators, all officers, fought as front line infantry soldiers. Major Nevins was recommended by Gavin for the Bronze Star for his meritorious service.[12, 13]

* * *

General Gavin continued in his report:

I feel very keenly that the glider pilot problem at the moment is one of our greatest unsolved problems. I believe that they should be assigned to airborne units, take training with airborne units and have a certain number of hours allocated periodically for flight training. I am also convinced that our airborne unit co-pilots should have flight training so as to be capable of flying the glider if the pilot is hit.

The Division could not have accomplished any one of its missions, nor its complete mission, but for the splendid, whole-hearted cooperation of the Ninth Troop Carrier Command. The drops and landings were the best in the history of this Division. The courageous performance of the pilots was magnificent and has been the subject of boundless favorable comment by all ground personnel. With all the sincerity at my command I would like to express to you my appreciation and that of every soldier of this division for the splendid performance of your command.

Sincerely,
James M Gavin
Brigadier General, US Army
Commanding[14]

* * *

General Gavin's letter of faint praise about the deployment of glider pilots on the ground would not have made for enthusiastic reading among some of those same pilots.

Gentlemen (*sic*) Jim Gavin . . . never did like glider pilots, and the reason is quite simple: He had no authority over us and could not control us. Once we got our payload in to the landing zones, our job was completed and we were strictly on our own with only one priority: to get back to our respective units as soon as possible. On the *Market Garden* mission, none of us glider pilots had any idea of where our outfits were, knowing only that they were supposed to be somewhere in France. Two of our guys in the 441st ended up in Rome, not getting back to our outfit in France until the last of October ... With no one to tow us home, we got lost.[15]

Fifty or sixty glider pilots had gathered around a couple of hundred members of the 82nd Airborne in a wooded area a few kilometers from Groesbeck when a courier arrived ordering the paratroopers to move out immediately. The pilots stuck with the paratroopers for a couple of days until they left in:

... the middle of a very dark night ... leaving us glider pilots all by our lone-somes in the middle of "wherever" still deep in enemy territory. After the paratroopers (left) none of us were really sure just exactly where we were and none of us had any idea of just exactly where any of the Krauts were, so, we just sort of lay around in the edge of that heavily wooded area that day.

Two days after the paratroopers left us my buddy and I decided to take off on our own for parts hitherto unknown to us. We decided to stay off the main roads and just head in the general direction of Belgium. The Dutch people that we met during the next eight days were farm families who welcomed us warmly and shared their food with us,

> with four of the families insisting that we spend the night with them. They knew when Krauts were in the vicinity and were delighted to steer us away from those areas. Only once did we enter into a Dutch village, and only then at their insistence. We were taken to a bakery where we remained for some two hours while one or two at a time from the village came to see us and to thank us for liberating them from the tyranny of Nazi occupation. It was a most emotional time for us. Those two hours in the bakery were the highlight of eight days of wandering in German occupied Holland.[16]

The Battle of Arnhem

It was planned that the Guards Armoured Division would spearhead the ground attack along the 40 miles of a long, single road that left little or no room for tanks and supply vehicles to maneuver. In advancing along the road the Division suffered heavy losses in tanks and men.

On the operation's D-Day, Sunday, 17 September 1944, a force of 10,095 men was flown to Arnhem, most being in the 356 gliders, the remainder of the division dropped by parachute.[17] The landing and drop zones were of necessity, seven miles from Arnhem. Late that afternoon near the old Dutch Reform Church at the outskirts of Oosterbeek, three miles east of Arnhem, a large explosion was heard—the Germans had blown up the railroad bridge crossing the Rhine.

The objective of the airborne troops now was to take and hold the automobile traffic bridge crossing the Rhine at Arnhem. They were successful in capturing the north end of the bridge, but due to very strong German opposition, it proved impossible to cross it and capture the southern end.

Waves of paratroops land in Holland. *Operation Market Garden* was the largest airborne operation in history, delivering over 34,600 men of the 101st, 82nd and 1st Airborne Divisions and the Polish Brigade. 14,589 troops were landed by glider and 20,011 by parachute. Gliders also brought in 1,736 vehicles and 263 artillery pieces.

The problem was that two Panzer divisions had been refitting at Arnhem and the British airborne troops were lightly equipped. The heaviest weapons at their disposal were14 pounder anti-tank guns carried in Horsas and 25 pounder guns brought in by Hamilcars. Other than these, the only anti-tank weapon was the PIAT (Personal Infantry Anti-tank). This was a short-range hand-held launcher that fired an armour piercing bomb and whilst it would take the track off any tank and so render it immovable, it would just bounce off the armour of the heavier tanks.

The Germans managed to recover from the first shock of surprise of the airborne landings and from areas as far as twenty-five miles north of Arnhem, strong armoured units were thrown into the fray. Their job: Stop the British and prevent the main force from linking up with their troops on the Arnhem bridge. Although there were additional British and Polish airborne landings on the 18th (in 297 gliders[18]) and 19th of September (in 44 gliders[19]), the Allied forces were given an increasingly hard time by the heavily armoured and experienced German units.

It was planned that the attacking force from the 1st British Airborne Division would take and hold the bridge and be relieved by advancing ground forces from the south in forty-eight hours; it was held for nine days. Unfortunately the relief columns never materialized. When the paratroopers holding the bridge ran out of ammunition, they were obliged to abandon their positions and make their way to the Hartenstein Hotel, in Oosterbeek.[20, 21]

Remembering their participation in *Market Garden*, glider pilots of the British Glider Pilot Regiment recount their experiences in this continuous narrative.[22]

Due to a shortage of tug aircraft, the landings had to be made in three lifts on successive days, the first on 17 September 1944. I flew on the second lift. After an almost uneventful flight I pulled off at 4,000 feet, four miles from my designated landing zone. My glider carried a Willy's Jeep, two trailers and four men. The trailers held a radar set, one of two that were sent, but the only one to arrive.

Having made a successful landing, my glider was unloaded. To do this, we pilots would go along the inside, to the rear of the fuselage, cut the cables that operated the elevators and rudder and release four bolts, two at the bottom and two at the top. These held the tail onto the glider, which would now fall off. Steel ramps were then placed from the open end of the fuselage to the ground for the jeep to be driven down—it had been loaded facing to the rear. Whilst we were doing this, the four men who flew with us, the live load, as we called them, freed the quick-release clamps holding the load to the floor of the glider. All this was done in a few minutes. The jeep and its 4-man crew drove away and I never saw them again.

* * *

I was on the third lift to Arnhem. My co-pilot and I had been led to believe that we would be carrying members of the 52nd Highland Division who, due to their mechanical expertise, were going to create a sort of runway near our landing zone. But, when we got to the Horsa we found we were carrying members of the Polish Anti-tank Brigade. Our load consisted of a jeep, a 6 Pound Anti-Tank Gun, 17 radio sets, some ammunition, 2 Polish gunners and an Alsatian dog called Bruno!

We were towed across the Channel at about 2,500 feet by a Halifax and discovered a thick screen of fog which we had been told wouldn't be there. We then had the situation where some pilots were trying to fly above it, some below it—needless to say it got quite interesting. We managed to hit the Dutch coast without any problems and expected shrapnel to start coming up at us, which it did of course. A shell hit the tow rope and that was that! "Well, that's made a mess of it."

In an instant adrenaline started to kick in and we knew we had to get out of the stream of fire. We put the nose down and turned 180°. It took both of us to pull the Horsa out, we were going down fast because of the heavy load we were carrying and you could just see the gun starting to move forward towards the cockpit.

It took the strength and efforts of both of us to eventually pull the glider out of the stream at an altitude not much more than above tree-top height. We thought we were out of trouble but whilst travelling in a straight line the glider, all of a sudden, pulled down towards the ground! We were doing about 130 mph when we hit the deck! The nose wheel had gone through the roof but we all got out without a scratch and the dog was running around asking 'What's next?' Within ten minutes of being down on the ground we were picked up because we were in the middle of a gun emplacement.

* * *

Another pilot also ran afoul of German flak:

The sea crossing was fine but as we were coming in across the Dutch coast a German flak ship opened up on us. It shot the tug pilot in the Dakota and his port engine was gone. He came on the blower to me through the communication line along the tow rope to say, "I've got to release you. Cheerio. Hope you get back and the same for us!"

I found a piece of land that was suitable and made a perfect landing. When we got out of the glider the Warrant Officer said to me, "We'll split up, I'll take one section and you take the other."

There were five or six guys with me when I spied a farmhouse and knocked on the door. It was answered by a great big Dutch woman and her husband. We explained our situation and they hid us there for 4 or 5 days. They fed us and allowed us to sleep in peace. It was marvelous. One morning the Dutchman said "We're going to take you out now." I replied, "Where to?"

"I'm going to take you to a fishing village and from there you'll be able to make your way home." He had enough bikes for all of us stacked out in his yard and we cycled down to the fishing port. When we got down there fishing boats were lined up on the water and they took us all in. When we got 4 or 5 miles out we were picked up by a British destroyer.

* * *

We pilots made our way, as planned, to Oosterbeek, a suburb three miles west of Arnhem and 'dug in'—fashioning slit trenches around the elongated horseshoe perimeter of the grounds of the Hartenstein Hotel. The hotel had been the HQ (headquarters) of the German General Walter Model but was later taken over by the airborne division who now claimed it for their HQ.

As we explored the area adjacent to the hotel for Germans we came across a barn. A young soldier came out, his braces (suspenders) down around his ankles, his hands on the waistband of his trousers trying desperately to pull them up. There was absolute terror on his face—"Do I drop my trousers and put my hands up, or do I hang on to them and get shot?" As he was trying to make up his mind, a young girl ambled out of the barn buttoning up her blouse. I guess young people will be young people even in war. We didn't know what to do with the soldier and one of the paras in our group said, "Shoot the bugger." Instead we took him prisoner until we could hand him off to the POW holding place behind the Hartenstein Hotel.

* * *

The following morning I was sent off on patrol with two other glider pilots and a captain in the South Staffs (Staffordshires) to determine the position and strength of the enemy. We had gone about a ¼ mile from the Hartenstein when we were surrounded. We had two choices, surrender or take cover. Needless to say, we took the second option.

We ran toward a church, pursued by two enemy soldiers. One of our chaps asked, "Do you think that they're going to invite us for a cup of tea?" "No," yelled another. "Then shoot the buggers!"

We disposed of them, ran into the church and climbed a winding staircase that led to the organ loft. We continued on past the belfry, to the roof of the church. There we found a catwalk leading to the east. The catwalk was shaky and narrow, approximately eight inches wide, and ran the entire length of the church to the far end where a window provided the only light.

Opening it very cautiously, we found it gave an excellent view, so we opened fire. Realising that the enemy did not know that we were there, we restricted our sniping to just a few rounds at irregular intervals, always aiming to wound rather than to kill, because, by wounding, three men would be taken out of action, the wounded man and the two needed to take him to an aid post; killing removed only one man. We kept this going for four days, during which time we had nothing to eat although we had managed to get some water.

By the end of this time we had used most of our ammunition. In the intervals between shooting, we went down to the organ loft and it was there that the captain was shot in the stomach. As a stomach wound is serious, he decided, quite rightly, to give himself up in order to get medical attention. He must have been in shock for he told the Germans that, "There are three more British soldiers up there."

German soldiers came into the church warning us in easily understood English, "We have men posted on the staircase and there was no way out. You have five minutes to surrender or we start throwing grenades."

We had no choice and made use made use of the time given us to render our weapons useless by breaking off the firing pins. We gave ourselves up and told the Germans that we had not eaten for four days; food was immediately provided.

We were sent off to an interrogation centre where I was given a fake copy of the Geneva Convention. It stated that a captured soldier could tell his captors the name of his CO (commanding officer) and the location of his unit. I didn't fall for this and would only give my name, rank and number. After a number of days spent in refusing to answer questions, I was sent to Stalag Luft 7, at Bankau, a POW camp for shot-down RAF aircrew.

* * *

Meanwhile at the Hartenstein Hotel the Germans had almost completely surrounded the British who had been reinforced by Polish paratroopers. In attempts to break through the German lines west of Arnhem and reach the airborne troops still holding on at the bridge, the British were beaten back. They were running out of ammunition, medical supplies, and food, and, 80 per cent of the re-supply airdrops by the RAF fell into German hands.

But most of all, it was sleep that they most lacked. They were exhausted by the intensive day-long fights from tanks, artillery, heavy mortars, machine guns and flamethrowers, as snipers took their toll among the defenders.

Eventually during the course of Monday, 25 September, the airborne troops were informed that they would be evacuated on that same night, with the exception of those who were wounded and the doctors and orderlies who would stay with them. The escape route led to the north side of the Rhine River where they would be ferried across to safe hands.

Right, then. This is the order we'll go to make our way to the river. We'll start at 2000 hrs. Those positioned furthest away will be the first to leave. To get to the river from the Hartenstein, follow a guide line with white tape markers laid through the woods by our glider pilots who will be at intervals to demand the password, 'John Bull.' Don't forget it! Muffle your boots any way you can and don't carry anything that will make a sound. You'll go straight through the woods, past or through German positions, then the next group will follow on down to the river bank. The soldiers holding on near the old Dutch church will be the last to leave. At the river you will be met by our chaps and Canadian Engineers from Nijmegen who will ferry you across the river. You'll have covering fire from our medium artillery boys from Nijmegen. Any questions?

It was a dark night and fortunately the pouring rain muffled the sounds of thousands of footsteps as the evacuees made their way through the woods. After they passed the old church on their way to the marshes and flat lands of the low meadows just before the river's edge, there was no cover apart from some dead cows.

> We crawled on our bellies to get to the river; it was an orderly retreat, no one pushing another out of the way and each taking his turn. As I was crawling along I hit someone's head with mine. He didn't move and I thought he was probably dead. It was the middle of the night, it was raining and I couldn't be sure. I had hit the head of a dead cow.
>
> The Germans started putting up parachute flares from the higher positions and firing on the marshes and low meadow near the river's edge.

* * *

> I led the last 15 chaps along the white tape trail to a hollow in the meadow just on the north bank of the river. "Just lay there until I say it's time to go."
>
> There was a mighty explosion and roar and I felt like I had been hit in the shoulder with a hammer. I fell backwards and was knocked out for a moment. When I came to and stood up there was a terrible ache in my shoulder and my hand was wet and

The white tape guideline recreated at the Airborne Museum, Hartenstein Hotel, Oosterbeek, The Netherlands. *Author's collection*

sticky. I looked at the others to tell them to move along and realised that they were all dead. I made my way to the river bank and found the major there waiting for us.

"Where are the others?"

"They're dead. I've been hit, but I'll survive."

"All right, then, let's get across."

At this point a dinghy came to the river's edge, the north side of the Rhine just below the old church. "We're here for the wounded." The major turned to me, "All right, Staff, in you go."

We started across the river and mid-way there was a horrible roar and splash of water. The boats were hit by enemy fire, some of them capsizing, most of the occupants drowning along with those who had tried to swim across. I was thrown into the water on my back and my left leg hurt terribly. I couldn't hear anything because my ears were under water. I began to wonder where my body would end up, flowing down the river to Rotterdam or to Amsterdam. I thought, "They won't find me and my mum won't ever know what became of me." About this time my right leg touched bottom and I heard a couple of Canadians yelling, "Hey, there's a body here!"

"I'm not a body, I'm alive!"

They pulled me up and put me on a stretcher and tended to my wounds, and one of them said, "You'll need proper care for this." They put my stretcher on a jeep, but before we got underway I asked, "Does anyone have a cigarette?" I had been hours without a cigarette! "No, now off you go."

When I got to the aid station they took proper care of me. "The bullet in your shoulder is in the bone and I'm going to leave it there until it can be removed proper." The shrapnel in my leg was awfully close to my private parts but the medic assured me, "You'll be alright."

"Do you have a cigarette?" The medic found a 20-pack and slipped it under my blanket. After I had been evacuated I reached under my blanket for the cigarettes and they were gone!

"Someone pinched me cigarettes! Does anyone have a cigarette?"

* * *

In the newspapers of London, headlines glared at the reader, "8000 IN—2000 OUT."[23] But despite these figures of loss and survival, readers were also told of 'heroic troops,' the 'immortal British stand,' and, about 'one of the most glorious pages in British Military History.'[24] A war correspondent for the BBC writing for the British service publication, *Union Jack*, told readers that 'They came out because they had nothing left to fight with except their bare hands ... They hated to go because they were not beaten, but they got ready the meager equipment they had left. At divisional HQ the padre said a prayer ... I don't think any one man who was not there could possibly believe it. There is surely nothing finer in the annals of the British race.'[25]

In the 28 September London edition of the US serviceman's newspaper, *The Stars and Stripe*, a reporter's article of the evacuation from Arnhem read as a tribute:

> Struggling through a hurricane barrage of fire from 88 mm guns, tank cannon and machine-guns, the last survivors of the band of British airborne troops who had held the Arnhem bridgehead for nine days at Arnhem were ferried over to our lines during the night.
>
> Bloody and mud-stained, exhausted, hungry and bearded, the remnants were brought to safety. They were beaten in body but not in spirit.
>
> The tragic yet heroic cavalcade returned from what one London sergeant described as "The kind of hell I never dreamed could exist on earth." As he spoke, groups of survivors, many stretcher cases, many wrapped in blankets, some hobbling with sticks, flooded like a tide of broken yet staunch-hearted humanity up from the river banks into our lines.[26]

* * *

Since that fateful time in September 1944 the Dutch remember and honor what happened in the fields and byways so many years ago during *Operation Market Garden*. But it is not the memorial services and laying of wreaths, nor the parades, nor the tour companies that specialize in visiting battle sites, nor the re-enactors who don the uniforms of the past and manage the vintage military motor vehicles on the streets of Oosterbeek during the annual recognition of those who fought on those same mean streets in 1944 that is important.

The Dutch remember because it is important that their children be taught about the men in maroon berets—those who came to earth in fragile aircraft or floated down dangling beneath silk parachutes, those who made sacrifices on behalf of their ancestors so long ago; it is the children who best honor the memory of those soldiers who were there and of the many who fell there.

> The sky was black with parachutes and they gave us hope. Although the battle was lost, they gave us hope.[27]

The importance in remembering is seen in the children, who during the Annual Remembrance of "The Battle of Arnhem" at the Arnhem-Oosterbeek War Cemetery move quietly through row on row of headstones, turn at the appointed time, raise the flowers they have brought with them, and quietly honor the veterans in attendance. It is the children who keep the memories alive when they turn to the 1,759 grave sites dedicated to the fallen airborne, bend down, and quietly read the name on the stone marker of a fallen soldier and then with care and tenderness arrange their floral gifts at each grave site as 4,000 adult attendees at the memorial service stand in respectful silence.

"They shall grow not old, as we that are left grow old;
age shall not weary them, nor the years condemn.
At the going down of the sun and in the morning,
we will remember them.
We will remember them."[28]

Dutch children remember the young airborne soldiers at the cemetery nearby their school in Den Dungen with words and symbolic air-spun pinwheels. Although dampened and limp from a rain shower common in the fall, their efforts embrace a sincerity of acknowledged sacrifice.

The children are taught about the sacrifices made by the glider-borne soldiers and by their elders, even today, at an elementary school with a specially prepared textbook, *The History of Dan Griffiths; A Premature Landing.*

From the children's textbook:

> An Exciting Event During the Liberation of the Netherlands
>
> 18 September 1944 . . . At six o'clock in the morning it is still quiet in the streets of the Dutch town of Den Dungen. A lot of people are still asleep. They don't know, that on airfields in England thousands of soldiers are preparing themselves for a flight to the German occupied Netherlands. Amongst the soldiers are glider pilots Dan Griffiths and Skip Evans on the airfield of Down Ampney. The plan is to depart early, but because of heavy fog the start has to be postponed for some hours ...[29]

A pinwheel of remembrance. *Author's collection*

22

Nuts!

> The heroic efforts of American forces in action at Bastogne during the Battle of the Bulge need no retelling. However, few historians give more than a casual mention of the part that gliders and glider pilots played in this important action during late December 1944. Flying their frail aircraft into a hail of enemy flak and ground fire, the glider pilots who participated in this battle carried to the besieged defenders badly needed ammunition and medical supplies that enabled them to hold out and secure the ultimate victory.[1]

Several iconic images and phrases emerged from the Second World War: the raising of the American flag on Mt. Suribachi on Iwo Jima; St Paul's Cathedral bathed in light through the smoke of nearby burning buildings following a German air raid on London in late December1940; the encouragement of the navy chaplain to his shipmates during the Japanese attack on Pearl Harbor, 'Praise the Lord and pass the ammunition;' Winston Churchill's speech to the British House of Commons, and to the world, that 'never was so much owed by so many to so few; and General Douglas MacArthur's declaration following his ordered departure from the Philippines, 'I shall return.' But, it is arguable that one of the most famous in this collection of war-time memories for the ages is the response to a demand to the American general, Anthony McAuliffe, that he surrender his garrison of beleaguered troops who, in late December 1944, were holding Bastogne against superior numbers of German forces that surrounded the town. The general's written response was terse and mystifying to its intended audience: 'Nuts!'

It was one of the coldest winters in years as Allied soldiers huddled to stay warm and somehow defend a front that stretched for eighty-five miles through the Ardennes forest. And, it was this very combination of foul weather and a thin line of enemy troops that persuaded Hitler to punch through and drive toward the prize of the port of Antwerp. Taking this seaport would shutter the supply line that was bringing men and materiel to the both the British and Americans who had made advances toward the German Siegfried Line.[2]

In the early morning hours of 16 December 1944 the Germans launched a massive offensive of 200,000 troops and columns of Panzer tanks that had been gathering unseen under cover of the forests of the Ardennes. The 83,000 Allied defenders along the Luxembourg and Belgium line were "too thinly dispersed to offer any great resistance against the powerful enemy attack and were forced to fall back."[3] By 21 December the German advances penetrated through to a depth of nearly sixty miles along a Panzer created thirty mile-wide bulge in the line of Allied defenses.[4, 5]

For fear of losing the gains the Allies had made since the Normandy landings on D-Day, Eisenhower brought in reserve forces including the 82nd and 101st Airborne Divisions who had only recently been fighting in the *Market Garden* campaign in Holland. But, by 20 December the Screaming Eagles of the 101st Airborne found themselves surrounded in Bastogne, a transportation center with seven highways and three rail lines spreading out from the village.[6]

> Because Bastogne was the key to the road-net not only to the northwest but to southwest and south as well, and since nobody knew for sure at the time which way the Germans wanted to go, the need to hold Bastogne never came into question.[7]

Supply drops to the forces in Bastogne by C-47s from England could hardly be considered a milk run since the weather and fog forced the pilots to fly low and on instruments, easy targets for German gunners on the ground. Although they brought in 300 tons of supplies at a cost of eight planes, what the ground forces needed most was gasoline and ammunition, items not conducive to successful parachute drops.[8]

Also desperately needed were medical supplies and doctors for the more than 400 wounded soldiers, their surgical and care needs unmet as the result of the Germans capture of a field hospital and its doctors and other medical personnel, a clear violation of Geneva Convention.[9] McAuliffe's Christmas Eve greetings to his troops answered the question many troops in the battered city may have asked: What's so Merry about this Christmas? *We have stopped cold everything that has been thrown at us from the North, East, South and West.* And to the German Commander's proposal that we surrender, my response was, "*Nuts!*"

C-47s drop supplies to the troops in Bastogne.

439th [TCG] [91st TCS] glider taking off for Bastogne resupply 27 December 1944. *Courtesy National Archives, NWWIIGPA Collection*

On the next day, Christmas, McAuliffe sent an urgent request for glider-delivered combat surgeons, gasoline and ammunition, the highest priority given to the medical teams. The first glider carrying two volunteer medical teams arrived on the 26th after about an hour's flying time from its base in Étain, France. This flight was soon followed by ten additional gliders carrying additional medical personnel, gasoline and artillery shells.[10] Fifteen minutes after the last glider touched down in its LZ, Patton's first tanks broke through from the south. On the following day, an additional fifty gliders were dispatched from Châteaudun, France to fly to Bastogne, this time meeting heavy ground fire and suffering multiple hits, from anti-aircraft guns and machineguns, rounds ripping through the canvas and pinging off the metal frame, some piercing the Jerry cans of gasoline.[11]

One of the pilots who flew into Bastogne remembers that:

> Orders quickly came for twelve gliders to be loaded with five gallon Jerry cans of gasoline stacked double decked. I was one of the "lucky guys" assigned to fly the gasoline tankers! One tracer bullet and KABOOM! Hey, someone had to do it, and by that time we had all heard about Gen. McAuliffe's one word reply to the Kraut's surrender ultimatum: "NUTS!" Our loaded gliders sat on the tarmac a couple of days when word came (that) the Gooney Birds could immediately take off for Bastogne towing our loaded gliders, including my lil ole gasoline tanker. At the moment I really had big time mixed emotions. I really wanted to fly into Bastogne, but I really wasn't all that excited about flying that gasoline tanker.[12]

Another pilot recalls that:

> The timing of the arrival was good. The sun had already set and the moon had not yet risen. We came in between five and six hundred feet which meant the enemy had difficulty in getting our range. Every glider landed with nearly all gasoline intact, although some of the cans of gasoline had been pierced by small-arms fire, none, fortunately, had been hit by incendiary bullets.'[13]

McAuliffe and the 101st Airborne got a monumental amount of well-deserved glory as did Patton and his 4th Armored Division for breaking through the Krauts to relieve Bastogne. But the volunteer combat glider pilots who flew into Bastogne received very

> little, if any, recognition for what they did, and no glory at all! But ask the troopers of the 101st whose gas tanks were empty and who were running out of ammunition and ask those medics who were in desperate need of medical supplies and they would tell you how they felt about those "unknown pilots" who wore the silver "G" wings.[14]

And in the final analysis, isn't it the thanks and admiration of your fellow soldiers that matter most? Isn't it satisfaction enough to know that you had been responsible for saving the lives of some of your comrades by flying in teams of medical personnel, and that you were just 'doing your job?'

During the Battle of the Bulge, two supply operations were flown with gliders; 11 were dispatched on 26 December 1944, 50 were sent on the 27th. Sixteen pilots of the 72 sent out were reported as missing in action, one was wounded, none were killed.[15]

The Ardennes, the Battle of the Bulge, Bastogne, *Operation Repulse*—the battles fought here were bloody and muddy. It was miserably cold, and it cost thousands of lives. The campaign:

> ... which delayed the Rhineland Campaign for six weeks secured no major terrain objectives for either side. The Germans who had employed some of their best remaining units, lost nearly 250,000 men, 600 tanks and assault guns, and about 1,600 airplanes. The Allies suffered 72,000 casualties.[16]

A correspondent for the U.S. serviceman's magazine, *Yank*, reported the grizzly side of the conflict at the Battle of the Bulge:

> The Ardennes campaign was more than a fight against the strongest German attack we had faced since the early days in Normandy. It was also a fight against almost daily snowstorms in near sub-zero temperatures and face-freezing winds which doubled the difficulty of rolling back the German advance.
>
> We learned a lot about winter warfare in the Ardennes. Some of it was learned the hard way, by frostbitten hands and feet, pneumonia, and even death by freezing. Besides physical difficulties, there was the added trouble of frozen weapons, equipment, and even food.
>
> ... (D)own the street is a US Army hospital, formerly a Belgian schoolhouse, which was evacuated this morning. The wounded and sick who slept there last night are now in ambulances and trucks, bouncing over that road which has just been bombed ... Our jeep stalls beside a bomb crater on the right side of the road ... in the muddy crater are two American bodies and an abandoned stretcher. They had been pushed off the road so that the passing vehicles would not run them over. An Army blanket covers each corpse. Beside one body is a helmet with a medic's red cross painted on it. There is a hole drilled clean through it.[17]

23

Operation Varsity—3 Hours, 20 Minutes

> (The) aerial invasion of Germany at Wesel, on the Rhine River, was the final European Theater of Operation glider mission. On that date some 1,348 American and British gliders crossed the river strongpoint and delivered the final fatal blow to the Axis Forces.[1]

Operation Varsity was the airborne component of the larger mission, code-named *Plunder*, that became known simply as the Rhine Crossing or the Rhine River Crossing. Field Marshal Montgomery was assigned the task of crossing both the Rhine and Issel Rivers, natural barriers to the heart of Germany's interior, the Fatherland. Monty had tried to break across the Rhine six months earlier at Arnhem, but the Germans kept that from happening at a significant cost of lives and materiel. For this attempt in addition to his ground forces, he would commit two airborne divisions, the British 6th Airborne Division and the US 17th Airborne Division.

The orders for the implementation of *Operation Varsity* were deceptively simple. For the British 6th Airborne Division: Take and hold ten road junctions, three road bridges including two that crossed over the Issel River, a rail bridge over the same river, two rail and road crossings and junctions, numerous buildings and capture and hold the town of Hamminkeln. The Glider Pilot Regiment was to land with their load of parachute brigade support elements and divisional headquarters in their assigned LZs near Hamminkeln and the Diersfordter Wald (Forest).

The orders for the US Airborne Division: Conduct a parachute drop in the Wesel area to assist the assault crossings of the Rhine River by the British 15th Division; elements of the Ninth Air Force will accompany the Airborne lifts to their DZs and LZs near Wesel; IX Troop Carrier Command will transport parachute and glider troops and perform air resupply. The 17th Airborne Division will take and hold the heights near the edge of the Diersfordter, take the bridge over the Issel River, and, contact and support Allied forces in the area.[2]

U.S. Army Air Force Douglas C-47 Skytrain transports and Waco CG-4A gliders lined up for *Operation Varsity* on 24 March 1945.

17th Airborne Glider Troops wait to board glider on 24 March 1945 for *Operation Varsity*.

Yet nothing that involved such a massive commitment of troops and equipment could ever be called simple. In preparation for the river assault:

> ... (T)he crossing of the Rhine was to rival D-day in Normandy in terms not only of number of troops involved (a million and a quarter), in the build-up of supplies, transport, and special equipment, in the amount of supporting firepower, in complexity of deception plans, and in general elaboration. A sampling of statistics provides a ready index to the immensity of what probably was the most elaborate assault river crossing operation of all time. The British, alone, marshaled 60,000 tons of ammunition, 30,000 tons of engineer stores, and 28,000 tons of other commodities, all in addition to normal daily requirements.
>
> The Ninth Army built up another 138,000 tons of supplies. More than 37,000 British engineers were to participate, and 22,000 American were to participate. Including attached Canadian units, the British had 3,411 artillery pieces, anti-tank and anti-aircraft guns, and rocket projectors; the Americans added another 2,070 pieces. The Ninth Army issued over 800,000 maps.[3]

From mid-February to 21 March Allied air forces initiated and continued a heavy bombing program

> ... against the (German) transportation system ... Allied bombardiers directed 31,635 tons of bombs. Heavy and medium bombers made 1,792 sorties against 17 rail bridges and viaducts along the arc encompassing the Ruhr. By 21 March ... 10 of the bridges were destroyed and 5 others too damaged to use. British and US fighters and fighter bombers flew 7,311 sorties directed against the rail and road systems of the Ruhr. In the last three days before the crossing, heavy bombers of the Eighth Air Force concentrated on enemy airfields and barracks, with particular attention to fields known to harbor jet aircraft. The heavies flew 3,859 sorties and during this same period 2,000 medium bombers of the US 9th Air Force hit communications centers, rail yards, and flak positions.[4]

Combined components of the British and U.S. Airborne brought 21,680 paratroopers and glidermen to join the battle aboard 1,696 jump planes. In addition 390 Horsas and 48 of the large British Hamilcar gliders, each carrying Bren-gun carriers, were added as part of the glider contingent of 1,348 gliders. This air armada, escorted by 889 Allied fighters, was followed closely by 240 four-engine Liberator bombers (B-24s) of the US Eighth Air Force dropping 5,820 tons of supplies. Another 2,153 fighter aircraft either maintained a protective umbrella over the target area or ranged far over Germany in quest of any German plane that might see fit to interfere. None did.[5,6]

As part of this preparation, someone, somehow managed to ensure that in addition to the steaks and eggs that were served at breakfast on the morning of the crossing, apple pie was also available.[7] And to insure that participants in this epic battle would rest comfortably at the end of a long day of battle, one of the canisters of the supply drop by the B-24 American Liberators landed very close to pilots from the British Glider Pilot Regiment dug in for the night in their fox holes. "(It) split open very near us as it hit the ground. Its contents spilt out over the earth—hundreds of pairs of pajamas!"[7]

> The action started on March 23rd when the British artillery units began a heavy barrage of the DZs (drop zones) and LZs (landing zones) and the far (west) banks of the Rhine. When the barrage was stopped an hour later the British assault boats started across the Rhine under an unannounced blanket of heavy black smoke, which later made the glider landings extremely difficult. By dawn the next day a 20 mile front consisting of nine small bridgeheads had been established on the other side of the Rhine by the British forces.
>
> The IX Troop Carrier Command made available 226 C-47s as gliders tugs, many of which towed two gliders each. Seventy-two C-46 planes carried American 17th Airborne Division paratroopers, the first time this aircraft had been used as a paratroop carrier. The Allied sky train flying out of air bases in England and France took three hours and twenty minutes to pass a given point on its way to the targeted area, the transports eventually merging over Wavre, Belgium to start their run on Wesel.
>
> Although the Germans took a heavy toll as the last of the 572 American gliders in the first serials either landed or crashed in their LZs the American glider pilots delivered 3,492 men, 202 jeeps, 54 trailers and a great deal of ammunition and artillery. German gunners hit 140 of the 295 planes towing gliders, 12 C-47s crashing in or near the LZs. Only 83 gliders landed outside their LZs. During the American paratrooper drop the Germans destroyed 19 of the 72 C-46 jump planes and damaged 38 others.[8]

The British were no less successful in their delivery of men and machines to the battlefield. The Glider Pilot Regiment delivered 4,844 troops, 342 jeeps, 348 trailers, 7 Locust tanks, 14 lorries and 76 guns of various sizes and calibers.

The entire force landed within 63 minutes, their mission objectives taken by 1300 hrs of 24 March. Four tug aircraft were shot down, three were missing, thirty-two were flak damaged and two ditched in the English Channel. Ninety-eight members of the Regiment were killed in action, fifty-eight of those former RAF pilots.[9]

The memories and reports of participants in *Operation Varsity* bring a more dramatic presence to the battle scene than do the numbers of aircraft and personnel involved. Their edited and adapted accounts provide a narrative flow of the action.

Hamilcar glider delivering troops and equipment during *Operation Varsity.*

WITH THE 17TH AIRBORNE DIVISION—(Delayed): "Now," said the sergeant, "is when you pray." Thirteen men in a glider were diving toward a smoky battlefield 700 feet below and somewhere behind the Rhine. The sergeant was well-meaning but a little bit tardy with his cue. The sky had been full of praying men ever since this glider and hundreds like it soared off toward its destination east of the Rhine. You prayed from the moment the silken rope stretched taut from the tail of the twin-engined C-47 up ahead and the flimsy fabric craft started breaking down the runway. And while you were praying you felt something akin to horror as you read the label on a case lashed by heavy rope to the floor—"Five—Anti-Tank Mines—Five." And you wondered why they had to go in this glider with a bunch of medics, a radio operator, a lineman, a photographer and a war correspondent.

You thought of landing and remembering pictures of gliders in Normandy and Holland, all smashed and splintered—and you prayed some more. You looked off to the left and watched the right wingtip of a sister glider, tied to the same C-47, swing perilously close. What would it be like, you wondered, if the two locked wings and you plummeted to the green fields below? You gritted your teeth and turned your head away as a man across the aisle vomited into his helmet, partly from the pitching of the glider and partly from nausea induced by a fear which he admitted unashamed.

Then things began happening—too fast. Above the sustained roar of wind ripping past the cloth-covered ribs of the glider you began to hear Crack! Pop! Snap! You glued your eyes on the pilot waiting for him to push the lever which would cut the glider loose from the tow-plane. Bursts of rifle fire were accompanied now by the popping of machine guns and the guttural whoomph of 88-mm flak shells.

You unconsciously lift off your seat and brace as if to meet hot metal singing through the smoke. You find yourself dodging and weaving from something you can't even see. The pilot's hand goes up and forward. "Going down," he shouts, and the nose pitches forward steeply. The speed slackens and the roar of the wind dies down and the battle noises suddenly are magnified into a terrifying din.

"Now," says the sergeant, "is when you pray." Everyone with a weapon has it cocked and across his lap. Then, before you know it, the ground is racing underneath. You are in a pasture, crashing through a fence, bounding across a gulley, clipping a tree with a wingtip. You've made it—landed and nobody hurt. You relax for a moment, but realize a split second later that that was a mistake. Bullets are ripping through the glider. "Get outta here! Get outta here!" someone shouts and prayers give way to curses and first one and then another kicks savagely at the door. Men spill onto the grass haphazardly and begin crawling toward a ditch just beyond the barbed fence. Lead whines overhead. Bullets uproot little cupfuls of green turf around you until you are digging your toes in and clawing the earth with your fingers to move forward.

Everyone is outside the glider. Two men are hit—both medics. One has a bullet through the top of his head—it went in and out through his helmet.

You're getting cold and uncomfortable by now—and take a cautious look around. Someone gets a jeep to take the wounded to an aid station and the rest of the party strikes out for the regimental command post. And you pray a prayer of thanksgiving and tell yourself—you are a common, ordinary flat-footed reporter—that you've had your first and only glider ride.[10]

* * *

In other gliders, pilots remembered that

the guys came into the glider like a bunch of piss-ants, skittering around, real cocky like. But they settled down in the glider. Some got airsick and they began thinking about what was ahead.[11]

* * *

Several slugs went through the glider fabric, sounding much like a dull drum beat, but no one was hit. My eyes darted about looking for a landing place, for high-

"Two men are hit—both medics." *Courtesy of the Silent Wings Museum*

tension power lines and for other gliders. We were down to a 100 feet, and out of the corner of my eye I saw a transmission tower, but no wires. Just ahead of us there was a pasture with barbed wire fences, and two gliders were touching down …

* * *

… (A) glider rolled to a stop, disgorging troops on the run. Just past it there was a burning glider with smoke and flames billowing into the air. Glancing to my right, I saw a small woods and approaching it, there were two gliders on the ground but rolling too fast. The first one hit the trees, crumpling the nose and stopping abruptly. The big tail lifted up and then dropped. The second glider pilot tried desperately to ground loop, but his right wing caught a tree and his glider was drawn into the woods, parts flying all over …

But I concentrated on our approach and landing. We flared, touched down, put it up on the skids, and quickly came to a stop. We had accomplished our primary mission. But while we were still moving, a rifle slug whined through the glider, and the airborne troops started scrambling out of the doors.[12]

* * *

When we stopped rolling we all got out as fast as possible and raised the tail with the two poles we carried for that purpose.

Dodging small arms fire I made my way to cover behind a hedgerow. It wasn't long after that that I had to make my way back to the glider to get the maps I had left behind in the cockpit. On the way back to the glider two young German soldiers came out of the bushes with their hands up shouting, "Kamerad, Kamerad." They thought that they would be killed and so gave themselves up to become my prisoners rather than die in battle. I made my way to a general's command post, turned my prisoners over to the MPs (Military Police) and eventually found the GP (Glider Pilot) checkpoint and reported in as we were instructed to do.[13]

* * *

We flew our gliders down to Chartres, France, the afternoon of March 23rd, and after supper gathered in a large room for our intelligence briefing. They showed pictures of our landing zones taken at 20,000 feet altitude and talked about hedgerows, which from that altitude looked like the harmless hedges in our front yards back home. I looked around the room that night and wondered who would get it the next day. Never once did I consider the possibility that I might be one of those who would get it the next day …

It was still very dark at 4:00 a.m. when the call came through the barracks for all Catholics to attend a special early Mass in preparation for the mission of the day.

I woke up from a deep sleep and for the first time in my life had an overwhelming awareness of the possibility of ME being killed that day! It felt as if the blood in my veins had turned to ice water, and when I couldn't shake that weird feeling, I turned over on my stomach, face down in my pillow, and for the first time since I was a little child, I prayed. The only prayer I knew was the child's prayer that my mother had taught me long ago. "Now I lay me down to sleep, and pray the Lord my soul to keep. If I should die before I wake, I pray the Lord my soul to take." Then I rattled off several things about making some changes in my life and doing better in the future if God would just see me through this one last combat mission. Feeling much better, I turned on my side and went back to sleep.

Breakfast was fantastic that morning, steak and eggs and biscuits and gravy. Everyone figured that this would be our last mission, so they were sending us off in style, and we really loved it. We were all on the flight line at least a couple or more hours before takeoff, getting acquainted with the 17th Airborne personnel who would be flying with us in our gliders. We were taking in a combat surgical team composed of a major, who was the surgeon, and three enlisted medics all of whom would be seated in their jeep, which was equipped to serve as a mobile surgical room. That jeep was piled high with all the medial equipment they would need for two days. We crawled over the jeep to get to the cockpit before it was loaded. They then stacked all their equipment and supplies in and on the jeep, tying everything down so stuff wouldn't be flying all over the place while in flight.

The three and a half hour flight from Chartres to the Rhine was uneventful, with turbulence building up from the prop wash from planes ahead in the miles-long serials of a "Gooney-bird" and glider. When things got bumpy for those of us who were at the back end of the train, the C-47 pilots just flew above the turbulence, creating a stair-step effect, with those in the back stacking up higher and higher. Those in front were flying at 500 feet actual altitude and those in the back flying at 1,000 or more feet altitude. While it made for a smoother ride for all, it would complicate things for those of us in gliders at the back when we arrived at our landing zones.

While the flight was uneventful, it always became spectacular when the P-51s, P-47s and the Limey Spitfires and Hawker Hurricanes arrived on the scene to escort us the last 30 minutes. Just seeing all those beautiful fighters buzzing all over the skies would get the adrenalin flowing. The adrenalin really started moving when we saw the clouds of smoke rising up from our landing zones!

The 17th paratroops had jumped just over an hour before we came in, and the Krauts knew that the gliders would be coming in shortly, so they were prepared to set fire to most anything that would give off a lot smoke. Just about all that we could see as we approached the landing zones were clouds of smoke.

When we cut loose at over 800 feet altitude, we could only get glimpses of the ground through small openings in the clouds of smoke. Little did we know that the 17th paratroopers were getting the hell kicked out of them at that moment and that we would be landing right in the middle of a fierce fire fight.

We were less than 300 feet altitude before we broke out under the smoke clouds to get a clear sight of places to land. At that altitude we were only a few seconds from landing and had to take pretty much what we could get. We wanted to get on the ground as quickly as possible because as long as we were in the air we were too big a target for the enemy on the ground, coming in low and slow as we always did.

We landed in a grassy field that had once been cultivated with the furrows 90 degrees to our approach, and when we were about 6 or 8 feet off the ground, it sounded as if a giant popcorn machine had exploded in the back of the glider. It was a "machine" alright, machine gun bullets literally ripped our fuselage to shreds. Just moments after our wheels touched down, we saw a paratrooper lying in the furrow just straight ahead of us, too late to even attempt to turn the glider or to stop it. It was a sickening sound when one of the wheels of our glider ran over the middle of his body. As we got the glider stopped, we were already aware that all hell was busting out all over the area, with grenades and mortars exploding, the Krauts and paratroopers mixing it up like mush, everyone shooting in all directions.

The moment we got our glider stopped, I had ripped my seat belt loose so that I could grab the hollow steel tubing above my head and lift my body up and turn so I could swing my feet to kick out the plexi-glass *(sic)* side window. I reached down got my trusty old Tommy gun and went out the window headfirst, catching one of the side pockets of my pants that was heavily loaded with double Tommy gun clips taped together. In that split second that I hung on the window frame, a burst of machine gun bullets split the air some two inches below my head. Had my pocket not caught on that window, I would have been minced meat forever! I managed to kick loose and drop to the ground and according to my co-pilot, covered the distance from the glider to the tree-lined road nearby on my all fours faster than he was able to run the distance standing upright!

When things settled down we got out of our hole and went back to find the surgical team that we had brought in and who had immediately driven back to check on the paratrooper that we had run over when we landed. They were still there at that spot surrounded by a number of wounded, both American and Krauts, with the major still operating on the wounded. When I inquired about the paratrooper we had run over, the major told me that he had been hit in the rectum while still in the air by a "dum-dum" bullet (a bullet that expands or fragments when hitting someone), the bullet literally exploding his guts out of his body, causing him to bleed to death long before we ran over him. That did relieve us somewhat, but neither I nor my co-pilot will ever forget that awful moment when we both thought that we had killed one or our own.[14]

* * *

Members of the British Glider Pilot Regiment remember that

we received our briefing for the Allies were going to push into Germany and cross the Rhine. Much opposition was anticipated. Composite units were to land together to become an efficient fighting force as quickly as possible. The bar in the mess was shut the day before we took off but on the day itself the pilots were served their morning cup of tea in bed!

The tug pilot navigated and after about two hours we were close to our landing area. We released the tow rope and after about five or six minutes of free flight we landed safely, as planned, in a ploughed field in the face of enemy fire. We landed near the haystack identified at the briefing. The artillery had bombarded the German positions earlier and everywhere you looked all was covered in smoke. It was perhaps because of this that some American paratroopers were dropped in the wrong area and we saw many dead. Some had been shot as their parachutes tangled in the trees and their bodies hung still.

The field was full of gliders, men and equipment. There was a lot of noise of gliders splintering, men shouting, engines running, weapons being fired. Not all of the gliders landed as successfully as ours. For a while it was chaos but the training kicked in and the soldiers rapidly got sorted and moved forward. We were armed with rifles which we fired at the enemy as we made our way as briefed to a farmhouse which was to be the headquarters of the lieutenant-general. We were to guard him which meant that we were away from the thick of the fighting and relatively safe. This was because pilots were a valuable resource and would be needed again.

* * *

The day before we took off we all got our equipment together and I remember that apart from a .303 rifle, ammunition, hand grenades, I was also given a 2-inch mortar with bombs. I did not get much sleep during the night of 23/24 March.

We had to be ready to go down to the runway at about 0600 hours. The gliders had all been marshalled at the end of the runway close together in two lines, one just in front of the other, and the tug aircraft were lined up on either side of the runway. At an appointed time a tug taxied out in front of our glider and we hitched up and were waved away. This went very smoothly with the combinations taking off quite quickly, one after the other.

We crossed the Rhine some three hours after take-off and immediately we were in an area of very bad visibility. I found out later that this was due to dust and debris that had been thrown up from the heavy bombing of Wesel.

Although we couldn't see the ground the tug pilot told me to release as he reckoned we were over the correct point and he wished us both luck. I thanked him for his good wishes and hoped he and his crew would enjoy their breakfast of bacon and eggs when they returned to Earls Colne. How I wished I was with them!

We couldn't see the ground and there were several gliders who had released and were turning aimlessly and we knew full well that we were meant to be landing by a farmhouse and we did not know where we were. I followed the glider in front of me and he did a turn to port of 360 degrees. While he was doing that there was a certain amount of flak coming up. I carried on, hoping I was going in the right direction and turning here and there so that I did not go too far into Germany and overshoot the landing zone.

I was down to about 250 feet when I first saw the ground and I recognised on my port side the village of Hamminkeln so I continued flying south looking for a field in which to land. I spotted a field where I thought we could land which I hoped would be somewhere near the farmhouse where we were meant to be. I operated the lever to bring the flaps down to lose height. I pushed the nose of the glider down and to my horror found that the speed built up to about 120 mph; the flaps had not come down. I think gunfire had pierced my compressed air bottle and so this put the flaps out of action.

It was impossible to get into the field without crashing so I decided the only thing I could do was to do a shallow dive into the field and aim between two trees at the far end, hoping that the wings would hit these trees and bring us to a standstill. I hit the ground and broke the nose wheel so the cockpit started digging into the ground.

At about this time I think a mortar bomb exploded under my starboard wing which turned the glider upside down. The nose broke away from the glider and rolled over and over like a ball for some time; eventually it came to rest.

I pulled the release on my safety harness but did not realise we were upside down until I fell on my head! Neither my co-pilot nor I were hurt so we crawled out of the cockpit and ran back to what was left of the glider. Amazingly no-one was hurt. One chap did have a graze on his thumb and that was all.

We came under fire from two Spandau machine guns which were situated near the trees which I had been aiming for. We kept very still under the wreckage of the glider and amazingly the firing soon stopped and I can only think the Germans thought that no-one could have got out of our glider alive.[15, 16]

* * *

An American pilot filed the following after-battle intelligence report of his participation in the glider landings of *Operation Varsity*. These edited narrative excerpts identify LZ and glider pilot assembly conditions, organization and command structure implementation following the death of the group leader.[17]

Formation en route as observed from number one glider: formation was all at same altitude and in two echelons to the right. Flying condition in flight was ideal. It was a bit rough for the first hour and forty-five minutes, but smoothed out near end of the flight.

Visibility from Rhine River to LZ "S" was very poor as smoke laid down by the British for protection on river crossing had drifted over LZ "S". Smoke from shell fire and burning aircraft also covered LZ "S". Altitude at LZ "S" was approximately 1200 feet indicated.

We encountered small arms and machine gun fire at the south border of LZ "W". Lead glider was hit at this point with machine gun fire—medium flak also observed in this area and some 20 mm fire. Glider in No. 2 position was shot off course at turn position at LZ "S", also flak had damaged wing to extent that pilot had to release. This was a simultaneous action.

From release point and on downwind approach, machine gun and rifle fire was very heavy—pilot was killed by 20 mm fire on base leg—at this point the undersigned (co-pilot) took control and completed 180° turn into a field visible from side. This landing was approximately 300 yards north of designated spot for landing.

Patterns for gliders were carried out as well as could be under such visibility conditions. All gliders were released too high.

Upon landing all airborne and glider pilots were under fire; rifle and machine gun from wooded areas and houses.

Little difficulty was found in assembling pilots. All squadrons of the group were in squadron assembly points within one hour after landing. Assembly and moving into defense areas as designated was carried out as planned and contact was established with Squadrons, Wing, and Regimental CPs (command posts). Personnel and glider loads were seventy-five per cent accounted for at 1800 hrs. Defense positions were made and held by all organizations; communications were maintained by runners. At 2300 hrs, 24 March 1945, enemy resistance was met. Two tanks with estimated one hundred infantrymen tried to make a road approach through our area. The Group made no attempt to join this attack. The TC (Troop Carrier) Group to our immediate left front and flank held off the attack. This information was dispatched to field artillery to our rear; at this same time the Regt. CP was shelled.

At 1700 hours, 25 March, the Group received marching orders for evacuation—at 1815 hours the Group had formed and proceeded on march to evacuation point. Orders were given to proceed to Corps Headquarters where further orders were received by runner to proceed to Rhine River crossing.

At 2330 hours we had completed our crossing via Dukw at the Stone River crossing (British) and were evacuated to Glider Pilot Rest Area and from there to the airdrome.

Glider pilot rest area ... "hotel was operated by the British. There were cots in the tents and we had a hot meal. I remember that the water was cold so I skipped a shower until I returned Orleans, France."[18]

Summary: Glider pilots were well aware of the conditions about them. Control was maintained throughout—weapons were adequate—chain of command was carried out.

> The unit functioned without the aid of airborne liaison officer who received a flak leg wound during the approach to the LZ. All wounded glider pilots and airborne were cared for on the spot and at temporary aid stations until they could be turned over to medical units. One German doctor was employed for this use.
>
> Recommendations: Glider pilots should be briefed a day or two earlier and be given time to study overlays, photo and terrain maps. More oblique photos should be furnished for study. Release altitude should be approximately 400 feet above terrain. Organization for control of glider pilots was excellent; the best that has been observed in any operation. Paratroopers should recede gliders by at least twelve hours.
>
> /s/ G. M. Slaughter[19]

One of the more unusual and fascinating exchanges between members of the German army and a number of those American glider pilots who had landed on the east side of the Rhine during *Operation Varsity*, occurred during the night of 24 March. After delivering their loads to LZ "S" just north of Wesel the glider pilot flight officers of the 435th Troop Carrier Group, became organized as the 435th Provisional Glider Pilot Infantry Company with the assignment of protecting the flank of the divisional headquarters. Shortly after midnight a large number German troops supported by a tank, a self-propelled artillery piece and two 20 mm flak guns, began a fire-fight with the pilots. Not far away, a glider pilot recalls that his co-pilot:

> … shook me awake while holding his hand over my mouth and saying, "shhh." Sure enough, a Kraut Tiger tank was rumbling right down the dirt road that ran beside our slit trench parachute-lined boudoir, shaking dirt all over us in our hole as it passed within ten feet of us. We didn't think about doing anything heroic for a moment and let it pass. After it rumbled away, I went back to sleep but was soon awakened again, this time to the sound of a fierce firefight not too far away from us. It sounded like all hell was breaking out, which in a real sense it was, with one of the most unique battles of WW II going on at a place that would become known as Burp-Gun Corner.[20]

The glider pilot flight officers fired into the night at the approaching German troops and tank. One of this officer-only group made his way to within yards of the tank and fired his bazooka at it. Although not damaged, the tank backed off the attack, the starch taken out of its forceful move towards the Americans.

The glider pilot who had the close encounter with the Tiger tank in his slit trench sleeping accommodations, observed that, "*While many American glider pilots were 'odd-balls,' we dead sure knew how to and could and would fight if the occasion merited it.*"[21] Although the Battle of Burp-Gun Corner might be considered a minor skirmish when looked at from the broader perspective of the entire Rhine River Crossing operation, it was the occasion for the display of bravery and courage that earned for its participants the recommendation for the Bronze Star. Unfortunately the recommendation for awarding the medal was lost in the maze of paperwork that accompanied the push towards ending the war. Fifty years after the battle, Congress authorized the presentation of the Bronze Star to every member of the company, a tribute that spoke loudly to *"the contributions and sacrifices of the glider pilots of the US Army Air Forces (which) aren't as well-known as those of many other flying units."*[22, 23]

Historians and arm-chair after-battle strategists have asked the question of whether or not *Operation Varsity* necessary?[24] Did the territory gained by the Allied airborne participants and the number of enemy forces that were killed or taken prisoner from engagement with Airborne units exceed gains that might have been made by traditional ground forces? One review of the operation and its outcomes has been provided by the Office of the Chief of Military History, of the United States Army:

> *Operation Varsity*, the airborne phase of the big Rhine assault, was an impressive success. All airborne troops were on the ground by 1230, along with 109 tons of ammunition, 695 vehicles, and 113 artillery pieces; and in a matter of hours both Americans and British had seized all objectives assigned for the first day ... The 17th Airborne Division claimed 2,000 prisoners, the 6th Airborne Division, another 1,500 ... By late afternoon supplies were moving across the Rhine in dukws in such volume as to eliminate the need for additional supply by air.
>
> Yet for all the success of *Operation Varsity*, the question remained whether under the prevailing circumstances an airborne attack had been necessary or was even justified. It unquestionably aided British ground troops, but at a cost to the 17th Airborne Division alone during the first day's operations of 150 men killed, 522 wounded, and 840 missing (though 600 of the missing subsequently turned up to fight again). The IX Troop Carrier Command alone lost 41 killed, 153 wounded, 163 missing. The airborne assault also cost over 50 gliders and 44 transport aircraft destroyed, 332 damaged. In the low-level supply mission flown directly after the assault by 240 Liberators (B-24s) of the Eighth Air Force, 15 aircraft were lost.[24]

* * *

The British 6th Airborne lost 347 men killed and 731 wounded. The combined losses of British and American airborne troops resulted in the war's most costly airborne operation.[25]

* * *

In view of the weak conditions of German units east of the Rhine and the particular vulnerability of airborne troops in and immediately following the descent, some overbearing need for the special capability of airborne divisions would be required to justify their use. Although the objectives assigned the divisions were legitimate, they were objectives that ground troops alone under existing circumstances should have been able to take without undue difficulty and probably with considerably fewer casualties. Participation by paratroopers and glidermen gave appreciably no more depth to the bridgehead at Wesel than that achieved by infantrymen of the 30th Division. Nor did the airborne attack speed bridge construction ... for not until 0915 the next day, 25 March, did engineers start work on bridges at Wesel.[26]

24

The Summer of '45

The commanding officer at Hollandia, New Guinea understood that from the beginning of the war one of the greatest problems affecting air operations in the Pacific area was that of morale and fatigue and that the highest rates of low morale and highest levels of fatigue occurred at base area sections where boredom, unrelieved by the stimulus of combat, was predominant. Medical staff used the term "morale" interchangeably to describe all manner of fatigue: environmental, operational, and tropical.

The tropics with the heat and humidity, mud, rain, dust, insects, the surrounding jungles and primitive natives, all contributed to deadly monotony. Illness from diseases, malaria, dengue, scrub typhus, bacillary dysentery, ulcers, fungus infections, boils and abscesses were common and the constant hammering at personnel—"take your atabrine," "use repellent" "dress properly," "dry out your clothes, blankets and shoes," "drink only chlorinated water," "stay out of the brush," "stay away from native villages," "don't walk here"—aggravated the hell out of everyone and were contributing factors to the bottom dwelling morale of his unit.[1]

The base commander had arranged for sight-seeing flights along the coastline of the island as a weapon against the calamitous enemy of his staff, boredom. Perhaps as a distant celebration of the end of the war in Europe or to take their minds off another Mother's Day away from home, he arranged for members of his command on this Sunday the best joy ride available, a trip to Hidden Valley, an area of mystery about who or what lived there.

The flight would allow passengers to look down from the windows of a C-47 at the place that had been the subject of wild speculation since it was discovered the previous summer by Col. Ray T. Elsmore, a command pilot who was making a survey flight of a proposed north-south route over the island of New Guinea. Maps of area in which the valley lay were left blank with notes of, "UNEXPLORED" and "Estimated 14,000 foot peak."[2]

Col. Elsmore was curious about the fertile valley he found and sent photo squadrons to take pictures of it. The valley, about 20 miles long, and four miles wide, lay beyond the hump of the Oranje Range at an altitude of about 5,000 feet. But reconnaissance photos revealed something more intriguing than the valley's geographical features—clusters of native huts and cultivated irrigated land. "According to Dutch and Australian authorities, no white man had ever penetrated that far into the Dutch New Guinea jungles." It didn't take long for stories to be told by some of the persons who had flown over the valley and romanticized about it that it was a land whose inhabitants were completely out of contact with the rest of the world, a real-life Shangri La.[3]

It was intended as a joy ride, a sight-seeing trip, an attempt to boost the morale of a commander's troops. It would become an incident in the war that received wide news coverage from both the civilian and military press. A *Yank* magazine staff correspondent, Sgt. Ozzie St. George, recorded the news-making story for his military readers.

> It was Sunday, May 13, 1945, at 2:15 in the afternoon when the C-47 took off from the Sentani Strip at Hollandia for a flight over the 14,000-foot hump of the Oranje Range, about 130 air-miles away. Counting the crew members there were 24 persons aboard, including eight WACs of the Far East Air Service Command, eight enlisted men and eight officers.
>
> The plane got over the hump and began its descent into the valley for a closer look at Elsmore's Shangri La. It crashed, nose on, 300 feet below the top of a ridge line, mowing through the jungle of New Guinea, fire breaking out, the tail section snapping off.
>
> Five managed to survive the crash and fire, one of the officers, 1st Lt. John McCollom, who was uninjured, an enlisted man, T/Sgt Kenneth Decker, a gash in his head, and three WACs, one of whom was able to make her way out of the crash despite having burns on her legs and having had her shoes burned off. The other two WACs were pulled from the wreckage, and administered morphine by Lt. McCollom for the pain from their burns, however their wounds were so grievous that they both died within two days of the crash.
>
> When the C-47 did not return to its base from the sight-seeing trip to Hidden Valley, base personnel at Hollandia checked other nearby airstrips but none reported that the plane had landed there. A search plane was sent out with no sightings of a downed C-47. Other planes joined the search on the following day.
>
> The three survivors, their only food hard candies from the crash and water from on-board canteens and a nearby creek could see search planes circling overhead. The native inhabitants of the area could be heard moving closer to their tiny encampment, the three survivors not knowing if they were head-hunters or cannibals. After spending two days at the crash site and seeing the search planes overhead they realized that if they were to have any chance of being seen by those looking for them from the air they would have to move to open ground. They started out for a clearing lower down the ridge, going slowly and eating the candies. It took a day and a half to

make the two and a half mile journey. An hour after their arrival they were spotted by a B-17.

Two life rafts were dropped as markers by the 17, whose crew charted the location before flying back to Hollandia. There they reported they had seen three people dressed in khakis waving from a small clearing on the uphill side of a ridge about 10 air miles northeast of the valley proper. But the weather closed in solidly over the hump and a return flight that day was impossible.

An hour after being spotted by the B-17 they were approached by the local natives. The universal language of the smile signaled both from the natives and from the crash survivors that for the moment at least that neither group was hostile against the other.

Communication between the native inhabitants of the valley and the pale skinned visitors progressed through sign language. The natives built a fire by rubbing sticks together like an Eagle Scout and put bananas and a variety of sweet potatoes to roast in the coals. When it began to rain the three survivors crawled under the tarps stretched over the life rafts dropped by the B-17 and were dismayed to see the natives leave, taking the chow with them. Their fourth night in the New Guinea jungle was cold and wet and they were hungry and in pain. They were greatly cheered by the fact that they had been found, but they had no idea how their ultimate rescue from the jungle was to be achieved.

On the Thursday after they were spotted, they received the first of what would become a regular parachute drop of supplies: first aid kits, a walkie-talkie and 10-in-1 rations (US Army field rations designed so that one unit could feed ten men). Later that same day a second supply drop included enough equipment to stock a good-sized country store including lipstick and bobby-pins for the WAC, shoes and walkie-talkie batteries. Before they were rescued and brought out of the valley, they would receive tents, mosquito bars, cots, signal panels, 20 pairs of shoes, 300 pounds of medical supplies, 14 .45 caliber pistols (the standard Army issue sidearm), six Tommy guns, 3,000 rounds of .45 ammunition, coffee, bacon, tomato juice, eggs that landed unscrambled, pineapple juice, 75 10-in-1 units; knives and machetes, clothes for the survivors, lap-laps (a waist/loin cloth) for the natives, stoves, canteens, water, gasoline, 75 blankets, magazines, rice, salt, shells for trading with the natives, mail, at least three cases of beer, and for the WAC, scanties (women's panties),[4] although she later denied having received any intimate apparel during her stay in the survivor's camp.[5]

Five days after the disaster, two medics of the First Filipino Reconnaissance Battalion volunteered to parachute into the valley and provide medical support for the three survivors. Two days later their battalion jumpmaster and eight paratroopers dropped into the main valley near the mouth of the canyon where the C-47 had crashed and established a base camp where they received by air drop 21 flags, twenty crosses and one wooden Star of David, used in the burial of the victims of the crash.

Thirty-five days after the crash another person joined the rescue team by parachute, a Canadian newsreel photographer, who worked for the Netherlands East Indies

Government, with the intent of making a documentary of the Hidden Valley crash, survival, and rescue. During this entire time suggestions for methods of rescuing the group, now numbering 15, were being evaluated in Hollandia, including an overland trek that was estimated to take up to a month each way and would have required the services of 150 natives.

Rescue by aircraft of various sizes and types were suggested but the terrain, distance from Hollandia, altitude and the unpredictable weather all worked against this rescue method. However, one air based rescue idea did emerge as possible, the use of gliders to snatch out the survivors and their rescuers. Work began at installing the snatch pickup equipment on a C-47 that would be used in the pick-up. Trial snatch flights began at an air base in Hollandia at the same time that a 400-yard glider landing strip was being prepared at the rescue site by burning off vegetation and marking the landing area with parachutes that had been used to drop in supplies to the Hidden Valley encampment.

A glider snatch at the altitude of Hidden Valley was a dicey operation at best—at over a mile in elevation, the lift required to bring the glider airborne was greater because of the thin air of the valley's location. And, the unstable weather over the hump of the surrounding mountains was a factor that would always be a factor that would threaten to cancel any glider pick-up or smack one down that was being attempted.

It was decided that it would take three flights in and three snatches out to bring the team back to civilization; bringing the entire group out at once would put too much weight in the glider and the snatch would not be successful. Everybody in Hidden Valley was ready to get the hell out of their alleged Shangri La.

On June 28th, the weather cleared, and a C-46 towed a CG-4A Waco glider to the valley where it released from its tow plane and landed without incident.

The glider was turned around, and immediately prepared for the next phase of the rescue, the snatch by the C-47equipped with the special snatch winch and pickup hook. The snatch was made, the C-47 pulling the glider off the floor of the valley and over the menacing mountain walls that marked its boundaries.

During the take-off a parachute that had been used as a field marker became snagged up against and through the floor of the glider. Lt. McCollom pulled the silk up through the hole in the floor of the glider, handful by handful, until it was completely inside the Waco and stowed. A little more than an hour later, the glider landed at the Sentani Strip, the same strip where the sight-seeing flight to Hidden Valley had begun.

They had made it. After 45 days in their Shangri La, Lt. McCollom said, "I want a shave." Sgt. Decker said, "I want a shower." And WAC Cpl. Margaret Hastings said, "I want a permanent."[6]

The three survivors met one last time nearly three decades later when they were made honorary members of the National World War II Glider Pilots Association at the group's reunion in 1974.[7]

Margaret Hastings with souvenir spears as she prepared to leave the valley.

* * *

Meanwhile, the war continued to rage on in the Pacific. The Okinawa campaign was declared ended on 2 July 1945. The cost of this 83 day campaign was staggering: 49,151 Army, Navy and Marine casualties of which 12,520 were killed or missing; 36,631 wounded. Thirty-six ships were sunk, 368 damaged; 763 planes were lost from 1 April to 1 July. Approximately 110,000 Japanese soldiers were killed; 7,400 were taken prisoner. Japan lost 7,800 aircraft and 16 ships were sunk.[8]

* * *

The Japanese were at the end of their rope in the Northern Luzon area of the Philippines in the latter part of June, 1945. The Japanese general had brought with his retreating troops enough food and ammunition to get them through to mid-September. After that, the Japanese would conduct one last banzai attack against the American forces.[9] The area in which General Yamashita, the "Tiger of Malaya"[10] had driven his troops for their last stand was in a

> ... vast mountainous area of northwestern Luzon. Barren is the word to best describe much of the country. Imposing in their grandeur, most of the steep-sided mountains are grassy sloped. [11]

Although Yamashita was planning a suicidal charge against the Americans, the US area commander of the operations in northern Luzon, General Walter Krueger, thought it was more likely that the Japanese would pull back to the small seacoast town of Aparri on the north shore of the island. From there they would be picked up by units of the Japanese navy and slip safely away, probably to the homeland for the inevitable invasion that seemed likely to be in the near future. To deny the Japanese this port of escape he ordered that Connolly Task Force march forward and take the coastal village as soon as possible. In addition:

> Despite reports to the contrary General Krueger had concluded that Japanese forces in the Cagayan Valley, upon the approach of (US forces) ... were fleeing "in wild disorder" toward Aparri. Actually, the general trend of Japanese movement had been southward for weeks, and certainly no Japanese force intended to hole up at Aparri, an indefensible, flatland cul-de-sac.
>
> In view of Krueger's estimate of the Japanese situation, "and in order to complete the annihilation of the enemy forces it was decided to make a vertical envelopment of airborne troops to close the trap and prevent the enemy from all possibility of escaping from Aparri. Accordingly, on 21 June, Krueger directed a battalion combat team to drop near Aparri on 23 June.
>
> On the very day that Krueger issued this order, Connolly Task Force entered Aparri unopposed. By evening of the next day elements of the task force had secured Camalaniugan Airstrip, three miles from Aparri. There was no trap for the 511th Parachute Infantry to close.
>
> Despite the successes of the reinforced Connolly Task Force, Krueger did not change his mind about the desirability and necessity for the airdrop. Instead, he concluded that the seizure of Aparri without opposition by elements of the Connolly Task Force on 21 June 1945, together with the almost unopposed advance of the 37th Division, indicated clearly that the time had come for airborne troops to block the enemy's retreat in the Cagayan Valley. It is not clear just what retreat Krueger expected to block.
>
> The airborne force totaled about 1,030 men, (including infantry and field artillery units), 54 C-47's, 14 C-46's, and six Waco CG-4A gliders, these being used for the first time in the Southwest Pacific Area, and one CG-13A glider, the first and only time a glider of this type was used on a combat mission. The DZ (drop zone) for the paratroopers and the LZ (landing zone) of the gliders was Camalaniugan Airstrip, which pathfinders, who arrived at Connolly Task Force headquarters on 22 June, marked with ease.
>
> Paratroopers and the Task Force glidermen were up at 4 a.m. for a breakfast of bacon and eggs, a rarity for troops in the Philippines, and made their way to the C-46 and C-47 aircraft waiting on the field for a 6 a.m. liftoff.[12, 13, 14]
>
> No untoward incident marked the flight of the troop carriers from Batangas in southern Luzon to the drop zone, and paratroopers began dropping on the morning of 23 June while Fifth Air Force bombers and fighters flew cover and other planes laid smoke screens to conceal the drop zone from the east and south. The paratroopers

> were greeted on the ground by men of the Connolly Task Force and the 11th Infantry. Once the paratroopers were down, gliders brought in artillery, communication jeeps and other types of heavy equipment; C-47's and C-46's dropped additional material.
>
> Jump casualties were 2 men killed and 70 injured, a rate of about 7 percent; one glider flipped after its skids dug into the ridge of a bomb crater.
>
> While Connolly Task Force held the Aparri area, other units started south to gain contact with forces moving north. Paratroopers saw only a few Japanese stragglers on their way south and on 26 June met the northbound units near the Paret River, thirty-five miles south of Camalaniugan Airstrip. The airborne operation had proved both useless and unnecessary.[15]

Three of the gliders were snatched, the rest, including the CG-13A were left at Camalaniugan Airstrip to rot in the sun. The last combat mission for gliders in the Second World War turned out to be 'much ado about nothing.'

Endnotes

PART I

Chapter 1

1. *'At the 11th hour'*: Harry R. Rudin, *Armistice 1918* (New Haven: Yale University Press, 1944), pp. 426-429.
2. *'The new Germany in size'*: Margaret Macmillan, *Paris 1919 (NY: Random House, Trade Paperback Edition, 2003), p. 161.*
3. *'Spelled out through'*: Adolph Hitler, translated by Ralph Manheim, *Mein Kampf* (Boston: Houghton Mifflin, a Mariner book, 1971), p. 214.
4. *'The US aviator remembers'*: Edward V. Rickenbacker, *Seven Came Through; Rickenbacker's Full Story* (Garden City, NY: Doubleday, Doran and Company, Inc., 1943), p. 104.
5. *'While the interwar years'*: Jonathan C. Noetzel, "To War on Tubing and Canvas: A Case Study in the Interrelations Between Technology, Training, Doctrine and Organization." (thesis, School of Advanced Airpower Studies, Air University, 1992), p. 3.
6. *'Glider clubs flourished'*: Frank Paul Wisbar, with Fred Allhoff, "Gliders For War" (*Liberty* magazine, April 11, 1942), p. 33.
7. *'I was always interested'*: Willi Gänzler in conversation with the author, 11 September 2013.
8. *'Göring immediately'*: Frank Paul Wisbar, with Fred Allhoff, "Gliders For War" (*Liberty* magazine, April 11, 1942), p. 33.
9. *'Hitler attended the games'*: Laura Hillenbrand, *Unbroken; A World War II Story of Survival, Resilience, and Redemption* (NY: Random House, 2010), p. 31.
10. *'A year later'* : Noetzel, p. 3.
11. *'And in two years'*: *ibid.*, p. 5.

Chapter 2

1. *'By comparison, the British combat glider'*: James E. Mrazek, *Fighting Gliders of World War II* (London: Robert Hale, 1977), p. 70.
2. *'None of these aircraft'*: William Green, *The Warplanes of the Third Reich* (London: MacDonald, 1970), p. 107.
3. *'Walter Cronkite, the American'*: Michael H. Manion, "Gliders of World War II: 'The Bastards No One Wanted.'" (thesis, School of Advanced Air and Space Studies, Air University, 2008), p. 2.
4. *'In February 1941'*: Noetzel, p. 6.
5. *'Missing from the recommendations'*: *ibid.*
6. *'Eventually doctrine led'*: Training Aids Division, Office of the Assistant Chief of the Air Staff, Training Headquarters Army Air Forces, "Glider Tactics and Technique." (NY: Commanding General, Army Air Forces, 1944), pp. 1-2.
7. *'And it seems'*: *ibid.*
8. *'Its overall length'*: Anon., *Pilot's Flight Operating Instructions for Glider, Army Model CG-41, British Model Hadrian; AN 09-40CA-1*, (USAAF, June 20, 1945), pp. 1-9.
9. *'Made of six-ply'*: Anon., *Air Force; The Official Service Journal of the U.S. Army Air Forces, Vol. 27, No. 10,* (NY: U.S. Army Air Forces, October 10, 1944), p. 45.
10. *'A training manual'*: *Pilot's Flight Operating Instructions for Glider, Army Model CG-4A, British Model Hadrian; AN 09-40CA-1* (USAAF, June 20, 1945), pp. 1-9.
11. *'It worked like a charm.'*: Charles L. Day and Leon B. Spencer (Edited by William T. Milanovits and Marion "Smokey" Miller, adapted from, *Development and Use of the Waco CG-4A Cargo Glider Deceleration Parachute* (Silent Wings Museum, Lubbock, Texas, vertical/archival files) pp. 6-8.
12. *'Many of these companies'*: Manion, p. 51.
13. *'Sub-contractors were also from'*: Gerald M. Devlin, *Silent Wings* (NY: St Martin's Press, 1985), p. 67.
14. *'Ford solved this problem'*: *ibid.*, p. 66.
15. *'In this area'*: Anon., Untitled notes from the archival/vertical files of the Silent Wings Museum (Lubbock, Texas) p. 1.
16. *'Chances are that if'*: Leon B. Spencer, *The Wizards of Crookham Common* (Silent Wings Museum, Lubbock, Texas, vertical/archival files,1998), p. 1-2.
17. *'Gentlemen, you can only'*: James Merkel, *Beer, Brats, and Baseball: St. Louis Germans* (St. Louis, MO: Reedy Press, 2012), p. 113.
18. *'The CG-4A plunged nose-first'*: Associated Press News Service, "St. Louis Mayor and Nine Others Die in Army Glider Crash," *The Independent* (St. Petersburg, Florida), p. 6.

19. *'The investigators determined'*: Anthony J. Mireles, *Fatal Army Air Forces Aviation Accidents in the United States, 1941–1945; Volume 2: July 1943–July 1944* (Jefferson, NC: McFarland, 2006), p. 459.
20. *'The investigators also found'*: David Gero, *Military Aviation Disasters; Significant losses since 1908* (North Yeovil, Somerset: Patrick Stevens Ltd., 1999), p.
21. *'The crashed CG-4A glider'*: Mireles, p. 459.

Chapter 3

1. *'It was conceived'*: Claude Smith, *The History of the Glider Pilot Regiment (Barnsley, South Yorkshire: Pen & Sword Aviation, 2007), p. 16.*
2. *'The first production model'*: Denis Edwards, *The Devil's Own Luck; Pegasus Bridge to the Baltic* (Barnsley, South Yorkshire: Leo Cooper, 2001), p. 22.
3. *'The British Glider Pilot Regiment'*: Noetzel, *The British Glider Pilot Regiment* p. 12.
4. *'The Airborne Forces': The British Glider Pilot Regiment*: www.gliderpilotregiment.org.uk
5. *'With a snub, bug-like nose'*: Alan Lloyd, *The Gliders; An Action Packed Story of the Wooden Chariots of World War II* (Leo Cooper with Secker & Warburg Ltd., 1982), p. 14.
6. *'With a snub, bug-like nose'*: George Boyle in discussion with the author, 6 February 2013.
7. *"I was conscripted'*: Joan Roberts, *Oral History, Factory worker responsible for Horsa construction, Wolesey Factory* (Used with permission of The Assault Glider Trust: www.assaultgliderproject.co.uk, 2011).
8. *'Kicking the trestle away'*: Louis Hagen, *Arnhem Lift; A German Jew in the Glider Pilot Regiment* (Stroud, Gloucestershire: Spellmount, 2012), p. 30.
9. *'Horsa data characteristics'* : Edwards, p. 22; Lloyd, pp. 19-20; James E. Mrazek, *Fighting Gliders of World War II* (London: Robert Hale, 1977), p. 75; *Pilot's Notes for Horsa I Glider* (Air Ministry, 1944), p. 9; Smith, p. 15.
10. *'The Hotspur was the first'*: Mrazek, p. 60.
11. *'Landing a large contingent'*: Smith, p. 44.
12. *'Despite numerous modifications'*: Manion, p. 32.
13. *'The Glider Pilot Regiment'*: Smith, p. 44.
14. *'Yes,' the massive result'*: *ibid.*, p. 84.
15. *'With their enormous'*: Frank Ashleigh in email communication with the author, 24 March, 2013.

Chapter 4

1. *'The first flight test'*: William Green, *The Warplanes of the Third Reich* (London: MacDonald, 1970), p. 104.
2. *'The Luftwaffe was no longer'*: Wisbar, p. 33.
3. *'It was this model'*: Green, p. 106.
4. *'Defensive muscle was also added'*: *ibid*, p. 252.
5. *'The overall length'*: Mrazek, p. 33.
6. *'With portable ramps'*: *ibid*, p. 42.
7. *'A single aircraft'*: Green, p. 648.

Chapter 5

1. *'Perhaps the most striking'*: Mrazek, p. 87.
2. *'Even though it was'*: Devlin, p. 72.
3. *'Although spoilers were found'*: Mrazek, p. 91.
4. *'With a reported 700'*: *ibid.*

Chapter 6

1. *'There were 10,692 C-47s'*: Anon., *The Beacon*, Newsletter of the Palm Springs Air Museum, (Palm Springs, CA: December, 2013), p. 3.
2. *'With a maximum weight load'*: David Polk, *The History of Army Airborne Troop Carriers of World War II*, (Paducah, Kentucky: Turner Publishing), p. 7.
3. *'General Dwight Eisenhower'*: Dwight D. Eisenhower, *Crusade in Europe*, (Garden City, NY: Garden City Books Edition, 1952), p. 190.
4. *'But this unassuming legend'*: Polk, p. 7.
5. *'These flights were often'* : Greg Goebel website in the public domain at: www.faqs.org/doc/air/sitemap.html.
6. *'Its wide double doors'*: Polk, p. 7.
7. *'Inexperience among some of'*: Nick Jacobellis, *G for Guts*, (Silent Wings Museum, Lubbock, Texas, vertical/archival files July 1, 2002), pp. 4-6.
8. *'(W)e were ready to go.'* : William F. Dawson, 'Coming in With a Glider and a Gulp', 82nd Airborne *All American Airborne Division newspaper, The All American Paraglide, European Final, VE Day,* (May, 1945), p. 3.
9. *'The tow ship and glider'* : Charles A. Cowing, *Flying; Standard Operating Procedure for Gliders (United States Army Air Corps, 17 August, 1943), pp. 1-4.*

PART II
Chapter 7

1. *'What were they like as'*: Raymond S. Hall, as cited in Cornelius Ryan, *A Bridge Too Far (NY: Simon & Schuster Paperbacks, 1995), p. 174.*
2. *'In their own words'*: The memories and recollections of this chapter, identified in an italics, have been shared with the author through private conversations or email messages, are quoted from published sources, or are oral histories from the Silent Wings Museums of Lubbock, Texas, and are used with permission. These sources are listed here in alphabetical order and where appropriate may be found in the bibliography: Frank Ashleigh, George Boyle, John Cason (son of Denis Cason, GPR member), Timothy Ferguson, M.D., Louis Hagen (*Arnhem Lift; A German Jew in the Glider Pilot* Regiment), Nick Jacobellis, Jack W. Lester, Lynton Hugh Martin, Jim Thomas, and James Harley Wallwork, from the death notice in the newspaper, *The Independent.*
3. *'They were seduced'*: Milton Dank, *The Glider Gang; An Eyewitness History of World War II Glider Combat* (Philadelphia: J. B. Lippincott, 1977), pp. 17-18.
4. *'This is a real flying'*: U.S. Army, *New Flying Opportunities; Be a Glider Pilot in the U.S. Army*, pp. 1-7.
5. *'One day I answered'*: Anon. *One day I answered the popular call,* (sung to the tune of: "The Daring Young Man on the Flying Trapeze," of the (Silent Wings Museum, Lubbock, Texas, vertical/archival files), p. 1.
6. *'And then there was the fellow'*: Anthony Coogan in discussion with the author, 6 June 2013.
7. *Ibid.*
8. *'Sixty thousand British civilians'*: *Instructions for American Servicemen in Britain, 1942* (Washington, D.C.: War Department, 1942), 6/7/10-11.
9. *'But, it was the men'*: Author/date unknown. The eight virtues are inscribed on the face of the double doors of the meditation chapel of the Luxembourg American Cemetery and Memorial.
10. *'It's not easy to make'*: Lynton Hugh Martin, personal memoirs.

Chapter 8

1. *'When you landed behind'*: As in the previous chapter the personal accounts of training have come from a wide variety of sources including personal communications with the author and from the archival vertical research files of the Silent Wings Museum, Lubbock, Texas. The memories of glider pilot veterans have in many cases been edited and combined in order to provide

for a coherence of content and continuity of experiences. Contributors are listed in alphabetical order: Frank Ashleigh, George Boyle, John Cason (son of Denis Cason, GPR member), Jack Lester, and Lynton Hugh Martin.

2. *'Additional words and phrases'*: McDonough, Doug (Editor), 'WW II Army glider cadets developed specialized lingo.' (*Plainview Herald*, Plainview, Texas, 19 October 2012), (e-article).
3. *'But questions arose'*: Michael J. F. Bowyer, *Action Stations; 6. Military Airfields of the Cotswolds and the Central Midlands* (Cambridge: Patrick Stevens, 1983), pp. 251-254.

Chapter 9

1. *'On our flight to Arnhem'*: Frank Ashleigh, personal communication.
2. *'One of our landings'*: Jack Lester, in discussion with the author, 30 November 2010.
3. *Ibid.*
4. *'Nothing that flies'*: Author/date unknown, *Glider Tactics Over Hostile Territory* (Silent Wings Museum, Lubbock, Texas, vertical/archival files), p. 1.
5. *'With hours of practice'*: Anon., *Composite P.O.M. File; Glider Pilot,* (314th Troop Carrier Sqdn., Pope Field, North Carolina (Silent Wings Museum Lubbock, Texas vertical/archival), p. 1.
6. *'In the spring of 1942'*: Leon B. Spenser, adapted from, *WW II U.S. Army Air Force Glider Aerial Retrieval System* (Silent Wings Museum Lubbock, Texas vertical/archival files), pp. 3-5.
7. *'I could hear the aircraft'*: Norman Wilmeth, Banquet presentation, 42nd Annual Reunion of the National WW II Glider Pilots Association, San Antonio, Texas, 26 October 2012.
8. *'Thirteen CG-4As were snatched'*: Spenser, p. 5.
9. *'Since the aircraft'*: N/a, *Flight nurses revolutionize military medical care,* (ww.af.mil), The official web site of the U.S. Air Force, Fort Meade, Md.), p. 1.
10. *'A decoration awarded'*: Woodford Agee Heflin, (ed.), *The United States Air Force Dictionary* (Washington, DC: Air University Press, 1956), p. 31.

PART III
Chapter 10

1. *'This afternoon, after two days'*: Jim Thomas, adapted from *Jim Thomas Diaries, 30 March 1944–12 April 12, 1944* (Lubbock, Texas, Silent Wings Museum, vertical/archival files), pp. 3-6.

Chapter 11

1. *'Arriving in Karachi'*: George E. Boyle, adapted from personal memoir/ scrapbook/letter, *Glider Guider Gladiator, unnumbered.*

Chapter 12

1. *'Described as a'*: James E. Mrazek, *The Fall of Eben Emael (Novato, California, Presidio Press: 1991), p. 169.*
2. *'For external defense'*: John L. Lowden, *Silent Wings at War; Combat Gliders in World War II (Washington, D.C.: Smithsonian, 1992), p. 32.*
3. *Mrazek, p. 32.*
4. *'Antiaircraft positions'*: Thomas B. Gukeisen, *The Fall of Fort Eben Emael: The Effects of Emerging Technologies on the Successful Completion of Military Objectives (Fort Leavenworth, Kansas: Unpublished Master's degree thesis, 2004), p. 14.*
5. *Ibid.* p. 15.
6. Mrazek, pp. 30-31.
7. *'The German High Command'*: Anon, *A Summary of Information About the American World War II Glider Pilots and the CG-4A Combat Glider* (Lubbock, Texas, Silent Wings Museum archival papers), p. 2.
8. *'The attack had to occur'*: William H. McRaven, *Spec Ops; Case Studies in Special Operations Warfare: Theory and Practice* (Novato, California: Presidion Press, 1996), p. 33.
9. *'The hohllandung was'*:Mrazek, p. 37.
10. *'Additional components of a'*: *ibid.* pp. 14-17.
11. *'Intelligence about the site'*: *ibid.* p. 43.
12. *'Intelligence about the site'*: Mrazek, p. 54.
13. *'It was a large assault'*: *ibid*, pp. 49-71.
14. *'despite taking enemy anti-aircraft fire'*: Manion, pp. 17-19
15. *'German sappers'*: *ibid*, p. 31.
16. *'The glider assault'*: *ibid.*
17. *'The attack on Fort Eben Emael'*: David Marley, editor, *The Daily Telegraph Story of the War; 1939–1941* (London: Hodder & Stoughton, 1942), p. 72.
18. *'Two days later'*: Stanley Glazer, compiler, *War Papers; Presenting a fascinating collection of historic newspaper front pages, 1939-45* (London: Fontana Paperbacks, 1989), unnumbered.
19. *'While the glider offers'*: Helmuth Reinhardt, committee chairman and principal author, *Airborne Operations; A German Appraisal* (Washington, D.C.: Center of Military History, United States Army, facsimile edition, 1982), p. 10.

20. *'While the glider offers'*: Albert Kesselring (contributor), *Airborne Operations; A German Appraisal* (Washington, D.C.: Center of Military History, United States Army, facsimile edition, 1982), p. 17.

Chapter 13

1. *'Three cruisers and six'*: Antony Beevor, *Crete; The Battle and the Resistance* (London: John Murray, paperback edition, 2005), pp. 346-348.
2. *'German losses were as'*: *ibid.*
3. *'German losses were as'*: John Weeks, *Assault From the Sky; The History of Airborne Warfare* (Newton Abbot, Devon: paperback edition, 1988), p. 39.
4. *In an after battle report'*: Alan Moorehead, "The Navy Brings 15,000 Troops Out of Crete," *Daily Express*, London, June 2, as reprinted in, *War Papers; Presenting a fascinating collection of historic newspaper front pages, 1939–45* (London: Fontana Paperbacks, 1989), unnumbered.
5. *'An attack plan was'*: Helmuth Reinhardt (principal author), *Airborne Operations; A German Appraisal* (Washington, D.C.: Center of Military History, United States Army, facsimile edition, 1982), pp. 10-11.
6. *'(A) plan in not'*: *ibid.*
7. *'The operational plan'*: Harry J. Potter, *The Battle of Maleme, Crete,* harrypotter@hellenicfoundation.com, adapted and used with permission.
8. *'The exceptionally unfavorable'*: Kesselring, p. 20.
9. *'The fact that the'*: Reinhardt, pp. 22-23.
10. *'They would be needed'*: Devlin, p. 47.
11. *'Members of the British armed forces'*: No author, "Message from London," as reprinted in, *Union Jack, A Scrapbook, British Forces' Newspapers, 1939–1945* (London: HMSO, 1989), p. 88.
12. *'Although the attack'*: Klaus Neetzow & Georg Schlaug, *Deutsche Lastensegler 1938–1945; Eine Chronik in Beldern,* (Weihuachzen, 1993)—from the private collection of Willi Gänzler, German glider pilot of Second World War.
13. *'the command post where'*: Jean Claude Mathevet, (translated by Glen Boudet), adapted from, "German Gliders over Vercours (also Vercors) (France)," *Silent Wings Museum Newsletter*; *From the Archives*, (Lubbock, Texas, Summer 2013), pp. 3-5.
14. *'The last seven of a'*: Neetzow & Schlaug.
15. *'Whenever it was impossible'*: *ibid.*
16. *'I flew my DFS 230'*: Willi Gänzler in conversation with the author, 12 September 2013. (Translator, Alexander Hug). *Ibid.*

Chapter 14

1. *Of the components necessary'*: Richard Wiggan, *Operation Freshman; The Rjukan Heavy Water Raid 1942* (London: William Kimber, 1986), p. 22.
2. *'The creation of heavy water'*: *ibid.*
3. *'Within a month of occupation'*: *ibid.*
4. *'A directive from* a': *ibid*, 57.
5. *'Although Operation Freshman failed'*: Anon., Operation 'Freshman', 19 November 1942, (n/p, n/d – envelope date stamped 19 Nov. 92) descriptive insert single page card, no author, copyright or publishing/printing data.

Chapter 15

1. *'252'*: Samuel W. Mitcham, Jr. and Friedrich von Stauffenberg, *The Battle of Sicily* (NY: Orion Books, 1991), p.80.
2. *'This was a bad time'*: Frank Ashleigh, in conversation with the author, 19 September 2013.
3. *'The battle for Sicily'*: Mitcham and Stauffenberg, 69.
4. *'The poor sanitary environment'*: Mae Mills Link and Hubert A. Coleman, *Medical Support of The Army Air Forces in World War II* (Washington, D.C.: Department of the Air Force, Office of the Surgeon General, USAF, 1955), pp. 423-24.
5. *'For some units'*: Link and Coleman, p. 428.
6. *'Due to insufficient numbers'*: Weeks, p. 55.
7. *'Despite being attacked by Ju 88 aircraft'*: Devlin, *Silent Wings,* p. 84.
8. *'Despite being attacked by Ju 88 aircraft'*: Lloyd, p. 34.
9. *By the middle of June'*: Devlin, *Silent Wings,* p. 82.
10. *'Their regimental motto would be'*: *ibid.*
11. *'Their regimental motto would be'*: Lloyd, p. 38. *Ibid.*
12. *'The villages on the southern'*: Mitcham and von Stauffenberg, p. 27.
13. *'The villages on the southern'*: Ernie Pyle, *Brave Men (NY: Henry Holt, 1944), p. 31*
14. *'These villages in the south'*: *ibid*, p. 58.
15. *'Once the bridge was secured'*: Weeks, p. 56.
16. *'This time period would give': Mitcham and von Stauffenberg, p. 11.*
17. 'From there they would give': Lloyd,p. 38.
18. *'Seven combinations failed to clear'*: Garland and Smyth, p. 115.
19. *'On the evening of the assault'*: Mitcham and von Stauffenberg, p. 78.
20. *'The British contingent'*: Garland and Smyth, p. 117.
21. *'To avoid radar detection'*: *ibid*, p. 115.
22. *'To avoid radar detection'*: Lloyd, p. 39.

23. *'Another lit up the sky'*: Mitcham and von Stauffenberg, p. 82.
24. *'Exactly how many gliders': Garland and Smyth, p. 117.*
25. 'Unable to make the coast': Mitcham and von Stauffenberg, p. 82.
26. *"As we landed'*: Thesis, www.ww2gp.org, used with permission.
27. *'from the moment I cut loose'*: *ibid.*
28. *'We had to capture'*: Bernard Halsall, Oral History, (Used with permission of The Assault Glider Trust: www.assaultgliderproject.co.uk, 2011).
29. *'"Sicily Invasion - Paratroopers in Action.'"* : Anon., *The Star*, London, 10 July 1943 as reprinted in, *War Papers; Presenting a fascinating collection of historic newspaper front pages, 1939–45* (London: Fontana Paperbacks, 1989), unnumbered.
30. *'One London daily reported'*: David Marley, editor, *The Daily Telegraph Story of the War; January–December 1943 (*London: Hodder & Stoughton, 1944), p. 138.

Chapter 16

1. *'They were about to be'*: Otto Skorzeny, translated from the French by Jacques Le Clercq, *Skorzeny's Secret Missions; War Memoirs of the Most Dangerous Man in Europe* (NY, E. P. Dutton, 1950), pp. 40-1.
2. *'Skorzeny was to locate'*: Charles Foley, *Commando Extraordinary; Otto Skorzeny's Remarkable Exploits and their urgent meaning urgent meaning for us NOW* (London: Longmans, Green, 1954), p. 42.
3. *'Only a limited number'*: *ibid.*
4. *'Skorzeny reminded Student'*: Robert Forczyk, *Rescuing Mussolini; Gran Sasso 1943* (Botley, Oxford: Osprey, 2010), p. 23.
5. *'No military map'*: Albert N. Garland and Howard McGraw Smyth, assisted by Martin Blumenson, *United States Army in World War II; The Mediterranean Theater of Operations; Sicily and the Surrender of Italy* (Washington, D.C.: Office of the Chief of Military History, Department of the Army, 1965), p. 536.
6. *'But because the planners of the abduction'*: *ibid.*
7. *'The general ordered twelve gliders'*: Greg Annussek, *Hitler's Raid to Save Mussolini; The Most Infamous Commando Operation of World War II* (Cambridge, Massachusetts: Da Capo, 2005), p. 215.
8. *'Other groups were'*: Forczyk, p. 26.
9. *Skorzeny's personal addition'*: *ibid., p. 27.*
10. 'It was during this delay': Foley, p. 56.
11. *'The rescuer had the Duce'*: *ibid*, p. 59.
12. *'The pilot of the tiny aircraft'*: Garland and Smyth, p. 538.
13. *'Paratroopers held the wings'*: *ibid.*

14. *'Operation Oak Scoreboard'*: Skorzeny, p. 98.
15. *'Honors accorded'*: Annussek, p. 240.
16. *'Mussolini's rescue was addressed'*: David Marley, editor, *The Daily Telegraph Story of the War; January–December 1943* (London: Hodder & Stoughton, 1944), p. 181.

Chapter 17

1. *'They were successful at attacking'*: Henry. H. (Hap) Arnold, "The Aerial Invasion of Burma," *National Geographic Magazine*, August, 1944 (Washington, D.C.), p. 129.
2. *Ibid.*
3. *'It was when I was visiting'*: Louis F. A. V. N. (Dickie) Mountbatten, *Personal Correspondence* (to President Franklin Roosevelt), 28 March, 1944 (South East Asia Command Headquarters), Franklin D. Roosevelt Library & Museum; Military Correspondence: 1944-45; Box 36, p. 1.
4. *'Large numbers of Allied'*: Arnold, p. 129.
5. *'All that was left'*: *ibid.*
6. *'Dislodge the Japanese;* : Julian Thompson, *Forgotten Voices of Burma* (Reading: Ebury Press), p. 152.
7. *"He ended the meeting'*: *ibid.*, p. 130.
8. *'In India there were work-filled'*: *ibid.*, 130-31.
9. *'I also enclose'*: Mountbatten, *Personal Correspondence*, p. 1.
10. *'This is how Phil Cochran'*: James W. Bellah, Lt. Col., Edited and adapted from, *The Password Was Mandalay*, (n/p, n/d, enclosure with letter from Lord Louis Mountbatten to President Franklin Roosevelt; used with permission from James Bellah's son, John Bellah), pp. 1-7.
11. *"Surprise: Sun Tzu'*: Sun Tzu, *The Art of War,* Edited by Dallas Galvin; translated by Lionel Giles, (New York, Barnes & Noble Classics, 2003), p. 9.
12. *'At General Wingate's advanced airfield'*: John E. A. Baldwin, Air Marshall, *Letter extract to Air Commander-in-Chief, South East Asia,* (10 March 1944, enclosure with letter from Lord Louis Mountbatten to President Franklin Roosevelt, Franklin D. Roosevelt Library & Museum; Military Correspondence: 1944–45; Box 36.
13. *'An American observer'*: Ed Cunningham, "Burma Air Invasion; An eyewitness report from a YANK correspondent who landed 150 miles behind the Japanese lines with Col. Phil Cochran's glider and transport fliers in one of the most daring airborne attacks of the war." *Yank*, Down Under edition, (2 June 1944).
14. *'One of those men'*: Boyle discussion, 6 February 2013.
15. *'Reprise'*: Bellah, p. 5.

Chapter 18

1. *The memories that are included'*: George E. Buckley, edited and adapted from, "Normandy; A Glider Pilot's Story" from the vertical/archival files of Silent Wings Museum, Lubbock, Texas, n/d, 1-11; Nick Jacobellis, edited and adapted from, "G for Guts," 2002, vertical/archival files of the Silent Wings Museum, 8-11; Jack Lester, edited and adapted from, "Saga of a Dust Bowl Legacy," n/d, 26-31; Jack Townsend, in discussion with the author, 28 June 2013.
2. *'There ain't nothing'*: Gus Martin in discussion with the author, 6 June 2013, a remembrance of a conversation with Senator Strom Thurmond during a visit to the Normandy battlefields on the 40th anniversary of D-Day.
3. *'I dragged my co-pilot'*: Jim Davison, edited and adapted from, "Jim Wallwork: Decorated glider pilot who took part in D-Day and *Operation Market* Garden," an obituary notice, *The Independent,* 30 January 2013. Internet edition; used with permission.
4. *'It turned out that'*: Frank Dougan, "Oral History," The Assault Glider Trust web site, www.assaultglidertrust.co.uk. Used with permission.
5. *'Wrecked gliders littered the'*: Leonard Mosley, edited and adapted from, "Behind the enemy lines in Normandy; Paratroop Reporter No. 1 Types His Dispatch in Battle," *Crusader; The British Forces' Weekly, 25 June, 1944, 1.*
6. *'They are very confident':* Doon Campbell, edited and adapted from "We have won battle of the beaches," *Union Jack; For the British Fighting Forces, 14 June, 1944, 2.*
7. *'Wallwork received'*: Davison, *ibid.*
8. *Ibid.*

Chapter 19

1. *'On 15 August 1944'*: George Theis, *Eight Missions–Southern France* (National World War II Glider Pilots Association web site, www.ww2gp.org) used with permission.
2. *'Around August 1'*: Lester discussion, 30 November 2010.
3. *'We had a bird's-eye'*: Theis, www.ww2gp.org, with permission.
4. *'Red, Red, we aren't'*: Leonard J. Stevens, adapted from *Personal Account*, (Silent Wings Museum, Lubbock, Texas vertical/archival files), pp. 1-2.
5. *'WITH A TROOP CARRIER COMMAND'*: Robert Meyer, Jr., cited from *Stars and Stripes, Rome Edition,* 17 August 1944, in *The Stars and Stripes Story of World War II,* (NY, David McKay, 1960), P. 268.

Chapter 20

1. *'It was learned later'*: Denis Cason, edited and adapted from, "*Operation 'Dingson'* and 'X' Flight," (n/d, n/p; used with permission from Denis Cason's son, John Cason), 1.
2. *'It was learned later'*: Lynton Hugh Martin, edited and adapted from, *Silent Wings*, personal communication with the author, 1May 2013. Used with permission. Two documents, pp. 1-10 and pp. 1-28.
3. *'On the next day'*: Cason, 1.
4. *'The next day'*: Martin, 15.

Chapter 21

1. *'There are several objectives'*: Anon., *A Summary of Information about the American World War II Glider Pilots and the CG-4A Combat Glider,* (Lubbock, Texas: Silent Wings Museum, vertical/archival files), pp. 7-8.
2. *'The Germans for their part': Frank Ashleigh, in email communication with the author, 2 April 2013.*
3. *'US glider missions for'*: Anon., *USAF Historical Division, Research Report; Training and Employment of Glider Pilots (Silent Wings Museum, Lubbock, Texas: vertical/archival files of the), p. 2.*
4. *'Drop zones for paratroopers'*: Anon., *A Summary of Information About The American World War II Glider Pilots and the CG-4A Combat Glider,* p. 7.
5. *'England: Our troop carrier group'*: Clyde Martin Litton, "Pilot Describes Airborne Landings at Nijmegen," *Los Angeles Times* (Los Angeles, CA: 27 October 1944), p. 6. Used with permission of the author.
6. *'A continued shortage'*: Jacobellis, p. 12.
7. *'Soon the sky was filled'*: Litton, 6.
8. *'A battle report marked SECRET'*: James M. Gavin, The following letter has been received from General GAVIN, Commander 82nd Airborne Division while in the field of *Operation "Market"* and is reproduced for your information, (APO 469, US Army, Holland/The Netherlands, 25 September 1944), pp. 1-5.
9. *'Some pilots wouldn't be seen'*: Jack Lester, in conversation with the author, 30 November 2010.
10. *'I got in the back of the jeep'*: Jim Townsend, in conversation with the author, 28 June 2013.
11. *'In this division'*: Gavin, pp. 1-5.
12. *'Note: Because of fierce'*: Jacobellis, p. 14.
13. *'Note: Because of fierce'*: Dank, 191-93.
14. *'General Gavin continued'*: Gavin, pp. 4-5.

15. '*"Gentlemen" (sic) Jim Gavin*': J. Curtis Goldman, edited and adapted from, *Tales of an Extinct Military Species: A World War II Combat Glider Pilot: Hybrids Like Mules, Who Will Never Reproduce Ourselves!* (Privately published), pp. 108-111.
16. '*the middle of a very dark*': *ibid.*
17. '*On the operation's D-Day*': Mike Peters and Luuk Buist, Glider *Pilots at Arnhem,* (Barnsley, South Yorkshire: Pen & Sword, Military, 2009), pp. 326-32.
18. '*Although there were*': *ibid.*
19. '*in 44 gliders*': *ibid.*
20. '*It was planned*': Anon., *A Summary of Information About The American World War II Glider Pilots and the CG-4A Combat Glider,* p. 7.
21. '*It was planned*': Ashleigh, April 2, 2013.
22. '*Remembering their participation*': Edited and adapted conversations or documents of the following, listed in alphabetical order and used with permission: Frank Ashleigh, Glider Pilot Regiment; Alan Austin, Glider Pilot Regiment, Oral history, Assault Glider Trust website, assaultglidertrust.co.uk, Norman Didsbury, Glider Pilot Regiment, Oral history, Assault Glider Trust website, H. A. Duinhoven, MBE, *The Old Church Oosterbeek; An Impression of the September days of 1944 and a "guided walk" in the church,* (Oosterbeek/Wolfheze, The Netherlands, Council of Churchwardens of the Dutch Reformed Community, n/d), 1-20, Mike Hall, Glider Pilot Regiment, Arthur Shakelton, Glider Pilot Regiment.
23. '*In the newspapers of London*': *The Daily Mail*, column headline, *8000 In – 2000 Out,* (London: 28 September 1944), p. 1.
24. '*But despite these figures*': *The Daily Sketch*, column headings/descriptors, (London, 28 September 1944), p. 1.
25. '*A war correspondent for the BBC*': Guy Byam, "Arnhem, Last Day," *Union Jack* (Wednesday, 28 September 1944).
26. '*Struggling through a hurricane*': Richard McMillan, "Bloody Arnhem Survivors Want to Fight Again," *The Stars Stripes*, (Wednesday, 28 September 1944), p. 1.
27. '*The sky was black*': Laurens Van Aggelen, in conversation with the author, 21 September 2013.
28. '*They shall not grow old*': Anon. *Program, Memorial Service at Arnhem Oosterbeek War Cemetery, 1944–2013, 69th Annual Remembrance, "The Battle of Arnhem", Sunday, 22 September 2013,* (Oosterbeek, The Netherlands, 22 September 2013), p. 7.
29. '*An Exciting Event During*': Anon. A History of Dan Griffiths; A Premature Landing, (Photo copy school textbook, Den Dungen, the Netherlands), p. 1. Used with permission.

Chapter 22

1. *'The heroic efforts'*: George Theis, *Eight Missions-Southern France* (National World War II Glider Pilots Association web site, www.ww2gp.org) Used with permission.
2. *'It was one of the'*: Devlin, pp. 284-85.
3. *'The 83,000 Allied defenders':* Kent Roberts Greenfield, (ed.), *United States Army in World War II; Pictorial Record; The War Against Germany: Europe and Adjacent Areas,* (Washington, D.C.: Office of the Chief of Military History, Department of the Army, 1951), p. 261.
4. *'By the 21st of December'*: Charles B. MacDonald, *United States Army in World War II; The European Theater of Operations; The Last Offensive,* (Washington, D.C.: Office of the Chief of Military History, Department of the Army, 1973), pp. 23-5.
5. *'By the 21st of December'*: Devlin, p. 285.
6. *'But by 20 December'*: Dank, p. 208.
7. *'Because Bastogne was the key'*: MacDonald, p. 24.
8. *'Although they brought in 300 tons'*: Dank, p. 209.
9. *'Also desperately needed': ibid.*
10. *'This flight was soon followed'*: Devlin, p. 292.
11. *'On the following day'*: *ibid*, p. 296.
12. *'Orders quickly came for'*: J. Curtis Goldman, *Tales of an Extinct Military Species: A World War II Combat Glider Pilot: Hybrids Like Mules, Who Will Never Reproduce Ourselves,* (Privately printed), pp. 122-3.
13. *'The timing of the arrival'*: Theis, (www.ww2gp.org) Used with permission.
14. *'But ask the troopers': Goldman, p. 123.*
15. *'Sixteen pilots of the 72 sent out'*: Anon., *USAF Historical Division, Research Report; Training and Employment of Glider Pilots* (Silent Wings Museum, Lubbock, Texas: vertical/archival files), p. 3.
16. *'The Germans who had employed'*: Greenfield, p. 262
17. *'The Ardennes campaign was'*: Ed Cunningham, *Yank, Battle of the Bulge*, 2 March 1945, (Reproduced in, *Yank, The Army Weekly, World War II From the Guys Who Brought You Victory,* (NY: St. Martin's Press), pp. 255-259.

Chapter 23

1. *'On that date'*: George Theis, *Eight Missions-Southern France* (National World War II Glider Pilots Association web site, www.ww2gp.org) Used with permission.
2. *'The 17th Airborne Division'*: Stephen L. Wright, *The Last Drop; Operation Varsity, March 24-25* (Mechanicsburg, PA, Stackpole, 2008), pp. 297-8.

3. *'(T)he crossing of the Rhine'*: MacDonald, pp. 296-7.
4. *'against the (German) transportation'*: *ibid.*
5. *'Combined components'*: MacDonald, p. 309.
6. *'Combined components'*: Wright, pp. 308-9.
7. *'(It) split open very near'*: John Dilworth, Glider Pilot Regiment, Oral history, Assault Glider Trust website, www.assaultgliderproject.co.uk, 2011), used with permission.
8. *'The action started on March 23rd'*: Anon, *A Summary of Information About the American World War II Glider Pilots and the CG-4A Combat Glider* (Silent Wings Museum, Lubbock, Texas: vertical/archival files), p. 9.
9. *'The entire force landed'*: Smith, p. 131.
10. *'WITH THE 17TH AIRBORNE'*:Howard Cowan, *A Summary of Information About the American World War II Glider Pilots and the CG-4A Combat Glider* (Silent Wings Museum Lubbock, Texas: vertical/archival files), pp. 9-10.
11. *'The guys came into'*: Jack Lester. In conversation with the author, 30 November, 2010.
12. *'... a glider rolled to a stop'*: Richard Redfem, *Eight Missions–Southern France* (National World War II Glider Pilots Association web site, www.ww2gp.org) Used with permission.
13. *'When we stopped rolling'*: George Theis, In conversation with the author, 11 September, 2013.
14. *'We flew our gliders down to'*: Goldman, 128-36.
15. *'We received our briefing'*: John Dilworth, Glider Pilot Regiment, "Oral History," (The Assault Glider Trust website, www.assaultgliderproject.co.uk, 2011), used with permission.
16. *'The day we took off'*: John Williams Rayson, Glider Pilot Regiment, Oral history, Assault Glider Trust website, www.assaultgliderproject.co.uk, 2011), used with permission.
17. *"This edited narrative'*: G. M. Slaughter, *Narrative Report of Interrogation Check Sheet,* (U.S. National Archives and Records; copy donated to author by Bruce Overman, October, 2013.
18. *'Glider pilot rest area'*: Theis in conversation with the author.
19. *'Paratroopers should precede'*: Slaughter, *Narrative Report ...*
20. *'shook me awake'*: Goldman, pp. 151-2.
21. *'While many American glider'*: *ibid.*
22. *'Fifty years after the battle'*: "Bellevue WW II veteran to get Bronze Star medal; Air Force officer helped repel German attack as part of infantry operation," *Bellevue Reporter.com* (newspaper e-edition), 2 August 2013.
23. *'... the contributions and sacrifices'*: George Theis, as cited in: "Bellevue WW II veteran to get Bronze Star medal; Air Force officer helped repel German

attack as part of infantry operation," *Bellevue Reporter.com* (newspaper e-edition), 2 August 2013. (Theis, used with permission.)

24. *'Operation Varsity, the airborne phase'*: MacDonald, pp. 313-4.
25. *'The British 6th Airborne'*: Gerard M. Devlin, *Paratrooper! The Saga of U.S. Army and Marine Parachute and Glider Combat Troops During World War II* (NY: St. Martin's Press, 1979), p. 626.
26. *'In view of the weak conditions'*: MacDonald, p. 314.

Chapter 24

1. *'Illness from diseases'*: Link and Coleman, 847-50.
2. *'The flight would allow'*: Ozzie St. George, *Hidden Valley, Yank*, 10 August 1945, Vol. 3, No. 2, Far East Edition, p. 6.
3. *'According to Dutch and Australian'*: *ibid.*
4. *'It was Sunday'*: *ibid.*
5. *'although she later'*: Mitchell Zuckoff, *Lost in Shangri-La; A True Story of Survival, Adventure, and the Most Incredible Rescue Mission of World War II,* (New York, HarperCollins, 2011), 227.
6. *'They had made it'*: *ibid*, 296.
7. *'The three survivors met'*: *ibid*, 316.
8. *'Meanwhile, the war continued'*: Roy E. Appleman, James M. Burns, Russell A. Gugeler, and John Stevens, *United States Army in World War II; The War in the Pacific; Okinawa: The Last Battle* (Washington, D.C.: Center of Military History, United States Army, 1948), pp. 473-4.
9. *'The Japanese were at'*: Devlin, *Paratrooper,* 643.
10. *'The area in which'*: Anon, *A Summary,* 9.
11. *'vast mountainous area'*: Robert Ross Smith, *U.S. Army in World War II; The War in the Pacific; Triumph in the Philippines,* (Washington, D.C.: Office of the Chief of Military History, Department of the Army, 1993), 543.
12. *'Paratroopers and the Task Force'*: *ibid*, pp. 569-71.
13. *'Paratroopers and the Task Force'*: Devlin, *Silent Wings,* p. 368.
14. *'Paratroopers and the Task Force'*: Anon, *A Summary,* p. 9.
15. *'The airborne operation had'*: Smith, p. 571.

Acknowledgements

It is an impossible task to write acknowledgements to the many who contribute to a writer's work—it is almost a certainty someone will be omitted who should have been recognized. From the outset, I recognize this and apologize for all of those, real or imagined, who I have slighted. What follows then, is a list of those who come to mind, a remembrance of things and people in the past several years who have contributed to this work.

The acquisition editor of Fonthill Media, Jay Slater, found me some years ago and has been there believing that I had something to contribute to the many volumes already in print about the Second World War. Jay, thanks for that allegiance because without it I wouldn't have written this volume. I owe you a pint.

Institutions or individuals—which is most important to a writer? Individuals by a long shot. The richest part of any non-fiction work such as *Silent Invaders: Combat Gliders of the Second World War*, is the journey taken by the author and the people he or she meets along the way. The people and the journey itself are the grist for a book by themselves. An acknowledgement, a thank you written on these pages, hardly seems sufficient for the indebtedness I feel for their contributions to the content. The persons listed here, in alphabetical order gave me their memories, often with emotions just below the surface, and just as often out in the open for me to feel. They gave me their personal papers, memoirs, letters, photos, and time, perhaps the most precious of all the personal gifts given to me. So thank you one and all:

Laurens Van Aggelen; Frank Ashleigh, GPR; John Bellah, son of James Bellah, USG (US Glider man); W. George E. Boyle, USG; John Cason, son of Denis Cason, GPR; H. A. Duinhoven, MBE; Tim Ferguson, M.D.; Willi Ganzler GGP (German Glider Pilot) and his translator-grandson; Alexander Hug; Charles E. Gibson; Mike Hall, GPR; Jack Lester, USG; Clyde Martin Litton, USG; Gus Martin, GPR; Lynton Hugh Martin, GPR; Frank Plebanek, USG; Arthur Shakelton, GPR; Kelly Stumpis, USG; George Theis, USG; Jack Townsend, USG; Norman Wilmeth, USG.

To the Silent Wings Museum and its staff in Lubbock, Texas, especially its head curator, Dr. Don Abbe, a most grateful 'Thank you'. Your opening of the museum archive files, photos, books, and materials with the freedom given to me to roam through them and absorb whatever I found useful and interesting, go beyond realms of courtesy. I don't even want to know what the cost was of the copier machine spitting out dozens and dozens of pages that I insisted had to be in my files. You simply said, 'go for it.'

Thanks also to the members of the National World War II Glider Pilots Association, Inc. who have graciously taken the time to talk with me at their annual reunion of veteran pilots. You are truly amazing.

The Assault Glider Trust in the UK likewise offered every long distance accommodation possible through several email correspondence sessions and ultimately gave their permission to cite the oral histories from their files. From those files my thanks to the following for sharing their personal histories: (Alan Austin; Norman Didsbury; John Dilworth; Frank Dougan; John Williams Rayson; and Joan Roberts.

To those who provided written permission to quote from their published works, I am most grateful and wish to remember here: the Tribune Media Services for the use of the *Life* magazine cover in Chapter 2, and for their permission to reproduce a strip from the series of *Terry and the Pirates*. In addition, thanks to Peter Chamberlain at Haddenham Airfield, for permission to cite images and works of George Cliff, Tim Hervey and Lawrence Wright. To Anthony Coogan, son of the late actor Jackie Coogan, thanks for the photos and your dad's memories. I am grateful to the following for use of their works, *National Geographic*, *Liberty* magazines, The Spellmount Press for use of material by Louis Hagen, *Arnhem Lift; A German Jew in the Glider Pilot Regiment,* Joanna Chaundy, syndication manager for the *independent.co.uk* for citations from the obituary of Jim Wallwork, the Celanese Corporation for use of their Second World War era magazine advertisements, and Harry J. Potter of the Hellenic Foundation to quote from their website material regarding the battle for Crete.

Thanks are extended to those associated with publications in the public domain by virtue of their contributions made as a part of their role, responsibility, and membership in the federal government of the United States or for service to various components of the government of the United Kingdom. Articles from these publications including, *The Stars and* Stripes, *Yank*, the *Union Jack* and the 82nd Airborne Division newsletter were edited and adapted to fit the story line of several sections of *Silent Invaders.*

Thanks also to Patricia and Bruce Overman for sharing their copy of the after battle report of G. M. Slaughter, and David and Tanya Mitchell for giving me photos and memories about Tanya's grandfather who was a German glider pilot during the war. Thanks to Clyde Martin Litton and Kelly Stumpis who provided their collection of photos taken during the war.

In September of 2013 I traveled to Britain to meet members of the Glider Pilot Regimental Association, an organization in the UK that "began as a tribute to the men of the Glider Pilot Regiment." The membership now includes family members and others who wish to be counted among those who admire and honor the role the GPR played in the Second World War. A long and mutually nourishing friendship between one of their members, Frank Ashleigh, evolved into an invitation to join the group on their annual pilgrimage to Arnhem and Oosterbeek, The Netherlands. The Dutch, each September, remember and celebrate the bravery and sacrifice made by the British Airborne in their attempt to free their country from German control. It is impossible to convey the warmth of welcome I received from the members of the Association as they included me in all of their activities during the week of recognition by the Dutch. I was particularly moved by the stories of the pilots as we visited various battles sites and landing zones.

Photo acknowledgements: Photos given to me by veterans and their families are much appreciated and are noted throughout the text as appropriate. Many of the photos and images in *Silent Invaders* do not have identified attributions. These photos and images are in the public domain as they are made available for use through Wikipedia Commons where the use of photos, maps and other images are provided to the public because: "This image or file is a work of a U.S. Air Force Airman or employee, taken or made as part of that person's official duties. As a work of the U.S. federal government, the image or file is in the public domain;" or, "This artistic work created by the United Kingdom Government is in the public domain;" or, "This file is licensed under the Creative Commons Attribution—Share Alike 3.0 Germany" with attribution to German Federal Archive (Bundesarchiv).

I ask that readers remember that the photos used in the text were often made under battle conditions, are seven decades old, and lack the clarity, color and precision available through digital photography today. But then, there are a good many of us who are "seven decades old (or older) and lack clarity, color and precision."

To the members of my "BES", Bent Ear Society, thanks again for listening to me go on and on about each new discovery I made during the long process of completing *Silent Invaders.*

And oh my dear Shirley—you have never been far away from my thoughts and affection.

Bibliography

Annussek, Greg, *Hitler's Raid to Save Mussolini: The Most Infamous Commando Operation of World War II,* (Cambridge, Massachusetts: Da Capo, 2005).

Appleman, Roy E., James M. Burns, Russell A. Gugeler, and John Stevens, *United States Army in World War II: The War in the Pacific; Okinawa: The Last Battle* (Washington, D.C.: Center of Military History, United States Army, 1948).

Arnold, Henry H., 'The Aerial Invasion of Burma,' *National Geographic Magazine*, (August, 1944).

Associated Press News Service, 'St. Louis Mayor and Nine Others Die In Army Glider Crash,' *The Independent* (St. Petersburg, Florida, August, 1943).

Baldwin, John E. A. Air Marshal, *Letter extract to Air Commander-in-Chief, South East Asia,* (10th March, 1944, enclosure with letter from Lord Louis Mountbatten to President Franklin Roosevelt, Franklin D. Roosevelt Library & Museum; Military Correspondence: 1944–45; Box 36.

Beevor, Antony, *Crete; The Battle and the Resistance,* (London: John Murray, paperback edition, 2005).

Bowyer, Michael J. F., *Action Stations: 6 Military airfields of the Cotswolds and the Central Midlands* (Cambridge, Patrick Stevens, 1983).

Campbell, David, edited and adapted from 'We have won battle of the beaches', *Union Jack; For the British Fighting Forces,* 14 June, 1944, 2.

Cowing, Charles A., *Flying; Standard Operating Procedure for Gliders* (United States Army Air Corps, 17 August, 1943).

Cunningham, Ed, 'Burma Air Invasion; An eyewitness report from a YANK correspondent who landed 150 miles behind the Japanese lines with Col. Phil Cochran's glider and transport fliers in one of the most daring airborne attacks of the war.' *Yank: Down Under Edition* (2 June 1944).

Cunningham, Ed, *Yank*, *Battle of the Bulge*, 2 March 1945, (Reproduced in, *Yank, The Army Weekly, World War II From the Guys Who Brought You Victory* (NY: St. Martin's Press, 1991).

Dank, Milton, *The Glider Gang; An Eyewitness History of World War II Glider*

Combat (Philadelphia: J. B. Lippincott, 1977).

Dawson, William F., 'Coming in With a Glider and a Gulp', *All American Airborne Division, The All American Paraglide, European Final, VE Day*, (May, 1945).

Day, Charles L., *Silent Ones; WW II Invasion glider Test and Experiment: Clinton County Army Air Field, Wilmington, Ohio* (Lambertville, MI: Charles L. Day, 2001).

Devlin, Gerard, *Paratrooper!: The Saga of U.S. Army and Marine Parachute and Glider Combat Troops During World War II,* (NY: St. Martin's Press, 1979).

Devlin, Gerald M., *Silent Wings* (NY: St Martin's Press, 1985).

Duinhoven, H. A. MBE, *The Old Church Oosterbeek: An Impression of the September Days of 1944 and a "Guided Walk" in the Church,* (Oosterbeek/Wolfheze, The Netherlands: Council of Churchwardens of the Dutch Reformed Community).

Edwards, David, *The Devil's Own Luck: Pegasus Bridge to the Baltic* (Barnsley, South Yorkshire: Leo Cooper, 2001).

Eisenhower, Dwight D. *Crusade in Europe*, (Garden City, NY: Garden City Books Edition, 1952).

Foley, Charles, *Commando Extraordinary* (London: Longmans, Green, 1954).

Forczyk, Robert, *Rescuing Mussolini: Gran Sasso 1943* (Botley, Oxford: Osprey, 2010).

Garland, Albert N. and Howard McGraw Smyth, assisted by Martin Blumenson, *United States Army in World War II; The Mediterranean Theater of Operations; Sicily and the Surrender of Italy* (Washington, D.C.: Office of the Chief of Military History, Department of the Army, 1965).

Gero, David, *Military Aviation Disasters: Significant Losses Since 1908,* (North Yeovil, Somerset: Patrick Stevens, 1999).

Glazer, Stanley, compiler, *War Papers: Presenting a Fascinating Collection of Historic Newspaper Front Pages, 1939–45* (London, Fontana, 1989).

Goldman, J. Curtis, *Tales of an Extinct Military Species: A World War II Combat Glider Pilot; Hybrids Like Mules, Who Will Never Reproduce Ourselves!* (Privately published).

Green, William, *The Warplanes of the Third Reich* (London: MacDonald, 1970).

Greenfield, Kent Roberts (ed), *United States Army in World War II; Pictorial Record; The War Against Germany: Europe and Adjacent Areas* (Washington, D.C.: Office of the Chief of Military History, Department of the Army, 1951).

Gukeisen, Thomas B., *The Fall of Fort Eben Emael: The Effects of Emerging Technologies on the Successful Completion of Military Objectives*, (Fort Leavenworth, Kansas: Unpublished Master's degree thesis, 2004).

Hagen, Louis, *Arnhem Lift; A German Jew in the Glider Pilot Regiment* (Stroud: Spellmount, 2012).

Hall, Raymond S., in Cornelius Ryan, *A Bridge Too Far* (NY: Simon & Schuster

Paperbacks, 1995).

Heflin, Woodford Agee (ed), *The United States Air Force Dictionary* (Washington, D.C.: Air University Press, 1956).

Hellmuth Reinhardt, *Airborne Operations; A German Appraisal* (Washington, D.C.: Center of Military History, United States Army, facsimile edition, 1982).

Hillenbrand, Laura, *Unbroken: A World War II Story of Survival, Resilience, and Redemption* (NY: Random House, 2010).

Hitler, Adolph, *Mein Kampf*, translated by Ralph Manheim (Boston: Houghton Mifflin, a Mariner book, 1971.

Instructions for American Servicemen in Britain, 1942 (Washington, D.C.: War Department, 1942).

Kennedy, Ludovic, *War Paper: Presenting a Fascinating Collection of Historic Newspaper Front Pages, 1939-45* (London, Fontana, 1989).

Kesselring, Albert (contributor), *Airborne Operations: A German Appraisal* (Washington, D.C.: Center of Military History, United States Army, facsimile edition, 1982).

Link, Mae Mills and Hubert A. Coleman, *Medical Support of The Army Air Forces in World War II* (Washington, D.C.: Department of the Air Force, Office of the Surgeon General, USAF, 1955).

Litton, Clyde Martin, 'Pilot Describes Airborne Landings at Nijmegen,' *Los Angeles Times* (Los Angeles, CA, 27 October 1944).

Lloyd, Alan, *The Glider: An Action Packed Story of the Wooden Chariots of World War II* (Secker & Warburg, 1982).

Lowden, John L., *Silent Wings at War: Combat Gliders in World War II* (Washington, D.C.: Smithsonian, 1992).

MacDonald, Charles B., *United States Army in World War II: The European Theater of Operations; The Last Offensive* (Washington, D.C.: Office of the Chief of Military History, Department of the Army, 1973).

Macmillan, Margaret, *Paris 1919* (NY: Random House, Trade Paperback Edition, 2003).

Manion, Michael H., *Gliders of World War II: The Bastards No One Wanted.* (thesis, School of Advanced Air and Space Studies, Air University, 2008).

Marley, David, (ed), *The Daily Telegraph Story of the War; 1939–1941,* (London, Hodder & Stoughton, 1942).

Marley, David, (ed), *The Daily Telegraph Story of the War; January–December 1943* (London: Hodder & Stoughton, 1944).

McDonough, Doug (ed.), 'WW II Army glider cadets developed specialized lingo', *Plainview Herald* (Plainview, Texas, 19 October 2012), (e-article).

McMillan, Richard, 'Bloody Arnhem Survivors Want to Fight Again', *The Stars Stripes*, (Wednesday, 28 September 1944).

McRaven, William H., *Spec Ops: Case Studies in Special Operations Warfare,*

Theory and Practice (Novato, CA, Presidio Press, 1996).

Merkel, James, *Beer, Brats, and Baseball: St. Louis Germans* (St. Louis, MO: Reedy Press, 2012).

'Message from London,' as reprinted in, *Union Jack, A Scrapbook, British Forces' Newspapers, 1939–1945*, (London: HMSO, 1989).

Meyer Robert, Jr., cited from *Stars and Stripes, Rome Edition,* 17 August 1944, in *The Stars and Stripes Story of World War II,* (NY: David McKay, 1960).

Miller, Robert, cited in, *Yank; Story of World War II as Written by the Soldiers: By the editors of Yank, the Army Weekly,* (NY: Greenwich House, 1984).

Mireles, Anthony J., *Fatal Army Air Forces Aviation Accidents in the United States, 1941–1945; Volume 2: July 1943–July 1944,* (Jefferson, NC: McFarland, 2006).

Mitcham, Jr., Samuel W. and Friedrich von Stauffenberg, *The Battle of Sicily* (NY: Orion Books, 1991).

Moorehead, Alan, 'The Navy Brings 15,000 Troops Out of Crete,' *Daily Express*, London, June 2, as reprinted in, *War Papers: Presenting a Fascinating Collection of Historic Newspaper Front Pages, 1939–45*, (London: Fontana, 1989).

Mountbatten, Louis F. A. V. N. *Personal Correspondence* (to President Franklin Roosevelt), 28 March, 1944 (South East Asia Command Headquarters), Franklin D. Roosevelt Library & Museum; Military Correspondence: 1944–45; Box 36.

Mrazek, James E., *Fighting Gliders of World War II* (London, Robert Hale, 1977).

Mrazek, James E., *The Fall of Eben Emael* (Novato, CA, Presidio Press, 1991).

Neetzow, Klaus and Georg Schlaug, *Deutsche Lastensegler 1938–1945: Eine Chronik in Beldern,* (Weihuachzen: 1993).

Noetzel, Jonathan C., *To War on Tubing and Canvas: A Case Study in the Interrelationships Between Technology, Training, Doctrine and Organization* (thesis, School of Advanced Airpower Studies, Air University, 1992.

Peters, Mike and Luuk Buist, *Glider Pilots at Arnhem* (Barnsley: Pen & Sword, Military, 2010).

Pilot's Flight Operating Instructions for Glider, Army Model CG-41, British Model Hadrian; AN 09-40CA-1 (USAAF, 20 June 1945).

Polk, David, *The History of Army Airborne Troop Carriers of World War II, (Paducah, KY: Turner, 1992).*

Pyle, Ernie, Brave Men (NY: Henry Holt, 1944).

Reinhardt, Helmuth, Airborne Operations: A German Appraisal (Washington, D.C.: Center of Military History, United States Army, facsimile edition, 1982).

Rickenbacker, Edward V., *Seven Cane Through: Rickenbacker's Full Story* (Garden City, NY: Doubleday, Doran,1943).

Rudin, Harry R., *Armistice 1918* (New Haven: Yale University Press, 1944).

'Sicily Invasion—Paratroopers in Action' , *The Star*, London, 10 July 1943 as reprinted in, *War Papers; Presenting a fascinating collection of historic newspaper front pages, 1939–45*, (London: Fontana, 1989).

Skorzeny, Otto, translated from the French by Jacques Le Clercq, *Skorzeny's Secret Missions; War Memoirs of the Most Dangerous Man in Europe* (NY: E. P. Dutton, 1950).

Slaughter, G. M., *Narrative Report of Interrogation Check Sheet,* (U.S. National Archives and Record).

Smith, Claude, *The History of the Glider Pilot Regiment* (Barnsley, South Yorkshire: Pen & Sword Aviation, 2007).

Smith, Robert Ross, *U.S. Army in World War II; The War in the Pacific: Triumph in the Philippines* (Washington, D.C.: Office of the Chief of Military History, Department of the Army, 1993).

St. George, Ozzie, 'Hidden Valley', *Yank* staff correspondent, *Yank*, Far East Edition, 10 August 1945.

Sun Tzu, *The Art of War,* Dallas Galvin (ed.); translated by Lionel Giles, (NY, Barnes & Noble Classics, 2003).

The Beacon, Newsletter of the Palm Springs Air Museum, (Palm Springs, CA: December, 2013).

Thompson, Julian, *Forgotten Voices of Burma,* (Reading: Ebury Press, 2010).

Training Aids Division, Office of the Assistant Chief of the Air Staff, Training Headquarters Army Air Forces, *Glider Tactics and Technique* (NY: Commanding General, Army Air Forces, 1944).

US Army, *New Flying Opportunities; Be a Glider Pilot in the U.S. Army.* (undated).

Weeks, John, *Assault From the Sky: The History of Airborne Warfare,* (Newton Abbot: David & Charles Military Book, 1978).

Wiggan, Richard, *Operation Freshman: The Rjukan Heavy Water Raid 1942* (London: William Kimber, 1986).

Wisbar, Frank Paul with Fred Allhoff, 'Gliders For War', *Liberty* magazine, (11 April 1942).

Wright, Stephen, L. *The Last Drop; Operation Varsity, March 24–25* (Mechanicsburg, PA: Stackpole, 2008).

Zuckoff, Michael, *Lost in Shangri-La: A True Story of Survival, Adventure, and the Most Incredible Rescue Mission of World War II* (NY: HarperCollins, 2011).

Index